What They're Saying about
Chicken Soup for the Teenage Soul II . . .

"The idea of teenagers writing about their experiences to help other teenagers is brilliant. It's about time a book came out that portrays teens as the intelligent, insightful people they are."

Will Friedle
actor, *Boy Meets World*

"The stories in this book are amazingly touching. It's great to see a book that can act almost like a friend— but I must say, even though it's for 'the teenage soul,' I think it's really for 'the human soul'."

Scott Vickaryous
actor, *Breaker High*

"**This is the perfect book for teenagers.** Every single story was a story I could have written about my own life. I loved reading about what other people did in the same situation and I loved the positive feelings that I felt after reading them."

Jim, 16

"I loved this book and I really didn't think they could do a sec ... first one. I was v ... ause this book is ... is better! This on ... :ionships and oth ...

Jamie, 18

"*Chicken Soup for the Teenage Soul II* was so good. I am just upset because I waited so long for this book to come out and now I have to wait for the next one. I read it in one sitting because I couldn't put it down. Please hurry up with the next one."

Carry, 14

"This book is filled with exactly the kind of stories teenagers want to read. They are written by other teenagers, which is great, and they are about things like boyfriends and friends. The stories are so good. I cried or laughed or both during each one."

Kristin, 15

"My favorite chapter was the one on relationships. It was interesting to read about what girls are thinking and feeling in relationships. I also like the stories that were written by guys. I was thinking while reading them that I might even write a story for the next book."

Jason, 16

"This is the kind of book you can read over and over again. I read it through completely and now I am going to go back to my favorites and read them again. I imagine I will like different stories at different times, depending on what I am going through."

Mitch, 17

"This book speaks directly to teenagers. It lets us know that we are all feeling the same kinds of feelings and going through the same kinds of things. It feels good to know that you're not alone."

Ashley, 14

CHICKEN SOUP FOR THE TEENAGE SOUL II

Chicken Soup for the Teenage Soul II
More Stories of Life, Love and Learning
Jack Canfield, Mark Victor Hansen, Kimberly Kirberger

Published by Backlist, LLC,
a unit of Chicken Soup for the Soul Publishing, LLC. www.chickensoup.com

Front cover artwork by Robbin O'Neill
Front cover redesign by Andrea Perrine Brower
Originally published in 1998 by Health Communications, Inc.

Back cover and spine redesign by Pneuma Books, LLC

Distributed to the booktrade by Simon & Schuster. SAN: 200-2442

Publisher's Cataloging-in-Publication Data
(Prepared by The Donohue Group)

Chicken soup for the teenage soul II : more stories of life, love and learning / [compiled by] Jack Canfield, Mark Victor Hansen, [and] Kimberly Kirberger.

    p. : ill. ; cm.

    Originally published: Deerfield Beach, FL : Health Communications, c1998.
    ISBN: 978-1-62361-122-4

    1. Teenagers--Conduct of life--Anecdotes. 2. Anecdotes. I. Canfield, Jack, 1944- II. Hansen, Mark Victor. III. Kirberger, Kimberly, 1953-

BJ1661 .C172 2012
158.1/28/0835   2012945867

PRINTED IN THE UNITED STATES OF AMERICA
on acid free paper

21 20 19 18 17   05 06 07 08 09 10

CHICKEN SOUP FOR THE TEENAGE SOUL II

More Stories of Life, Love and Learning

Jack Canfield
Mark Victor Hansen
Kimberly Kirberger

Backlist, LLC, a unit of
Chicken Soup for the Soul Publishing, LLC
Cos Cob, CT
www.chickensoup.com

Contents

2. ON FRIENDSHIP

3. ON LOVE AND KINDNESS

4. TOUGH STUFF

5. ON FAMILY

6. LEARNING LESSONS

7. MAKING A DIFFERENCE

8. GROWING UP

Introduction

Dear Teenager,

Shortly after the release of *Chicken Soup for the Teenage Soul,* we began to receive hundreds of letters a day. Those letters contained submissions of stories and poetry, wonderful thank-yous, and, last but not least, a request for a second book "as soon as possible." We heard you and we have responded!

We are, of course, proud of the success of the first book. In fact, it made a *Chicken Soup* record for being the first book to reach sales of 3 million copies in its first year. But our real happiness lies in our admiration and appreciation of you, the teenagers, who bought the book. You were the ones who showed the world that if a book is written that honors and respects you, you will respond in a positive way. We think that says a lot about who you are.

As was the case in the first book, we have included stories that deal with issues that concern you. Even though we couldn't use all the stories that were sent to us, we did pay attention to the issues that were contained in them. You wrote to us about losing a boyfriend or girlfriend and the recovery that followed; you wrote about how painful it is when a friendship ends or friends move in different directions. You wrote about the death of loved ones and the painful process of learning about and dealing with a friend being diagnosed with cancer.

You wrote about performing acts of kindness and how wonderful you felt afterwards and about how others' acts of kindness toward you touched you deeply. And, of course, you wrote about growing up—you are growing and learning so fast that it takes writing it down, or reading someone else's account of it, to see who you are and where you are going.

These are the stories you will find in this book. They are your stories—your triumphs and your tragedies, your heartaches and your breakthroughs, your insights and your discoveries, and your awareness that being a teenager is a journey. It is a journey of becoming your best self.

It is our hope that you will love this book as much, if not more, than the first. It is your book, there for you to read when you need some cheering up or when you simply need to be reminded that you are by no means alone on the journey.

How to Read This Book

Read this book however you want to, from beginning to end or jump around. If there is a particular chapter that speaks to your concerns or that you have a special interest in—such as On Relationships or On Family—feel free to go there first.

We encourage you to return to this book again and again, much like the way you would call on a friend. We received the following e-mail from *Iwilhelm@aol.com* after he had finished *Chicken Soup for the Teenage Soul.*

> *I just wanted to tell you how grateful I am for this great book. I read it all the time and it really has become my best friend.*

While we hope the book as a whole will touch you deeply, you may find that one story in particular will change your life. Kim Price wrote to us about a story that touched her that way.

> The story, "I Love You Dad," deeply touched my soul. Never had anything made me think how important my dad is to me.

Kim wrote him a letter after reading the story and he wrote back a beautiful reply that she says,

> ... boosted my confidence in myself and my love toward my family. . . . I haven't been afraid to tell people how much I care about them. I hope your stories have touched other people's lives in the way they have touched mine.

Let These Stories Help You Grow

Many of the letters we received told us how you changed something about yourself after reading a story. Diana Yarmovich wrote to us about an incident she was involved in at her school. She told us how she and some of her friends were teasing a fellow classmate and calling her gay. They were given the "punishment" of going around to different classrooms and talking about words ending in -ism, (i.e., racism, ageism and sexism). She went on to say,

> The story "Betty Ann" helped me realize how the other girl felt. I now realize how wrong I was.

In another letter, Melissa Moy writes,

> Every day the world looks different to me. In the morning I wake up feeling sure of myself, something that I have never experienced before. Remarkably, this book has also expanded my compassion for others.

Share These Stories

This is a great book to read with others. We've heard stories about classrooms reading it together, youth groups using it to begin their meetings, and teens passing the book around and reading to each other at parties or sleepovers. Lauren Antonelli wrote to us about a slumber party she went to. All the girls had fallen asleep except Lauren and her friend, Mary Beth. They had been reading the book together and sharing which ones were their favorites. She writes,

> *After we put the book away, we talked. We didn't gossip though, we had a very serious heart-to-heart. . . . We talked about life, love and stuff like that. We grew closer that Saturday night and I'm not sure what happened or how it happened. But one thing is for sure, we will never look at life the same way and that is all because of a book called* Chicken Soup for the Teenage Soul.

This Is Your Book

Once again, this is your book. We are thrilled that this book contains more stories actually written by teenagers than the first one. We were so impressed with the stories and poems that were sent to us. They contained such honesty and wisdom. What touched us the most, however, was the desire by every person who submitted something to help others. We heard over and over, "I hope that my story can help someone else the way these stories have helped me." Even if your story isn't in here, it still has helped others, because each and every letter, story and poem we received helped make this book what it is.

We were 100 percent committed to having teenagers decide what went into this book. We learned early on that to ensure a great book, we needed to include teenagers in all the decision making. There were count-less teenagers who read our final two hundred stories and some who read the final copy. We had high school students, middle school students and a youth group help us select the stories, poems and cartoons that appear in this book. They did a great job!

So here it is, another book, from our hearts to yours, just for you.

1

ON RELATIONSHIPS

Love is a fruit in season at all times, and within reach of every hand.

Mother Teresa

Starlight, Star Bright

When I was five years old, I took an extreme liking to my sister's toys. It made little difference that I had a trunk overflowing with dolls and toys of my own. Her "big girl" treasures were much easier to break, and much more appealing. Likewise, when I was ten and she was twelve, the earrings and make-up that she was slowly being permitted to experiment with held my attention, while my former obsession with catching bugs seemed to be a distant and fading memory.

It was a trend that continued year by year and, except for a few bruises and threats of terrifying "haircuts" while I was sleeping, one that my sister handled with tolerance. My mother continually reminded her, as I entered junior high wearing her new hair clips, that it was actually a compliment to her sense of style. She told her, as I started my first day of high school wearing her clothes, that one day she would laugh and remind me of how she was always the cooler of the two of us.

I had always thought that my sister had good taste, but never more than when she started bringing home guys. I had a constant parade of sixteen-year-old boys going through my house, stuffing themselves with food in the kitchen, or playing basketball on the driveway.

I had recently become very aware that boys, in fact, weren't as "icky" as I had previously thought, and that maybe their cooties weren't such a terrible thing to catch after all. But the freshman guys who were my age, whom I had spent months giggling over at football games with my friends, suddenly seemed so young. They couldn't drive and they didn't wear varsity jackets. My sister's friends were tall, they were funny, and even though my sister was persistent in getting rid of me quickly, they were always nice to me as she pushed me out the door.

Every once in a while I would luck out, and they would stop by when she wasn't home. One in particular would have long conversations with me before leaving to do whatever sixteen-year-old boys did (it was still a mystery to me). He talked to me as he talked to everyone else, not like a kid, not like his friend's little sister . . . and he always hugged me good-bye before he left.

It wasn't surprising that before long I was positively giddy about him. My friends told me I had no chance with a junior. My sister looked concerned for my potentially broken heart. But you can't help who it is that you fall in love with, whether they are older or younger, taller or shorter, completely opposite or just like you. Emotion ran me over like a Mack truck when I was with him, and I knew that it was too late to try to be sensible—I was in love.

It did not mean I didn't realize the possibility of being rejected. I knew that I was taking a big chance with my feelings and pride. If I didn't give him my heart there was no possibility that he would break it . . . but there was also no chance that he might not.

One night before he left, we sat on my front porch talking and looking for stars as they became visible. He looked at me quite seriously and asked me if I believed in wishing on stars. Surprised, but just as serious, I told him I had never tried.

"Well, then it's time you start," he said, and pointed to the sky. "Pick one out and wish for whatever you want the most." I looked and picked out the brightest star I could find. I squeezed my eyes shut and with what felt like an entire colony of butterflies in my stomach, I wished for courage. I opened my eyes and saw him smiling as he watched my tremendous wishing effort. He asked what I had wished for, and when I replied, he looked puzzled. "Courage? For what?" he questioned.

I took one last deep breath and replied, "To do this." And I kissed him—all driver's-license-holding, varsity-jacket-wearing, sixteen years of him. It was bravery I didn't know I had, strength I owed completely to my heart, which gave up on my mind and took over.

When I pulled back, I saw the astonished look in his face, a look that turned into a smile and then laughter. After searching for something to say for what seemed to me like hours, he took my hand and said, "Well, I guess we're lucky tonight. Both our wishes came true."

Kelly Garnett

Seven Minutes in Heaven

People say you change many times in the course of your teenage years, and that your time in school will teach you lessons you will never forget. I think they were referring to classrooms and football fields, but one of my greatest learning experiences began in a parking lot. It was as I was waiting to be picked up one day that I met my first girlfriend.

Her name was Brittany. She was pretty, outgoing and two years older than I was—it seemed too good to be true that she was interested in me—but not long after we met, we became an official couple. At our age, "going out" meant that we talked on the phone every night, and saw each other at school in between classes. We never really had a lot of opportunity to see each other or get to know one another very well. But, never having been in a relationship before, I thought that this was what they were like. It didn't seem like a big deal that we weren't that close, that I didn't get butterflies in my stomach when I saw her.

Not long after we got together, she called me and told me that she was going to a party with some friends, and that she wanted me to go with her. I said I would, and waited somewhat nervously that night for her to pick me up. When the small car packed with teenagers arrived, I squeezed in and wondered what I was getting myself into.

An hour into the party, I was feeling less self-conscious and a lot more comfortable. Though the people at the party were all older than me, they were people I knew, or had seen around school. It all seemed innocent enough—we just sat around eating popcorn, watching a movie and having a good time—until the movie ended.

Someone suggested a game of "Spin the Bottle," and my heart began to beat a little faster. *It can't be that bad,* I thought to myself. *It's just kissing even if it is in front of a bunch of other people.* But after a while, some people wanted to take the game a little further. I heard somebody say "Seven Minutes in Heaven," and everyone answered "Yes!" with knowing smiles. I had no idea what it was, and looked at Brittany for help, but she just smiled and agreed that it was a good idea.

After the first few couples spent their seven minutes in heaven, I figured out what the object of the game was—going into a closet and kissing. My stomach flip-flopped and I felt dizzy as I waited for the inevitable, when it would be my turn with Brittany. I was scared. I had no experience with this kind of thing, and I was about to jump into it head first with a girl two years older than I was. I didn't know what she expected, or what she would tell the other older kids when we got out. I could see a sad reputation of being a lame boyfriend looming in the near future.

I really didn't have a lot of time to think about it, because our turn came, and Brittany pulled me after her into the closet. As it turned out, she was an experienced kisser—I didn't have time to think, or react, she just kind of took over. I was relieved and glad when it was over. When she took me home later, neither one of us said much. I don't know what she was thinking about, but I was still trying to let everything sink in. It wasn't as much fun as I had thought it would be—there was no romance or feeling in it.

It was never talked about, but in the weeks that followed the party, my relationship with Brittany slowly ended, and I returned to doing normal things with kids my own age. I thought it was strange that I didn't feel sad about it. It was almost a relief to not have to worry about another party or situation where I would feel out of my league.

I was at the beach with friends several months later when I started talking to a girl. As we talked, I realized I was strangely happy just listening to her and watching her smile while she told me about her life. There was something about her that made me enjoy just being with her. With no thoughts of what it meant, I knew I wanted to see her again so we planned to meet the following week, same time, same place.

I was completely comfortable as we sat on a blanket that night filling each other in on the events of the long week that preceded our reunion. We sat next to the bonfire and laughed, and suddenly, I wanted to kiss her . . . and I did. A pure, sweet, innocent kiss, one that made me feel warm and happy. And though it was nowhere near seven minutes, it was definitely a piece of heaven.

Andrew Keegan
As told to Kimberly Kirberger

Practical Application

He's teaching her arithmetic,
He said it was his mission,
He kissed her once, he kissed her twice and said,
"Now that's addition."
And as he added smack by smack
In silent satisfaction,
She sweetly gave the kisses back and said,
"Now that's subtraction."

Then he kissed her, she kissed him,
Without an explanation,
And both together smiled and said,
"That's multiplication."
Then Dad appeared upon the scene and
Made a quick decision.
He kicked that kid three blocks away
And said, "That's long division!"

Dan Clark

A Geek, a Nerd, a Bookworm

Love is not what we become, but what we already are.

Stephen Levine

Stand straight, shoulders back, chin up, eyes forward, smile, I mumbled to myself. No, it was an impossible task. I put my glasses back on and slouched into my usual character. I immediately regretted this decision as I slid discreetly into my desk. His eyes did not even flicker at my entrance. Clearing my throat in an effort to be acknowledged seemed hopeless.

As I pulled out my organized binder neatly labeled "History," I stole a glance at him as he sat at the desk beside me. He appeared just as he had in my dream last night: flawless. Everything about him was right—his smile, the way a strand of hair always fell in his eyes and, oh, those eyes. He must have felt me staring because suddenly, he turned and looked at me. I quickly dropped my gaze back to my binder and pretended to be intently interested in finding a worksheet. I didn't dare peek to see if he was still studying me. Instead, I shifted my eyes toward the window. The light from the sun made me squint.

Ironically, I'm spending my summer in school. I didn't fail this class, unlike every other student here. I just have an incredible yearning to learn and want to get the most out of my high school career. More simply put, I am a geek. A nerd. A bookworm.

Out of the corner of my eye, I caught his hand ready to tap my shoulder. Every muscle in my body tensed. His touch was so light that I barely felt his fingers. I faced him with my eyes fixated on the tiled floor. I could not bring myself to look at him. In that instant, I just didn't feel worthy.

"The homework, from last night—did you finish it?"

Of course I finished it! I also finished tonight's assignment. Don't you know who I am? I am only the single most intelligent person in this school. Every night of the week, I spend countless hours in front of a computer screen. The force behind me is pushing me with an even greater force. Someday, I will be so far in the land of outcasts that I will want to carouse with my laptop. No, I have not entered that kingdom yet. For now, I am content knowing that there is something I don't know—what you are thinking right this second.

I cleared my throat. "Yes, I did the homework."

"Well, I was a little stumped on question thirteen. Do you know the answer?" With one smooth movement he put his pencil behind his ear.

"Me," I said.

"What? You are the answer?" he asked, confused.

"Uh, no." I could feel my cheeks burning. *Ugh! If I am such a brain, how did I just make such an error? I have practiced what I would say to him a thousand times over.* Supposedly, the conversation would lead to an invitation for a rendezvous. He would laugh at my wit and think that no one was more interesting than I.

I took a deep breath. "Franklin Roosevelt's Brain Trust."

"Thanks," he said, taking the pencil from behind his ear. I watched him sloppily jot down the answer and turn from his worksheet to the blond behind him. He tried to impress her by using his humor. She barely chuckled. I would have laughed uproariously. But then I remembered that the joke was not intended for me. I studied her body motions as she leaned forward toward him, twirling strands of her hair around her finger. Any closer and their noses would have touched. I nonchalantly pushed my pencil off the desk.

Distracted, he shifted his attention from her eyes to the floor. He bent down and picked up the pencil that was half gnawed by my nerves. He came up, his nose closer to mine than hers had been to his. My hand brushed against his as I reached for the pencil. Goosebumps ran down my arms and my heart raced. Never before had he shown so much interest.

As if that moment were just a figment of his imagination, without a word, he turned back to his beauty queen. Disappointed, I hunched forward and leaned on my hand, watching in awe as she brought out her lip balm. With much exaggeration, she moistened her lips and pressed them together firmly. He couldn't take those perfect eyes off her. I wanted to scream and shake him and make him wake up. This girl is a complete flake! Behind her beauty queen exterior is wasted, empty space.

Someday we will save each other, I silently vowed. *In an unconventional way, we are similar. Both of us are in dire need of being rescued from a fantasy world. This alone is grounds for building a relationship.*

Tonight I could go to Wal-Mart and buy hair dye and lip balm. Or maybe search around the mall until I found the halter top she was wearing. I should take advantage of the summer weather and get a bronze skin tone. Instead, I will end up doing homework.

No, tonight I will practice: practice standing straight, shoulders back, chin up and smiling. Then maybe tomorrow, he will ask me for the answer to number twelve . . . and my name.

Kimberly Russell

My Angel Has a Halo

You always were a daredevil. Flying eight or more feet through the air on your bike (your pride and joy), swinging high on a rope swing or flipping head first into the lake below.

I think that is what gives you both your wonderful character and your extraordinary inner strength. What amazes me most about you is the fact that no matter what, your determination pushes all your fears away. You never let fear stand in the way of accomplishing your goals.

But despite all your dangerous stunts, I never thought that this day would come. (Maybe in the back of my mind I did, but only there.)

You were away on a trip to the coast and I eagerly awaited your call. It came the morning of the third day of the seven days you'd be gone. Your voice was normal—but your words were not—"I broke my neck."

Right then every fear in the world hit me. My mom quickly reminded me that I needed to stay strong for you. I didn't talk much. I just quietly cried as you explained to me your ordeal and the halo you would have to wear for two months to keep your neck stabilized as it healed.

You seemed okay considering the situation, but in pain

and in low spirits. I hung up the phone and finally the tears could, and did, flow freely. Throughout this whole day I came to terms with the fact that you would be in a cast, with the exception of your arms, for two entire months. At first I was selfish and thought of how this would affect me. *He can't drive, so we'll see each other less often. He can't take me to school on the first day. I can't even give him a real hug.* But then I remembered and told myself: *Amanda, be glad that he's still alive and here for you to hug at all, no matter what form it's in. And be thankful for the fact that he can walk.*

I went and saw you tonight. You looked good but no smiles—no smiles, that is, until you saw a video of your biking stunts. I saw the determination in your eyes and it brought tears to mine. I know you're scared, but I also know that you're going to be okay. Because that determination inside of you is once again going to push those fears away, and you'll be 110 percent. You helped me be less afraid for you. I stopped thinking about what you cannot do and concentrated instead on what you can do, or what you will do again. Two months is a very short time in exchange for a lifetime of living.

I want to thank you. You have taught me more about inner strength and determination in this one day than I've learned in my whole life. I love you, Logan. We all do. Don't ever lose heart. Just let your wonderful self shine through. You're going to pull through this with flying colors, pushing yourself all the way, because that's who you are: a fighter. I feel so much better now that I'm not thinking about what I won't have and what I won't get from you. Instead, I feel grateful and so happy that you are who you are.

All I have for you now is faith and determination. I always knew that you were a blessing to me, my angel. Now, for two months, you'll have a halo to prove it.

Amanda Johnson

A Cool Drink of Water

After brushing my teeth, I stooped to drink the cool water streaming from the faucet, drifting back to that unforgettable summer. It was the summer when life began—the summer I turned sixteen. I had my own car, along with a brand-new soul. It was not the memory of a new privilege that rushed back to me, but that of him looming over me with a laughing grin painted across his lips as he watched me drink from the faucet. It was that memory that rushed back to me.

Our relationship was everything it should have been, almost as if our time together had been written for a novel. We came together through friends of ours, as do most typical high school relationships. We grew closer and closer during the school year, spending time together on weeknights rehearsing for the school's musical production and on the weekends with friends. Soon, with permission from the weather and sometimes despite it, we traveled to the beach with our friends and a cooler of colas. It was on the way home from the beach one Saturday that I realized I was falling for him. Every sign showed love. I could hardly sit still in class just anticipating the next time I would see him and the upcoming weekend we would spend together. Being in his arms were some of the happiest times I had ever experienced. I could look deep into his eyes and be enchanted forever.

Being with him changed my soul. I shared everything with him, even things I kept from my family and my best friend. I felt his love prying apart the hard shell of shyness that encircled me. His trust, his love and his support for me lifted me from the earth and gently sent me into the clouds. He cast off the chains I had given myself. Through him I learned a new insight about the world. It was as if a tall, dark mountain had stood in front of me and, out of nowhere, he provided the wings to fly over it.

Unfortunately, all good things must come to an end. Yes, even for my first love. I had matured a great deal during our time together, which possibly brought me to a clearer understanding of what true love is. Over time, the clouds floated away, replaced with a new sinking feeling that what I was doing was wrong. The eyes that had so lovingly enchanted me soon became those of a dear friend. Somehow, the spell was broken. I wished so dearly that I could return to the long summer nights we had spent together, embracing under the moonlight. But as I longed for those nights, I also longed for a new freedom. The adventure had somehow become a routine.

Sadly, we both acknowledged the separation. We held each other tighter than ever, both roughly accepting the reality that it would be best to say good-bye. He wiped away my tears and held me until it was time for him to leave. My heart was yearning to kiss him good-bye, but my mind and my lips told me no. He walked down the stairs to his black convertible and left. I watched through tear-stained eyes from the window as he pulled out of my

driveway. As his headlights faded in the distance, I turned off the light to my first love.

Having satisfied my thirst, I stood up and dried my mouth and chin with the towel at my side. I smiled, once again remembering how he stood by me and protected me in more ways than one. It is impossible to sum up seven-and-one-half months of pure joy and apprenticeship, but if there is one way to do it, a cool drink of water from the faucet would be sufficient.

Camden Watts

"He gave me a copy of *The Declaration of Independence*, then he got a tattoo that says *Give Me Liberty Or Give Me Death*. I think my boyfriend wants his freedom."

Reprinted by permission of Randy Glasbergen.

Unrequited Love

Nothing spoils the taste of peanut butter like unrequited love.

Charlie Brown
from Peanuts *by Charles Schulz*

"Guess what?"

I look at Sarah, my best friend since halfway through second grade. We've been through this routine before, and both of us know what's coming. "What?" I ask. I really don't like guessing.

We're walking home together after school. We usually do. It's freezing.

"Guess," she prompts me.

I study her face and then think for a second. What could be making her so happy? "You got another A in biology?"

"Nope."

"Your sister dropped dead?" I suggest.

"I wish," she replies, but shakes her head. "Guess again!"

"Just *tell* me!" I whine.

Her smile grows even broader, and I can see all her

braces-covered teeth. "Xander kissed me."

My jaw drops and I turn to her. "Get out!" I gasp. I hit her shoulder. "Don't tell me stuff like that!" But then curiosity gets the better of me, so I meekly ask, "Lips?"

"Cheek."

I hit her shoulder again. "What's wrong with you?" she demands loudly.

I glare at her. I've liked Xander since halfway through eighth grade. Ever since he turned to me one day in class and said, "Alyson, right?" I'd given him my usual witty reply of "Yun-hun." After that we spoke, like, once or twice.

Then this year, Sarah became friends with him and his group. I never used to hang out with Sarah during recess or lunch—her friends were all straight-A students, and I was one of those has-real-potential-but-won't-apply-herself types, so I mostly got Cs. Usually I hung out with my other best friends, Darcy and Mara. But neither Darcy nor Mara had very many friends who were guys, and I wanted some. Sarah did, so I tried to spend lunch with them at least two times a week.

"Why are we still calling him 'Xander'?" she asks, her voice breaking into my thoughts. I look at her, surprised. I had almost forgotten she was there. "No one we know is around here so even if we said his real name, no one would know!"

I shrug. "It's fun."

Xander's name isn't really Xander. I came up with that as a code name for him. All my friends do that. That way they can talk about their crush in front of people and no one will know. I chose to call him "Xander" because I have a deep respect (most people call it an obsession—I can't imagine why) for the TV show *Buffy the Vampire Slayer*. Xander is the name of one of the lead characters. Only three people know that my crush is referred to as "Xander": Sarah, Mara and Darcy. I call him Xander so much, sometimes I think that's his real name. When I talk about him I sometimes have to say "Xander—the untelevised version" so my friends know I'm not talking about Xander from *Buffy the Vampire Slayer*.

"Are you coming with us to see the movie Saturday?" she asks.

I smile. "Is Xander coming?" She gives me a look but says nothing. "Then I'm there!" I say. The last time I went with them to see a movie, I ended up sitting next to Xander. For an hour and forty-three minutes, I thought I'd died and gone to heaven. Okay, maybe heaven is a bit much, but I did feel very, very happy.

But now I think of something and my smile disappears. Nervously I tuck a strand of hair behind my ear. "Sar?"

I begin to crack my knuckles, which I do whenever I'm nervous. Aw, who am I kidding? I crack my knuckles all the time. I really need to stop because it's annoying and it'll give me arthritis when I'm older. "What does he think of me?" I ask.

I hear a click as Sarah turns off her Walkman. I know she'll tell me the truth. Sar isn't the kind of friend who, when you tell her you just messed up in public speaking, says, "I'm sure nobody noticed!" Instead, she'd just laugh. At you. Mockingly. Loudly. So I nervously wait for Sarah to answer.

"He . . . he says you're kinda weird. Like, a depressed, poetry-writing nut. But, like, a nice one," she adds to make it sound better.

"Really?" I sigh, feeling as though fifty midgets have found a way into my chest and have decided to simultaneously perform cartwheels, jumping jacks and handstands on my heart.

"That's a bit harsh," she says. "Look, he likes you—he just thinks you're a bit morbid."

I try to look at the positive, "Nice is good!" I tell her. She nods her head and turns her music back on.

I begin to feel worse every time I think about what Xander had said. "Nice is good," I repeat dejectedly. I stare straight ahead for a moment and then squint because the sun is so bright it hurts my eyes. Nice but insane is probably what he meant. *I am not insane,* I tell myself, *I am depressed. There's a difference.* I kick at a bit of snow on the ground.

"You are not depressed," Mom always tells me. "Right," I reply, "I am just deeply unhappy!" "There is a difference, Alyson," she tells me, then ships me off to therapy.

I pinch Sarah the way she taught me to, back in fifth grade. It's the best way to pinch 'cause it really, really hurts. She squeals and looks at me, annoyed. "What?"

"Am I depressing?"

"Yes, you're negative, morbid, cynical. . . ."

I sigh.

She puts her arm around my shoulders, "But that's why we love you."

I'm also known around school as being depressed.

That's not to say I actually *am* depressed. I'm not; I'm a complete and utter sucker for corny, happy endings (I practically live on films like *While You Were Sleeping* and *Addicted to Love*). A movie can be incredible, but if the ending is sad, I'll immediately despise it. But when people want to know about you, they usually ask certain questions, and my answers sometimes feed their "depressed poet" image of me. *Fave color?* Black. *Hobby?* Writing poetry and stories. *Oh, what kind of poetry? Sad?* Usually.

Of course, I don't exactly dissuade them from the tortured writer concept they have of me, because at least I'm known for something. Maybe it's negative, but it's better than nothing, right? So let them think me forlorn. I have my own friends and I don't really care what any of them think. Except *him.* . . .

But a long time ago, I really was depressed. I'd just been

dumped by my first boyfriend and felt really crappy. I thought about death and suicide a lot. I know it was dumb, but I'd never been dumped before and it just . . . hurt. That's the only word I could think of to describe it. And I know it sounds clichéd and all, but my heart actually felt as though it had been broken in two. But I got over it (with the help of my therapist, school guidance counselor, my parents and a really long letter to Mara that I never gave her and ended up gluing into my diary). And now when I think of Xander, I feel so miserable. . . .

Sarah and I reach the street where we split. We stop and I turn to her, "This is where I get off," I say. "I'll call ya later," I begin crossing the street.

She continues on. "Alright. Bye!" she calls.

I turn onto my street and look down at the ground. The snow around here is all white and beautiful. It reminds me of cream cheese. Not like the snow in front of our school. That snow is all gray and dirty and yuck. This snow is nice. Nice. Like how he thinks of me. Nice. The chances of Xander ever liking me are about as good as me passing math. I know that!

I giggle. But hey, maybe I'll get a few poems out of this unrequited love thing. Ya think?

Rachel Rosenberg

Gray

When I was a child
I saw in black and white.
Everything was obvious
Either wrong or right.
No arguments, no pros and cons
Choices were precise.
Pure and joyous clarity
Gave me a simple life.
So I grew and learned to face the world
Living life that way.
And now I feel so unprepared
'Cause black and white turned gray.
My unfaltering vision failed
Focus left my eyes.
Where choices were once obvious
I can't tell wrong from right.
Because today I am a teenager
And nothing's quite so clear.
I'm seeing through an adult's eyes
A child's biggest fear.

Constance Ananta Sobsey

Starting a New Path

"But I love you, Jessie," he says as we sit on the couch in my living room, his voice quivering and unstable. His pleading eyes look directly into mine, begging my forgiveness. I don't recognize these eyes that once provided me with a sense of comfort and security. The warm blue of his eyes that used to reassure me of a love that would last forever is replaced with a colder gray. I shiver and look away.

Tears cloud my eyes as I feel him breathing next to me on the edge of the couch. My mind wanders to a time a year earlier, a happier time, when I had also been acutely aware of his breathing as we sat in silence on that same couch. My heart had pounded that day as I glanced nervously into his eyes, unable to hold my stare, yet unable to look away. It was that particular day that my heart decided to surrender itself to the magic of first love. And as I sat beside him, overwhelmed by the certainty of my love for him, I struggled to say the words out loud for the first time. I wanted to scream to the world that my heart felt bigger than my whole body, that I was in love and nothing could ever take away that feeling, but no sounds came out of my mouth. As I fidgeted with the edge of a pillow, he gently placed his hand on my arm and looked directly into my eyes. His soft stare soothed my nerves. "I love you, Jessie," he told me, his eyes holding my stare. A small smile formed on my face as my heart began to beat quickly and loudly. He had known that night, just as I had—and he had felt the power of the realization of love, just like I had.

But that power is gone now, I remind myself. That returns me from that distant memory to the present moment like a slap in the face.

"Doesn't it mean anything to you that I love you?" he asks. "Please, I'm so sorry." His hand reaches for my face to brush the hair out of my eyes. I duck my head to avoid his touch. It has become too painful since I found out. He had told me two days before that he had kissed another girl. I had sat in stunned silence, unable to move or speak.

I sit now in silence, not because I don't know what to say, but because I am afraid that my voice will deceive me and begin to quiver. As I start to speak, I look into his eyes and stop myself, wondering if I will be making a mistake. *Maybe it can work*, I think, and I imagine his arms around me, hugging my head tightly to his chest, making everything okay like he had done so often in the past when I was in need of his comfort. Now, more than ever, I ache for the comfort of his arms and for the reassurance of his warm blue gaze. But it is not possible, for the trust is gone and our love has been scarred. His gaze is no longer a warm blue and his arms no longer provide comfort.

Now I struggle to find the words that I know must come out of my mouth, not like before when I knew the words would lead us to a place of magic on the path of our relationship. I now struggle to find the words that will end that path. It's not that my love for him has been taken away, it's just that I know my heart can never again feel bigger than my whole body when I am with him. When he gets up from the couch to leave, the pain in my heart feels too strong to endure, and I have to stop myself from calling after him. I know that I have done the right thing. I know that I am strong, although at this moment I feel anything but strong.

I sit frozen on the couch for a long time after he has left; the only movement in the room is the tears that run down my cheeks and soak the thighs of my jeans. I wonder how I can possibly go on when it feels like half of me is missing. And so I wait. I wait for time to heal the pain and raise me to my feet once again—so that I can start a new path, my own path, the one that will make me whole again.

Jessie Braun

"Kenny hasn't spoken to me in six months, he won't return my calls and he goes out with all my friends. Do you think I should break up with him?"

Reprinted by permission of Randy Glasbergen.

Discovery

My class was two weeks away from the opening night of our play when Sherry walked into my classroom and in a hesitant voice announced that she would have to quit.

Hundreds of reasons for such a declaration rushed through my mind—tragic illness, death in the family, a terrible family crisis.

The expression on my face prompted a further explanation. Sherry stammered, "My boyfriend Dave wants me to quit. The rehearsals are taking too much time away from our being together. I bring him sandwiches after football practice."

Her boyfriend was a football player who later went on to play in the pros. He was the opposite of his brother Dan, who also played on the high school team. While Dan was easygoing, had a terrific sense of humor and was liked by nearly everyone, Dave seemed to always be angry and in need of someone to boss around.

"Sherry," I said, "we're only two weeks from opening. You're outstanding in your role. I'd never be able to replace you."

"Really?" She beamed.

"Really," I said, and I meant it. "Everyone should be

allowed to do the things they are good at. You're a good actress. Dave should realize that. I know you know how much he loves football."

"Yes," she agreed. "But I still have to quit."

"I'll bet you're his best fan."

She measured the words. "I am," she said.

"Has he ever been to a Saturday morning rehearsal to see how good you are?"

"No."

"He should," I told her. "He should be your number one fan."

The next day after sixth hour, my door flew open with a thud. Dave thundered toward me, looking twice as big as his 260 pounds. His arms dangled by his side, his large fists clenched as if around my neck.

He leaned across my desk, veins popping, face red as a beet. "You . . . you . . . you . . ." he stammered.

"Can I help you, Dave?" I asked, hoping that my voice wouldn't shake the way my knees were.

He never got beyond "you" before he turned and stomped out the door. I listened until the heavy footsteps started down the stairs to the first floor.

Sherry did continue with the play, and I can honestly say starred in her art. I also noticed that she smiled more, and I occasionally saw her interacting with other students with a great deal of poise.

Dave, I heard, found another girlfriend.

Eugene E. Beasley

"We've been spending too much time together.
I think it's time we start hating other people."

Reprinted by permission of Randy Glasbergen.

Hopscotch and Tears

I watched the blue Toyota speed down my street and listened to the sound of the diesel engine fade. Tears collected in my eyes and trailed down my cheeks until I could taste them. I couldn't believe what had just happened. Making my way into the house, I quickly ran up the stairs, hoping that my brother wouldn't see the frozen look of terror in my eyes. Luckily that rainy day, his eyes were glued to the TV.

Plopping down on my unmade bed, I buried my face in my pillow. Light sniffles turned into cries, and cries into hysterics. I couldn't bear it; the pain was too strong, and my heart was broken.

We had been seeing each other for three months and two days (not that I had been counting). I had never been so happy. We had brought out the best in each other. But that day he threw it all away, out the window of his rusty blue Toyota, in a speech that still rings in my ears.

"I don't think we should see each other anymore. . . ." his voice had trailed off. I wanted to ask him why, I wanted to scream at him, I wanted to hold him, but instead I whispered, "Whatever," afraid to look him in the eyes because I knew I would break down.

I lay there crying all afternoon and into the night, feeling so alone, so upset, so confused. For weeks I cried myself to sleep, but in the morning I'd put a plastic smile on my face to avoid having to talk about it. Everybody saw right through it.

My friends were concerned. I think they thought I would recover sooner than I did.

Even months after the breakup, when I heard a car drive up my street I'd jump up to the window to see if it was him. When the phone rang, a chill of hope would run down my spine. One night as I was cutting out magazine pictures and taping photos on my wall, a car came up my street, but I was too preoccupied to notice that it was the car I'd been listening for over the last two months.

"Chloe, it's me, it's . . ." It was him, calling me to come downstairs! On my way down, my heart was pounding and my thoughts were of a reconciliation. He had seen the error of his ways. When I got outside, there he stood, gorgeous as always.

"Chloe, I came to return your sweater. You left it at my house. . . . Remember?" I had forgotten all about it.

"Of course. Thank you," I lied. I hadn't seen him since the breakup and it hurt—it hurt a lot. I wanted to be able to love him again.

"Well, I guess I'll just see ya around then," he said. Then he was gone. I found myself alone in the darkness, listening to his car speed away. I slowly walked back to my room and continued to tape photos on my wall.

For weeks, I walked around like a zombie. I would stare at myself for hours in the mirror, trying to figure out what was wrong with me, trying to understand what I did wrong, searching for answers within the mirror. I'd talk to Rachel for hours. "Rachel, did you ever realize that when you fall in love, you only end up falling. . . ." I'd say before breaking down in tears. Her comforting words did little but give me a reason to feel sorry for myself.

Pretty soon my sadness turned into madness. I began to hate him and blame him for my troubles, and I believed he had ruined my life. For months I thought only of him.

Then something changed. I understood I had to go on, and every day I grew a little happier. I even began to see someone new!

One day, as I was flipping through my wallet, I came upon a picture of him. I looked at it for a few minutes, reading his face like a book, a book that I knew I had finished and had to put down. I took out the picture and stuck it in a cluttered drawer.

I smiled to myself as I realized I could do the same in my heart. Tuck him away in a special place and move on. I loved, I lost and I suffered. Now it was time to forgive and forget. I forgave myself also, because so much of my pain was feeling like I did something wrong. I know better now.

My mom used to tell me, "Chloe, there are two kinds of people in this world: those that play hopscotch and sing in the shower, and those that lie alone at night with tears in their eyes." What I came to understand is that people have a choice as to which they want to be, and that each of us is a little of both.

That same day, I went outside and played hopscotch with my sister, and that night I sang louder than ever in the shower.

Becca Woolf

Inside

Bottled up inside
Are the words I never said,
The feelings that I hide,
The lines you never read.

You can see it in my eyes,
Read it on my face:
Trapped inside are lies
Of the past I can't replace.

With memories that linger—
Won't seem to go away.
Why can't I be happier?
Today's a brand-new day.

Yesterdays are over,
Even though the hurting's not.
Nothing lasts forever,
I must cherish what I've got.

Don't take my love for granted,
For soon it will be gone—
All you ever wanted
Of the love you thought you'd won.

The hurt I'm feeling now
Won't disappear overnight,
But someway, somehow,
Everything will turn out all right,

No more wishing for the past.
It wasn't meant to be.
It didn't seem to last,
So I have to set him free.

Melissa Collette

Lost Love

Love is the extremely difficult realization that something other than oneself is real.

Iris Murdoch

I don't know why I should tell you this. I'm nothing special, nothing out of the ordinary. Nothing has happened to me my whole life that hasn't happened to nearly everybody else on this planet.

Except that I met Rachel.

We met at school. We were locker neighbors, sharing that same smell of fresh notebook paper and molding tennis shoes, with clips of our favorite musicians taped inside our locker doors.

She was beautiful and had that self-assurance that told me she must be going with somebody. Somebody who was somebody in school. Me—I'm struggling, trying to stay on the track team and make good enough grades to get into the college my folks went to when they were my age.

The day I met Rachel, she smiled and said hello. After looking into her warm brown eyes, I just had to get out and run like it was the first and last run of my life. I ran ten miles that day and hardly got winded.

We spent that fall talking and joking about teachers, parents and life in general, and what we were going to do when we graduated. We were both seniors, and it was great to feel like a "top dog" for a while. It turns out she wasn't dating anybody—which was amazing. She'd broken up with somebody on the swim team over the summer and wasn't going out at all.

I never knew you could really talk to somebody—a girl, I mean—the way I talked with her.

So one day my car—it's an old beat-up car my dad bought me because it could never go very fast—wouldn't start. It was one of those gray, chilly fall days, and it looked like rain. Rachel drove up beside me in the school parking lot in her old man's turquoise convertible and asked if she could take me somewhere.

I got in. She was playing the new David Byrne CD and singing along to it. Her voice was pretty, a lot prettier than Byrne's—but then, he's a skinny dude, nothing like Rachel. "So where do you want to go?" she asked, and her eyes had a twinkle like she knew something about me I didn't.

"To the house, I guess," I said, then got up the guts to add, "unless you want to stop by Sonic first."

She didn't answer yes or no, but drove straight to the drive-in restaurant. I got her something to eat and we sat and talked some more. She looked at me with those brown eyes that seemed to see everything I felt and thought. I felt her fingers on my lips and knew I would never feel any more for a girl than I did right then.

We talked and she told me about how she'd come to live in this town, how her dad had been a diplomat in Washington and then retired and wanted her, all of a sudden, to grow up like a small-town girl, but it was too late. She was sophisticated and poised and always seemed to know what to say. Not like me. But she opened up something in me.

She liked me, and suddenly I liked myself.

She pointed to her windshield. "Look," she said, laughing. "We steamed up the windows." In the fading light of day, I suddenly remembered home, parents and my car.

She drove me home and dropped me off with a "See you tomorrow" and a wave. That was enough. I had met the girl of my dreams.

After that day, we started seeing each other, but I wouldn't call them dates. We'd get together to study and always ended up talking and laughing over the same things.

Our first kiss? I wouldn't tell the guys this, because they would think it was funny, but she kissed me first. We were in my house, in the kitchen. Nobody was home. The only thing I could hear was the ticking of the kitchen clock. Oh, yeah, and my heart pounding in my ears like it was going to explode.

It was soft and brief; then she looked deep in my eyes and kissed me again, and this time it wasn't so soft and not so brief, either. I could smell her and touch her hair, and right then I knew I could die and be happy about it.

"See you tomorrow," she said then, and started to walk out the door. I couldn't say anything. I just looked at her and smiled.

We graduated and spent the summer swimming and hiking and fishing and picking berries and listening to her music. She had everything from R&B to hard rock, and even the classics like Vivaldi and Rachmaninoff. I felt alive like I never had before. Everything I saw and smelled and touched was new.

We were lying on a blanket in the park one day, looking up at the clouds, the radio playing old jazz. "We have to leave each other," she said. "It's almost time for us to go to college." She rolled over on her belly and looked at me.

"Will you miss me? Think of me, ever?" and for a nano-second I thought I saw some doubt, something unlike her usual self-assurance, in her eyes.

I kissed her and closed my eyes so I could sense only her, the way she smelled and tasted and felt. Her hair blew against my cheek in the late summer breeze. "You are me," I said. "How can I miss myself?"

But inside, it was like my guts were being dissected. She was right; every day that passed meant we were that much closer to being apart.

We tried to hold on then, and act like nothing was going to happen to change our world. She didn't talk about shopping for new clothes to take with her; I didn't talk about the new car my dad had bought for me because that would be what I drove away in. We kept acting like summer was going to last forever, that nothing would change us or our love. And I know she loved me.

It's nearly spring now. I'll be a college sophomore soon. Rachel never writes.

She said that we should leave it at that—whatever that meant. And her folks bought a house in Virginia, so I know she's not coming back here.

I listen to music more now, and I always look twice when I see a turquoise convertible, and I notice more things, like the color of the sky and the breeze as it blows through the trees.

She is me, and I am her. Wherever she is, she knows that. I'm breathing her breath and dreaming her dreams, and when I run now, I run an extra mile for Rachel.

Robby Smith
As told to T. J. Lacey

Why Guys Like Girls

One day while reading my e-mails, I came across one of those that you have to scroll down for an eternity just to get to the letter part because it is sent to hundreds of people.

Well, normally, I automatically delete those. But this one intrigued me. It was titled, "A Few Reasons Why Guys Like Girls." The instructions were to read it, add to it and then forward it to at least twenty-five people. If you did not forward it, you would have bad luck with relationships, but if you did send it to twenty-five people or more, you would be the lucky winner of romantic bliss.

After reading the reasons why guys like girls, I had an idea. If I could attain romantic bliss by sending this e-mail to twenty-five people, imagine how lucky I'd be if I sent it to millions. My husband and I are looking forward to marital perfection thanks to each and every one of you who reads this.*

[*References to chain letter results are not meant to be taken seriously.]

A Few Reasons Why Guys Like Girls

1. *They always smell good, even if it's just shampoo*
2. *The way their heads always find the right spot on your shoulder*
3. *The ease with which they fit into your arms*
4. *The way they kiss you and all of a sudden everything is right in the world*
5. *How cute they are when they eat*
6. *The way they take hours to dress, but in the end it's all worthwhile*
7. *Because they are always warm, even when it's minus thirty degrees outside*
8. *The way they look good no matter what they wear*
9. *The way they fish for compliments*
10. *How cute they are when they argue*
11. *The way their hands always find yours*
12. *The way they smile*
13. *The way you feel when you see their names on the caller ID after you just had a big fight*
14. *The way they say "Let's not fight anymore," even though you know an hour later . . .*
15. *The way they kiss when you do something nice for them*
16. *The way they kiss you when you say "I love you"*
17. *Actually, just the way they kiss you . . .*
18. *The way they fall into your arms when they cry*
19. *Then the way they apologize for crying over something silly*
20. *The way they hit you and expect it to hurt*
21. *Then the way they apologize when it does hurt (even though we don't admit it)*
22. *The way they say, "I miss you"*
23. *The way you miss them*
24. *The way their tears make you want to change the world so that it doesn't hurt them anymore*

Yet regardless of whether you love them, hate them, wish they would die or know that you would die without them . . . it matters not. Because once they come into your life, whatever they are to the world, they become everything to you. When you look them in the eyes, traveling to the depths of their souls, and you say a million things without a trace of a sound, you know that your own life is inevitably consumed within the rhythmic beatings of their very hearts.

We love them for a million reasons. It is a thing not of the mind but of the heart. A feeling. Only felt.

Kimberly Kirberger

"Everything about girls makes me really, really nervous. I flunked my algebra test because algebra has the word 'bra' in it!"

Reprinted by permission of Randy Glasbergen.

Love Is Never Lost

If our love is only a will to possess, it is not love.

Thich Nhat Hanh

They say it's better to have loved and lost, than never to have loved at all.

That thought wouldn't be very comforting to Mike Sanders. He had just been dumped by his girlfriend. Of course, she didn't put it quite that way. She said, "I do care about you, Mike, and I hope we can still be friends." *Great*, Mike thought. *Still be friends. You, me and your new boyfriend will go to the movies together.*

Mike and Angie had been going together since they were freshmen. But over the summer, she had met someone else. Now as he entered his senior year, Mike was alone. For three years they shared the same friends and favorite hang-outs. The thought of returning to those surroundings without Angie made him feel—well, empty.

Football practice usually helped him take his mind off his troubles. Coaches have a way of running you until you are so tired, you can't really think of anything else.

But lately, Mike's heart just wasn't in it. One day it caught up with him. He dropped passes he wouldn't normally miss and let himself get tackled by guys who had never been able to touch him before.

Mike knew better than to have the coach yell at him more than once, so he tried a little harder and made it through the rest of the practice. As he was running off the field, he was told to report to the coach's office. "Girl, family or school: Which one is bothering you, son?" asked his coach.

"Girl," Mike responded. "How did you guess?"

"Sanders, I've been coaching football since before you were born, and every time I've seen an all-star play like a J.V. rookie, it's been because of one of those three."

Mike nodded. "Sorry, sir. It won't happen again."

His coach patted him on the shoulder. "This is a big year for you, Mike. There's no reason why you shouldn't get a full ride to the school of your choice. Just remember to focus on what's really important. The other things will take care of themselves."

Mike knew his coach was right. He should just let Angie go and move on with his life. But he still felt hurt, even betrayed. "It just makes me so mad, Coach. I trusted in her. I opened myself up to her. I gave her all I had, and what did it get me?"

His coach pulled out some paper and a pen from his desk drawer. "That's a really good question. What did it get you?" He handed Mike the pen and paper and said, "I want you to think about the time you spent with this girl, and list as many experiences, good and bad, that you can remember. Then I want you to write down the things that you learned from each other. I'll be back in an hour." With that, the coach left Mike by himself.

Mike slumped in his chair as memories of Angie flooded his head. He recalled when he had first worked up the nerve to ask her out, and how happy he had been when she said yes. Had it not been for Angie's encouragement, Mike wouldn't have tried out for the football team.

Then he thought of the fights that they had. Though he couldn't remember all the reasons for fighting, he remembered the sense of accomplishment he got from working through their problems. He had learned to communicate and compromise. He remembered making up after the fights, too. That was always the best part.

Mike remembered all the times she made him feel strong and needed and special. He filled the paper with their history, holidays, trips with each other's family, school dances and quiet picnics together. Line by line, he wrote of the experience they shared, and he realized how she had helped shape his life. He would have become a different person without her.

When the coach returned, Mike was gone. He had left a note on the desk that simply read:

Coach,

Thanks for the lesson. I guess it's true what they say about having loved and lost, after all. See you at the practice.

David J. Murcott

David's Smile

David could make me deliriously happy or crazy with anger, quicker than anyone I'd ever known, and when he smiled everything else disappeared and I could not help but smile back. He had a million smiles, but there was one in particular that I could even hear in his voice across the phone from miles away. It was playful and knowing and cynical and sincere and secretive and assertive and a thousand other paradoxical things all at once. That smile made me laugh when I was hurting, forgive him when I was angry and believe him even when I knew he was lying. That smile made me fall in love with him—and that was the last thing I ever wanted to do.

When he was mad or hurting or thinking or listening, his face was stone. When he smiled, though, I felt like I was looking right into his soul, and when I made him smile, I felt beautiful inside and out.

David was the first guy I ever really loved. Sometimes when he held me and my head was resting on his broad shoulder I felt that he could hear my deepest, darkest thoughts. He always knew how to say exactly what I needed to hear. He would touch my face and look into my eyes and say he loved me with such warmth that I couldn't help believing.

From the first time we touched, he dominated my thoughts. I would try to concentrate on school, church, my family or my other friends, but it was no use. I would tell myself over and over again that he wasn't the kind of guy I needed in my life, but with each passing day, I only wanted him more. I felt so out of control, so scared and so excited. I would fall asleep at night thinking about his kisses and wake up in the morning with his soft, magical words ringing in my ears. Sometimes when I was near him I trembled. Then, he would put his arms around me and I would relax and feel safe again.

My instincts were in constant conflict. *Trust him. Don't trust him. Kiss him. Don't kiss him. Call him. Don't call him. Tell him how you feel. No, it will scare him off.* And then finally I would wonder if maybe that would be the very best thing that could happen.

If he was scared or insecure, I only saw it once or twice. Like the rest of his emotions, I could never tell how much was an act for my benefit and how much he really felt. He fascinated me. I would stare into his brown eyes and wonder if he had any idea how much control he had over me. If he knew, he never let it show.

Then, one day it all came crashing down around me. He was gone and, as I hurt, I wondered if he had ever really loved me. I had so many questions—and so much to tell him. It was like an alarm had gone off too soon and now my dream was over. He was gone, and all that was left of all we had shared were a few letters and some memories that I was too proud to dwell on. My heart cried out for him, but my mind warned me to move on. In the end, that is what I did.

I learned more from David than from any other guy, with the single exception of my father. When the time and the strength finally came, I was forced to take those lessons and move on without him. Time passed, life con-tinued and I think of him less and less. But, sometimes my mind drifts back to the sweet dream of my first love, and I am haunted by images of his smile. I loved his smile.

Cambra J. Cameron

2

ON
FRIENDSHIP

*Each friend represents a world in us, a
world possibly not born until they arrive,
and it is only by this meeting that a new
world is born.*

Anaïs Nin

The Rift

I sit perched on the edge of my bed, faint smiles drifting across my face, as I sift through all my old photographs. My sleeves pushed up over my elbows, I dig down into all the old memories. I hold each memory briefly in my hands before dropping it onto the pile in my lap and searching for the next happy moment to remember. Each picture evokes feelings long gone, but deep within me. I'm not exactly sure what has prompted this sudden trip to my past, but I feel like I need to stop, and look back.

As I continue to relive the memories, I can't help but notice one photo in particular buried deep in the box. I pluck it from the sea of snapshots and hold it in my hands. The picture at first glance is lovely. The sun was shining with not a cloud to be seen in the bright blue canopy that hung high over my head. I was sitting with my arm around a happy-looking girl, her arm rested casually on my shoulders. As I focus in on the person's face, the warm smile that covers my face is replaced by an agitated frown. It is Amy Soule, my now ex-best friend. A terrible pang of regret flashes through me, and I feel the familiar constriction in my throat.

I'm not sure exactly how, or when our decline as friends started, but it started small. A simple crack that flourished in our awkward adolescence and shameful neglect. It began with simple differences in interest. She wanted to go to the mall and scout for guys, while I wanted to spend the evening watching old movies and talking about nonsense gossip. Suddenly after-school activities took up our usual time together and weekends were spent doing other things. Soon the only time I saw her was when we exchanged a hurried hello in the busy school halls between classes. A far cry from the whispered conversations behind my half-open locker at every spare moment. No more notes were passed behind the teacher's back, and my parent's phone bill became considerably cheaper. She found a new group of friends, and so did I. Before I had a chance to patch the crack between us, she moved away from me, causing the crack to become an uncrossable rift.

I tried to make excuses for not keeping in touch. I couldn't visit, it was too far and I couldn't ask Mom to drive me all that way. I even tried to convince my nagging conscience with the notion that people change, I matured, and that is why. I knew that was not the answer, but I was too nervous to pick up the phone and call. The rift grew too large to bridge. Amy had left, and she had taken a huge chunk of my heart with her.

I stand up and stretch my cramping limbs. Pulling myself back into the now, I let the picture fall from my hand onto my cluttered desk. I glance up at my calendar and remember that Amy's birthday is around the corner. In fact, we were born in the same room, two days apart. It had always been a good-natured joke between us that she was two days older than I. We started so close, and ended up so far. This bittersweet memory causes me to smile despite my feelings of regret. I suddenly have an idea. I hastily drop to my knees and begin to rummage through my desk drawers. At last I lay my hands on an old picture frame I have had around forever. I pick up the fallen photo of Amy and me, and snap it into the frame. I quickly pen a note, and for lack of anything better to say, I simply write,

Happy Birthday Amy!
Erica

I stick the piece of white paper under the edge of the frame and search for Amy's address. I hold the frame tightly in my arms. I am not going to let this golden chance slip through my fingers. It's not much, but it is a beginning and the space between us has already gotten smaller. Maybe this time I will be strong enough to build a bridge.

Erica Thoits
Teen People *contest winner*

The Right Thing

The counselor was late for our appointment. I sat in one of the hard plastic chairs in her office that, despite a few squirming attempts to rearrange myself, continued to be uncomfortable. I glanced at the boy who sat beside me, my partner in crime. He looked upset and unsure, wounded by the decision that we had finally made out of desperation. Friends for many years, we now offered each other little comfort as we sat lost in our own thoughts and doubt.

My tingling nerves heightened my senses, and I took in everything around me. From the smell of freshly sharpened pencils to the sight of the overly organized desk, the room oozed with the aura of a disciplined junior high school counselor and I found myself again questioning our judgment in choosing this complete stranger to help save our friend.

She entered in a cloud of smiles and apologies for being late. Sitting down across from us, she looked at us expectantly. I felt as if she were waiting for us to announce that she had just won the lottery rather than tell the story of pain and frustration we had both been holding in for so long.

I was overcome for a moment by the fear that had nested in my stomach. It was hard to imagine how my best friend Suzie would react when she found out that the two people she had trusted most in the world had betrayed her. But selfishly, I was also concerned about how this betrayal would affect me. *Would she hate me? Would she even speak to me?* As much as the pain that she would feel, I contemplated whether or not I would have a best friend the next day.

"Why don't you begin, Kelly, by telling me why you're here?" the counselor suggested. I cast one more glance at my friend; his sad eyes confirmed that we were doing the right thing.

As I began to tell Suzie's story, my uncertainty gave way to a feeling of relief. Carrying the emotional burden of a friend who was slowly killing herself was a lot for a fourteen-year-old to handle, and more than I could stand any longer. Like an exhausted runner, I was passing on the baton for someone else to carry.

By way of my emotional and broken telling, Suzie's story came out. How we laughed at her strange habit of breaking all her food into tiny little pieces, not realizing that by splitting her food up, she could take more time to eat less. How we went along with her self-deprecating jokes about how overweight she was, without realizing that deep inside, she wasn't joking.

The guilt rose in my throat as I related fact after fact, knowing now that all these things should have made us aware months earlier that Suzie actually had a very serious problem. We had pushed it away as she had deteriorated a little at a time. It wasn't until it was almost too late that we had finally understood the big picture.

I explained that the depression that typically walked hand-in-hand with anorexia had closed in on Suzie a few weeks earlier. I had sat by her side, avoiding the sight of her dark-circled eyes and gaunt cheekbones as she told me that she now ate practically nothing at all, and that for no explainable reason, she would often cry for hours.

It was then that I too began to cry. I couldn't stop my tears as I explained how I hadn't known how to stop my friend's tears, either. She had reached a point that terrified me, and the terror in my voice was plain as I revealed the last thing I knew, the thing that had cemented my determination to tell someone: She was looking for an escape from the pain, sadness and feelings of inadequacy that were now constant for her. She thought that killing herself might be that way out.

My part completed, I sat back in disbelief. I had just poured out secret after secret that I had been told with the understanding that I would never speak them again. I had shattered the most sacred aspect of our friendship: trust. A trust that had taken time, love, and good and bad experiences to build had just been destroyed in ten minutes, broken out of helplessness, desperation and the burden that I could no longer bear. I felt weak. I hated myself at that moment.

So did Suzie.

She needed no explanation when she was called to the office. She looked at me, at her boyfriend sitting at my side, at the concerned look of the counselor. The tears of fury that welled up in her eyes said that she understood. As she began to cry out of anger and relief, the counselor gently sent Aaron and me back to class, shutting the door behind us.

I didn't go back to class right away, but instead walked the hallways of the school trying to make sense of the emotional ramblings going through my head. Though I had just possibly saved my friend's life, I felt less than heroic.

I still can recall the overwhelming sadness and fear that

surrounded me, as I was sure that my actions had just cost me one of the best friends I'd ever had. But an hour later, Suzie returned from the counseling office, and with tears in her eyes, headed straight into my arms for a hug that I, perhaps even more than she, needed.

It was then that I realized that no matter how angry she was at me, she would still need her best friend to help her get through what was going to be a very difficult journey. I had just learned one of my first lessons of growing up and being a true friend—that it can be hard, and even terrifying, to do what you know is the right thing.

A year later, Suzie handed me my copy of her school picture. In it, she had color in her cheeks again, and the smile that I had missed for so long spread across her face. And on the back, this message:

> *Kel,*
>
> *You were always there for me, whether I wanted you to be or not. Thank you. There's no getting rid of me now—you're stuck with me!*
>
> *I love you,*
> *Suzie*

Kelly Garnett

Donna and Claudia

Donna is my sister, and I always thought of her as beautiful. Our father called her his princess. When Donna entered high school, with her long blond hair and incredible blue eyes, she caught the attention of the boys. There were the usual crushes and school dances, phone calls and giggles, and hours of combing and brushing her hair to make it glow. She had eye shadow to match the perfect blue of her eyes. Our parents were protective of us, and my father in particular kept close watch over the boys she dated.

One Saturday in April, three weeks before Donna's sixteenth birthday, a boy called and asked her to go to an amusement park. It was in the next state, about twenty miles away. They would be going with four other friends. Our parents' first answer was a firm no, but Donna eventually wore them down. On her way out the door, they told her to be home by eleven, no later.

It was a great night! The roller coasters were fast, the games were fun and the food was good. Time flew by. Finally one of them realized it was already 10:45 P.M. Being young and slightly afraid of our father, the boy who was driving decided he could make it home in fifteen minutes. It never occurred to any of them to call and ask if they could be late.

Speeding down the highway, the driver noticed the exit too late. He tried to make it anyway. The car ripped out nine metal guardrails and flipped over three times before it came to a stop on its roof. Someone pulled Donna from the car, and she crawled over to check on her friends. There was blood everywhere. As she pulled her hair back from her eyes so she could see better, her hand slipped underneath her scalp.

The blood was coming from her. Practically the entire top of Donna's head had been cut off, held on by just a few inches of scalp.

When the police cruiser arrived to rush Donna to a nearby hospital, an officer sat with her, holding her scalp in place. Donna asked him if she was going to die. He told her he didn't know.

At home, I was watching television when a creepy feeling went through me, and I thought about Donna. A few minutes went by, and the telephone rang. Mom answered it. She made a groaning noise and fell to the floor, calling for my father. They rushed out the door, telling my sister Teri and me that Donna had been in a car accident, and that they had to go to the hospital to get her. Teri and I stayed up for hours waiting for them. We changed the sheets on Donna's bed and waited. Somewhere around four o'clock in the morning, we pulled the sofa bed out and fell asleep together.

Mom and Dad were not prepared for what they saw at the hospital. The doctors had to wait until our parents arrived to stitch up Donna's head. They didn't expect her to survive the night.

At 7:00 A.M., my parents returned home. Teri was still sleeping. Mom went straight to her bedroom and Dad went into the kitchen and sat at the table. He had a white plastic garbage bag between his legs and was opening it up when I sat down at the table with him. I asked him how Donna was and he told me that the doctors didn't think she was going to make it. As I struggled to think about that, he started pulling her clothes out of the bag. They were soaked with blood and blond hair.

Some of the hair had Donna's scalp attached to it. Every piece of clothing she had worn that night was soaked with blood. I can't remember thinking anything. All I did was stare at the clothes. When Teri woke up, I showed them to her. I'm sure it was an awful thing to do, but I was in such shock that it was all I could think of.

At the hospital later that morning, Teri and I had to wait outside for a long time before we could see Donna. It was an old hospital and it smelled old, and Teri and I were afraid of it. Finally we were allowed in to see our sister. Her head was wrapped in white gauze that was stained with blood. Her face was swollen, which I couldn't understand because she had lost so much blood. I thought she would look smaller. She reached up and touched my long brown hair and started to cry.

The next day, I called a neighbor who was a hairdresser and asked her to cut my hair. It's a funny thing—I loved my long brown hair and it curled just right, but I never, ever missed it or wanted it back. All I wanted was for Donna to come home and sleep in the clean sheets that Teri and I had put on her bed.

Donna was in the hospital for two weeks. Many of her friends went to see her, especially Claudia, who was there a lot. Mom and Dad never liked Claudia—maybe because she seemed "fast," maybe because she spoke her mind; I don't really know. They just didn't like her being around.

Donna came home with the entire top half of her head shaved. She had hundreds of stitches, some of which came across her forehead and between her left eye and eyebrow. For a while she wore a gauze cap. Eventually she had our hairdresser neighbor cut the rest of her hair. It had been so soaked and matted with blood that she couldn't get it out. The hairdresser was such a kind person. She found Donna a human hair wig that perfectly matched her hair.

Donna celebrated her sixteenth birthday and went back to school. I don't know where rotten people come from, and I don't know why they exist, but they do. There was a very loud-mouthed, self-centered girl in some of Donna's classes who took great pleasure in tormenting my sister. She would sit behind her and pull slightly on Donna's wig. She'd say very quietly, "Hey, Wiggy, let's see your scars." Then she'd laugh.

Donna never said anything to anybody about her tormentor until the day she finally told Claudia. Claudia was in most of Donna's classes, and from then on kept a close eye on my sister. Whenever that girl got close to Donna, Claudia would try and be there. There was something about Claudia that was intimidating, even to the worst kids in school. No one messed with her. Unfortunately, though, Claudia wasn't always around, and the teasing and name-calling continued.

One Friday night, Claudia called and asked Donna to come spend the night at her house. My parents didn't want Donna to go—not just because they didn't like Claudia, but because they had become so protective of Donna. In the end, they knew they had to let her go, even though they probably spent the whole night worrying.

Claudia had something special waiting for my sister. She knew how awful Donna felt about her hair, so Claudia had shaved off her own beautiful long brown hair. The next day, she took Donna wig shopping for identical blond and brown wigs. When they went to school that Monday, Claudia was ready for the teasers. In a vocabulary not allowed inside school walls, she set them straight so that anyone ready to tease my sister knew they would have to mess with Claudia. It didn't take long for the message to get through.

Donna and Claudia wore their wigs for over a year, until they felt their hair had grown out enough to take them off. Only when Donna was ready did they go to school without them. By then, she had developed a stronger self-confidence and acceptance.

My sister graduated from high school. She is married and has two great kids. Twenty-eight years later, she is still friends with Claudia.

Carol Gallivan

A Friend for Life

I have had the privilege through my career to meet many amazing people, people who have been my idols, my crushes and my inspirations. But the greatest honor came last fall when I had the chance to meet a fourteen-year-old girl named Nicole.

I had been contacted by the Children's Wish Foundation of Canada, an organization that tries to make the dreams of young people suffering from potentially terminal illnesses come true. Nicole had been battling cancer for over two years, and her request to the Foundation had been a simple one: She asked if she could meet me. The foundation granted her wish by flying her here to Los Angeles, and arranging for us to spend the day at Universal Studios.

It was impossible not to like Nicole from the very first moment I met her. Her outgoing personality and incredible energy swept me up and immediately boosted my energy level. Her up-front attitude about dealing with her disease amazed me. When I mentioned during our initial meeting that I was very sorry that she should have to go through something so difficult, she thanked me, but replied that she did not want me to feel bad—she wasn't looking for anyone to feel sorry for her. A strength I had never known before shone in her eyes.

As our day went on, I realized how true it was. She didn't want sympathy, she just wanted to hang out and do things that friends do together. We ate junk food and gossiped about guys. The more we giggled over silly things, the more our newfound friendship grew, and I began to realize that I was just as lucky as she was to have this opportunity because I had made this incredible friend—a friend who was a brave, courageous and extraordinary person. I knew that my time with Nicole would affect me forever.

I will never forget the day I spent with Nicole at Universal Studios. We continued to be good friends after Nicole returned home to Canada, and spoke frequently on the phone. About two months ago, I received word from Nicole's father that she had passed away.

The devastation and sadness I feel about Nicole's death are soothed by my strong belief that Nicole is now my Guardian Angel. I know that no matter where she is, or where I go, she will be with me in spirit. And when I think about that first day we met, I can't help but see the irony in it. What began as one person's wish being fulfilled ended as an experience shared and loved by two people that words can never fully describe. Nicole will always remain in my life, as my inspiration, and as my friend.

Jennifer Love Hewitt

Speechless

True friendship multiplies the good in life and divides its evils. Strive to have friends, for life without friends is like life on a desert island. . . . to find one real friend in a lifetime is good fortune; to keep him is a blessing.

Baltasar Gracian

I glance in my cousin Hope's direction as we sit on the hill. We sit outside on the same exact spot every day; it's become our tradition. She eats her turkey on white while I nibble at a Sun Chip. It's her senior year and all I can think is, *Who am I going to find to sit out on the hill with me next year?* I like it this way, not having to say anything. She hands me half her sandwich, knowing I'll want it.

"Did you call your mom yet?" she asks, cutting through the silence. "Do they know what it is?" She bites her lip, not looking at me. I don't know what to say. Her mom had just gone into the hospital where my mom is an R.N. My mom hears everything. The second the doctors know it, so does she, and in this case, so did I. *Do I tell her the truth? Yes, they said that your mom has a malignant tumor. They said she's dying*. It echoes in my mind; my mouth feels numb.

"Well," I find the courage to say, "they did find something It's a tumor on her ovaries. They think it's . . . malignant."

"Oh," she mumbles, wiping the backs of her legs as she stands waiting for the bell. She pulls me to my feet and acts like what I've just said doesn't bother her. But she can't hide it. We both can feel it there like a shadow looming between us.

"I called her before third hour," I offer. She glances around me, waiting for the bell. I can see her hand moving toward the lighter in her pocket.

"Ovarian cancer, huh?" she says, looking at me. "That might not be too bad." She stares me straight in the eyes, waiting for my reassurance. But we both know what "ovarian cancer" means: It means death. We know the facts—that most women die as it spreads to vital organs. And yet she stands there, waiting for me to answer her, to tell her that it's not so bad.

"I don't know. Just because it can spread, doesn't mean it will. She's strong; she'll make it through this." I can't look at her. The bell rings, sending us into a crowd of people, pulling in all directions.

* * * *

We head toward Chicago and the hospital. Her mom went into surgery today to remove the tumor. They're going to tell us how bad it is.

The car feels heavy. An invisible barrier pushes against our chests. No one says anything while the radio plays stupid, happy songs. "YMCA" comes on the oldies station and she savagely pushes the preset buttons on the radio. "Why can't they play anything good?" she mutters, as she leaves it on the jazz station. The car is still weighted as we pull into the parking lot.

Aunt Catherine's room is nice, not drab like other

hospitals. The walls are a soft shade of light green, with cheerful wallpaper borders. The window reveals a full view of the parking lot and spring sky. My mother and her father stand at either sides of the bed, looking down at Aunt Catherine. My uncle holds one of her hands as she sleeps, his thumb moving in tiny circles along her smooth skin. They look up as we come in. My mother puts a finger to her lips, motioning for us to be quiet. Catherine opens her eyes and says Hope's name in greeting. Her voice sounds hoarse and deep. I look over at her new I.V. machine and read the label. Morphine.

Moments later the doctor comes in and my mom and I go to down to the cafeteria. After getting our dinner, we find a clean white table off in the corner.

"It's horrible," she says, looking at me. "They opened her up to see how much cancer there was and remove it. It was everywhere. Everywhere," she reiterates, as she loses most of her composure. Her clinical poker face is gone, and her eyes are filled with something I haven't seen before: uncertainty and anguish. "It spread so fast," she half whispers, "they had to remove everything. Her ovaries, womb, fallopian tubes, everything. The cancer is well beyond the second stage. They couldn't get it all out. Even with chemo, they can't. . . ." Her voice fades as she looks over at me, knowing that she's probably said too much. Her eyes tear and she dabs at them with a napkin. I am dazed. *Why did you have to tell me?* I wonder.

The room is dark when we come back and the air is thick, hanging around us like a fog. "Let's go," Hope says, taking my arm and handing me my jacket. Her keys jiggle as she slips the key ring around her finger.

My mom looks at her with concern. "Why don't you go down to the cafeteria and get something to eat? Here." She hands her a twenty.

"I'm not hungry," Hope mumbles, pushing past me

through the door and pressing the twenty into my palm.

"Shawna, I think I'm going to stay here tonight. Why don't you stay over at Hope's? Get her to eat something, will you?"

"Sure, Mom. See you tomorrow," I reply, kissing her on the cheek.

She drives mechanically, her eyes glued to the road. Silence hangs in the air. I flip the radio to the local rock station and put the volume on low. I see a McDonald's along the road. "Hey, why don't we get something to eat? You haven't had anything yet. You know, you just can't starve yourself. You need to eat."

"What is your problem?" she says, her voice with an edge. "Why don't you just stop worrying about me and mind your own business? I'm fine, okay? I knew what to expect and I'm fine. Why can't you people just quit worrying and nagging all the time?!"

"Look, Hope, I was just trying to get you to . . ." She reaches out and turns the radio up.

"It's my favorite song," she yells over the music. She hates Prodigy.

* * * *

Her hands don't seem to be working as she tries to slip the key into the door. I gently take them away from her and jiggle the lock. The door swings open. She goes to the bathroom while I fix her a turkey sandwich and orange slices in the kitchen. I hear the TV go on in the living room. She flips it to Comedy Central as I walk in.

"Here," I say, pushing the plate across the coffee table toward her. She takes a bite and looks at me with her are-you-happy-now? look. I can't help but smile.

The comic on TV is horrible and tells one bad joke after another. She laughs a little too hard at them. But by the time the second comic comes on, Hope is dozing.

"C'mon," I say, pulling her to her feet. "Let's go to bed.

I'm tired, too." She hands me some pajamas and I take my spare toothbrush out of its little holder in the medicine cabinet. She beats me to the bathroom and by the time I'm done, she's already curled up under the covers. I roll out my sleeping bag on the floor underneath her. If I look up I can see her sleeping and the clock on the opposite dresser. I steal a pillow and try to sleep. I check the clock and see that Hope isn't sleeping. She's staring straight ahead, her eyes wide open.

"Hope?" I say, trying to get comfortable.

"What?"

"Good night."

"Night, Shawna, you moron," she says. "Now go to sleep and quit waking me up." She closes her eyes. Within a few minutes, she gets out of bed. Another bad joke is heard coming from the living room.

* * * *

I buy Hope a turkey sandwich and a bag of chips for myself and start down the hill. She's waiting in our spot. I hand her the sandwich and sit down. The events of the last twenty-four hours play over in my mind. Aunt Catherine started chemotherapy a week after surgery. Yesterday afternoon she was readmitted as she went into remission. She was doing fine, except for the nausea that comes with chemo. She had even amassed a collection of wigs and could go from brunette to blonde in minutes.

My mom told me this morning that the cancer missed the kidney but was growing now on her liver. Doctors can take out a kidney, but livers they can do nothing about. It took us all by surprise. I was still in aftershock. Hope tried her best to act like she knew it would happen and that it didn't bother her. But I could tell how much pain she was feeling by the way her eyes glazed and the fact that she couldn't remember her locker combination or count her money while we waited in line for the sandwich.

And yet she sits there, taking slow bites of her sandwich while I crunch away at my Sun Chips. The sun is brighter now, as the school year winds down. The beams seem to play with the shadows on her curved cheeks and catch, ever so slightly, on those chocolate pupils. She stares off into space, trying to look cold, but I can see that she is fighting back her fears. All I think is how it shouldn't have to be this way, no one saying anything. I find myself wishing that I could tell her how I feel, that I love her. Instead I move closer to her and sit right next to her. She doesn't even glance in my direction.

"Hope?" I say looking at her.

"What?"

"I just . . . look, Hope, it's . . ." I look into her eyes and watch as a tear runs down her cheek.

"So do you think she'll be all right?" she asks, cutting me off, her eyes pleading for reassurance. I can't think of a thing to say, and this time I don't have to. I hold her in my arms as she begins to sob, and Hope finally lets go.

Shawna Singh

I Need You Now

My friend, I need you now—
Please take me by the hand.
Stand by me in my hour of need,
Take time to understand.

Take my hand, dear friend,
And lead me from this place.
Chase away my doubts and fears,
Wipe the tears from off my face.

Friend, I cannot stand alone.
I need your hand to hold,
The warmth of your gentle touch
In my world that's grown so cold.

Please be a friend to me
And hold me day by day.
Because with your loving hand in mine,
I know we'll find the way.

Becky Tucker

Choices

Hold a friend's hand through times of trial,
Let her find love through a hug and a smile;
But also know when it is time to let go—
For each and every one of us must learn to grow.

Sharon A. Heilbrunn

When I first met Molly, she instantly became my best friend. We enjoyed the same things, laughed at the same jokes and even had the same love for sunflowers.

It seemed like we had found each other at the right time. Both of us had been in different groups of friends that didn't get along or we didn't feel comfortable in. We were thrilled to find each other.

Our friendship grew very strong. Our families became friends, and everyone knew that wherever you found Molly, you found me, and vice versa. In fifth grade, we were not in the same class, but at lunch we both sat in nearby assigned seats and turned around to talk to each other. The lunch ladies did not like this. We were always blocking the aisle, talking too loudly and not eating our lunches, but we didn't care. The teachers

knew we were best friends, but we were also a distur-
bance. Our big mouths got us into trouble, and we were
warned that we would never be in the same classes
again if we kept this up.

That summer, Molly and her brother were at my house
quite often. My mom took care of them while their mom
worked. We went swimming, played outside and practiced playing our flutes. We bought best-friend charms
and made sure to wear them as often as possible.

Summer went by very quickly, and middle school
began. As the teachers had warned us, we were not in the
same classes. We still talked on the phone, went over to
each other's houses, sang in choir and practiced our flutes
together in band. Nothing could destroy this friendship.

Seventh grade started and, again, we were not in the
same classes and could not sit near each other at lunch. It
seemed as if we were being put to a test. We both made
new friends. Molly started to hang out with a new group
of people and was growing very popular.

We spent less time together, and we rarely talked on the
phone. At school, I would try to talk to her, but she would
just ignore me. When we did take a minute to talk, one of
her more popular friends would come up and Molly would
just walk away with her, leaving me in the dust. It hurt.

I was so confused. I'm sure she didn't know at the
time how badly I felt, but how could I talk to her if she
wouldn't listen? I began to hang around with my new
friends, but it just wasn't the same. I met Erin, who was
also a friend of Molly's. She was in the same situation I was
with Molly. She and Molly had been close friends, and
lately Molly had been treating Erin the same way as me.
We decided to talk to her.

The phone call was not easy. Talking and saying how I
felt was difficult. I was so afraid that I would hurt her feelings and make her angry. It was funny, though—when it

was just the two of us talking on the phone, we were friends again. It was the old Molly.

I explained how I was feeling, and she did, too. I realized I was not the only one hurting. She was alone without me to talk to. What was she supposed to do, not make new friends? I didn't think about this before, but she was feeling left out by me and my new friends. There were times when I didn't even notice I was ignoring her. We must have talked for a long time, because once we were finished I had used a handful of tissues for my tears, and felt as if I had lifted a heavy weight off my heart. We both decided that we wanted to be with our new friends, but we would never forget the fun and friendship we had shared with each other.

Today, I look back on all of this and smile. Molly and I are finally in the same classes, and you know what? We still get in trouble for talking too loudly. Molly is not my best friend anymore, but more like my sister. We still enjoy the same things, laugh at the same jokes and share the same love for sunflowers. I will never forget her. Molly taught me something very important. She taught me that things change, people change, and it doesn't mean you forget the past or try to cover it up. It simply means that you move on, and treasure all the memories.

Alicia M. Boxler

"You're my friend, Katie, but we just don't
fight enough to be *best* friends."

Friends Forever

It seemed as if Chrissy and I had been friends forever. Ever since we'd met on the first day of fourth grade, we had been inseparable. We did almost everything together. We were so close that when it came time to pick partners, it was just assumed that we'd pick each other.

In ninth grade, however, things changed. We had been in the same classes for the last five years, but now we were going to different schools. At first we were as good friends as ever, but eventually we found we had no time for each other. Slowly but surely, we were drifting apart. Promises were broken and important get-togethers postponed. I think both of us knew we were breaking apart, but neither of us wanted to admit it.

Then one day, I finally faced the fact that Chrissy and I weren't close anymore. We'd both grown up, and didn't have much in common any longer. I still missed her, though. We had shared five incredible years together—years I will never forget. Years I don't *want* to forget.

One day, as I was thinking of our great times together, I wrote a poem about our friendship. It was about letting go and growing up, but never forgetting friends.

I still talk to Chrissy sometimes, though now it's hard because we both have such busy schedules.

To this day, I still think of Chrissy as one of my best friends . . . even though by some definitions we aren't. But when I'm asked to list my friends, I never hesitate to add her name. Because as she would always say: "Real friends are forever." When I gave her this poem we both cried, for it's changes like these that make growing up so difficult.

Changes

"Friends forever," you promised.
"Together till the end."
We did everything with each other.
You were my best friend.

When I was sad, you were by my side.
When I was scared, you felt my fear.
You were my best support—
If I needed you, you were there.

You were the greatest friend,
You always knew what to say:
You made everything seem better.
As long as we had each other,
Everything would be okay.

But somewhere along the line,
We slowly came apart.
I was here, you were there,
It tore a hole in my heart.

Things were changing,
Our cheerful music reversed its tune.
It was like having salt without pepper,
A sun without its moon.

Suddenly we were miles apart,
Two different people, with nothing the same.
It was as if we hadn't been friends;
Although we knew deep in our hearts
Neither one of us was to blame.

You had made many new friends
And luckily, so had I
But that didn't change the hurt—
The loss of our friendship made me cry.

As we grow older, things must change
But they don't always have to end.
Even though it is different, now,
You will always be my friend.

Phyllis Lin

I Remember Gilbert

It's been seven months since I last saw the light in Gil's room. Mrs. Blithe waved at me from his bedroom window next door. I smiled, but inside I was numb.

I will never forget the first day I met Gil and his mom. I was seven, and Mom and Dad were taking me to our new house in the suburbs. My mother's employer transferred her, so we'd had to move and leave everything behind.

I missed my room and my best friends back home. I could not believe how my parents were torturing me. The idea of going to a new school was frightening. I didn't have any friends to talk to, and I did not want to make new friends either.

My grandparents were at the new two-story house to welcome us, and I noticed a lady hugging my mother. It turned out that Mrs. Blithe was Mom's best friend from high school and our new next-door neighbor.

Mom took me to my room upstairs, and I let myself fall onto the bed. I must have fallen asleep because the next thing I knew, it was getting dark. The huge window in my room was open, and I could hear loud music coming from outside. I looked out the window, and across from me was another window. A boy in dark clothes was looking through his telescope and into the glittering night sky. Right away, I noticed the white Christmas lights on his ceiling.

"Hi, I'm Gilbert Jim Jonathan Blithe. Call me Gil." He startled me.

"I'm Katharine Kennedy—Katie for short," I shouted back.

It was our beautiful beginning. I realized then and there that I liked this weird neighbor of mine. Gil was like a brother to me. We spent countless hours just talking and telling stories to each other. My dad put a fire escape ladder on my window. After that, Gil used it as an entrance to my room. Funny, he never used the front door. And he had lights on his ceiling because the stars and planets fascinated him.

When school started, we biked there together. He kept me safe and held me back from hurting myself. Sometimes, *I* had to keep *him* out of trouble. Afterwards, we would go to the park and play on the monkey bars. Most of the time my family's backyard was our playground, and the big acacia tree, which had boards nailed to its trunk, held our tree house. It was home, and nobody was allowed in there except us.

Summers passed and I turned thirteen. Gil gave me April blossoms. Then Mrs. Blithe told Mom and me that Gil was sick and needed a heart transplant. When I heard that, I was so distressed, I felt I needed one, too.

The hospital was gloomy. A white-walled prison that had disgusting food. Every day, Gil had to eat mushy-looking meals. I promised him I'd bring chocolate-covered peanuts the next day, and I knew I made him happier.

Whenever Gil sensed I was anxious or about to cry, he would tell me to look out my bedroom window. "Let the light in my room tell you I'm always there," he said softly.

He always found a way to make me smile.

After a month in the hospital, Gil came home. It was the first time I had ever been in his room, and it felt peculiar. It was unexpectedly neat. After jumping onto his bed and throwing me a pillow, he said he missed his room. I said I missed him more. It troubled me that things might never be the same, but Gil was up and about after a couple of weeks. I knew he was all right when he climbed up to my room and ate pizza with me.

Before we knew it, Gil and I were in high school. School and girls kept him occupied, but he was always there. Despite our jobs, we spent sunny summers together. As usual, the days hanging out with him passed quickly. But then he got sick again.

During the first semester of our senior year, Gil was taken to the hospital for the second time. At first I thought it was a false alarm, but it was worse than I could imagine. All I could do was hope and pray that he would get better. The unlit room across from mine was the constant reminder of his being away. I visited him in the hospital as often as I could, even though I never knew what to say. To tell him that everything would be all right was a fallacy, yet it comforted us both.

Christmas was spent in a cold hospital room. He was determined that we would go to our graduation together. I assured him we would. I held his hand and looked into his eyes until they stopped looking into mine. No words were uttered; we both knew what we were feeling. He looked peaceful when he said his last good-bye.

I locked his face at that moment in my thoughts, but it wounded my soul. He went away even though I tried my best to keep time from slipping.

How could a friend, someone who was with me and kept me happy, be the one person who would leave me now, forever? There was no one now to console me.

Now, as I stood looking at his bedroom window and the stars and planets on his ceiling, I knew he would always be there—in my room, in my heart and in my memories. I wiped away the tears on my cheek, and I saw a little boy waving at me. Until this day, I cannot figure why I could not say "I love you" to Gil, even at the last second. Maybe because I knew he felt the same way.

I'm leaving for college soon, and I am sad he won't be there to laugh at my jokes or comfort me when I'm blue. But because of a little boy looking through a telescope into the infinite night sky, I now know that friendship goes beyond time. I will always remember Gilbert, and the light of his love tells me he's always there.

April Joy Gazmen

The Tragic Reunion

I almost dropped the phone when I heard the words. "Julia's father died today." After I hung up, I walked to my room in a daze and fumbled with my CD player, hoping that the sound of my favorite songs would provide some comfort.

Although I had known this day was coming, I still felt as if the wind had been knocked out of me. As I sat on my bed, the tears came. My mother came quietly into the room and held me in a gentle embrace.

As I sat cradled in my mother's arms, I thought about last summer. I had gone with Julia and her parents on a trip to an island off the coast of South Carolina. We'd had a great time together, sharing breathtaking sunsets on the beach, eating at posh restaurants and biking along the rugged coastline. Julia's dad had taken it upon himself to fulfill our every desire.

Now I knew that beneath all the laughter and fun, Mr. Yolanda must have been suffering. One night, as Julia and I were getting ready to go out, Mrs. Yolanda came into our room looking upset. She told us that Mr. Yolanda was sick and was not up to coming with us. Julia didn't seem alarmed, and we went out as we had planned without her father.

The next day Mr. Yolanda appeared to be his usual self: soft-spoken, generous and on the go. Since his illness was not mentioned again, I didn't think about it any more for the rest of that wonderful trip.

When school started, my friendship with Julia began to change. I watched as she became caught up in making new friends. She didn't include me in her new plans, and I felt left in the dust. Pretty soon, we were no longer best friends. In fact, we were barely friends at all.

One day, my mother sat me down and told me that Mr. Yolanda had terminal pancreatic cancer. Shocked, my thoughts turned to Julia. At school she seemed a happy-go-lucky teen. Her sunny exterior displayed no sign of any turmoil, but now I knew it had to be present somewhere within her. Not wanting to upset Julia in school, and still feeling separate from her, I didn't say anything to her about her father. But inside, I wanted to run up to her in the hallway, give her a hug, and let her know that I was there and that I cared.

Now I wondered, as I walked nervously into the funeral home, if it was too late. Wakes make me uncomfortable, probably because they make death so real. And the thought of seeing Julia in this setting, knowing what a very private person she was, also made me uneasy. As my friends and I got in line to pay our respects to Mr. Yolanda, I noticed pictures of the Yolandas surrounding the casket. One photograph in particular jumped out at me. It was of Mr. Yolanda and Julia on our vacation in South Carolina.

The photograph triggered an overwhelming sadness in me, and I began to weep. I simply could not understand why God would take a parent away from his child. Julia found me then and seeing me in tears, she too began to cry.

Even though I told her how sorry I was about her father, I realized I could never fully understand what she was going through. What was it like to come home every day to a house where someone you loved was dying, or to head off to school each morning not knowing if your father would be alive when you got home? I couldn't imagine. But I did know how to express support and compassion. It wasn't too late.

Julia apologized for her neglect of our friendship, and we vowed to be friends again. A funeral is a strange place to make up with a friend, but I guess a tragic reunion is better than none at all.

Amy Muscato
Submitted by Olive O'Sullivan

3

ON LOVE AND KINDNESS

One kind word can warm three winter months.

Japanese Proverb

Bobby, I'm Smiling

Little deeds of kindness, little words of love, help to make Earth happy.

Julia Carney

When I was ten years old, my grade school closed, and I was transferred to a school in a nearby town. In each classroom, the teachers would seat my classmates and me alphabetically, thus seating me beside the same boy, time and time again. His name was Bobby, and he was as out-going as I was shy. I didn't make friends easily, but Bobby managed to reach beyond my shyness, and eventually, we became friends.

As the years passed, Bobby and I shared all the normal school experiences—first loves, double dating, Friday night football games, parties and dances. He was my friend. My confidant. My devil's advocate. It didn't matter that we were so different—he the popular, handsome, self-assured football star who had a beautiful girlfriend; me the overweight, inhibited and insecure teenage girl. We were friends, regardless.

One morning during the spring of our senior year, I

opened my locker and, to my surprise, there was a beautiful flower. I looked around to see who might have left it for me, but no one stood by waiting to take credit.

I knew that Gerry, a guy in my history class, had a crush on me. *Had he left it?* As I stood wondering, my friend Tami walked by.

"Nice flower," she said.

"Yes, it is. It was left in my locker without a note, but I think I know who gave it to me," I said. "I'm just not interested in dating him, but how do I tell him without hurting his feelings?"

Tami said, "Well, if you're not interested in going out with him, tell him *I* will. He's awesome!"

"But Tami," I said, "you know that Gerry and I aren't anything alike. It would never work out."

At that, Tami laughed and said, "Gerry didn't give you that flower. Bobby did."

"Bobby? Bobby Matthews?"

Then Tami explained.

Earlier that morning, she had passed Bobby in the school's parking lot. Noticing the flower and unable to resist, she had asked him who it was for. His only reply had been that it was for someone special and meant to brighten their day.

I was touched by Tami's story but was certain that the flower had been intended to be given anonymously.

Later that morning, I carried the flower to class and set it on my desk. Bobby noticed it and said nonchalantly, "Nice flower."

I smiled and said, "Yes, it's beautiful."

Minutes later, while we stood to recite the Pledge of Allegiance, I leaned over to Bobby and whispered "Thank you," then proceeded to finish the pledge.

As we were retaking our seats, Bobby said, "For what?"

I smiled. "The flower."

At first, Bobby feigned ignorance, but then he realized I had discovered his secret. "But how did you know?"

I simply smiled and asked why he had given it to me.

He hesitated only briefly before answering. "I gave it to you, because I wanted you to know you're special."

In retrospect, as I look back over seventeen years of friendship, I don't believe that I ever loved Bobby more than I did at that moment. The flower itself paled in comparison with his unexpected and purely giving act of kindness. That kindness meant the world to me then—and still does.

As Bobby had hoped, I did feel special—not only on that day, but for many days to follow. To paraphrase Mark Twain, a person can live a month off a compliment. It's true. I've done it.

When my lovely flower finally wilted and died, I pressed it in a book.

In the years that followed, Bobby and I remained good friends, and although our lives took different paths, we kept in touch.

When Bobby was twenty-five, he was diagnosed with terminal cancer. Shortly before his twenty-seventh birthday, he died.

Since then, I've lost track of the times I have recalled that spring day so long ago. I still treasure my pretty pressed flower, and when I hear the old cliché, "Remember with a smile," I'm certain that it was coined by someone who understood the meaning of a friend's love, and the lasting impression of a kind gesture.

Bobby, I'm smiling.

E. Keenan

An A for Mrs. B

I was sitting next to Missy in my ninth-grade world history class when Mrs. Bartlett announced a new project. In groups, we were to create a newspaper around the culture we were studying.

On a piece of paper, we wrote the names of three friends we wanted in our group. After collecting all the requests, Mrs. B. informed us that she would take into consideration the names we chose and would let us know the results the next day. I had no doubt I would get the group of my choice. There were only a handful of sociably decent people in the class, and Missy was one of them. I knew we had chosen each other.

The next day, I anxiously awaited the class. After the bell rang, Missy and I stopped talking as Mrs. B called for our attention. She started to call out names. When she reached group three, Missy's name was called. *So I'm in group three*, I thought. The second, third and fourth members of the group were called. My name was not included. There had to be some mistake!

Then I heard it. The last group: "Mauro, Juliette, Rachel, Karina." I could feel the tears well in my eyes. How could

I face being in that group—the boy who barely spoke English, the one girl who was always covered by skirts that went down to her ankles, and the other girl who wore weird clothes. Oh, how badly I wanted to be with my friends.

I fought back tears as I walked up to Mrs. B. She looked at me and knew what I was there for. I was determined to convince her I should be in the "good" group. "Why. . . ?" I started.

She gently placed a hand on my shoulder. "I know what you want, Karina," she said, "but your group needs you. I need you to help them get a passing grade on this assignment. Only you can help them."

I was stunned. I was humbled. I was amazed. She had seen something in me I hadn't seen.

"Will you help them?" she asked.

I stood straighter. "Yes," I replied. I couldn't believe it came out of my mouth, but it did. I had committed.

As I bravely walked to where the others in my group sat, I could hear the laughter from my friends. I sat down and we started. Different newspaper columns were assigned according to interests. We did research. Halfway through the week, I felt myself enjoying the company of these three misfits. There was no need for pretending—I grew sincerely interested in learning something about them.

Mauro, I found out, was struggling with the English language and his lack of friends. Juliette was also alone, because people didn't understand that she was only allowed to wear long skirts or dresses because of her religion. Rachel, who had requested to do the fashion column, wanted to be a fashion designer. She had a whole barrel of unique ideas. What a walk in another person's shoes did for me! They weren't misfits, just people that no one cared enough about to try to understand—except

Mrs. B. Her insight, vision and thoughtfulness brought out the potential in four of her students.

I don't recall what the newspaper's headline was or even the culture we wrote about, but I did learn something that week. I was given a chance to see other people in a new light. I was given the opportunity to see in myself a potential that inspired my actions in later years. I learned that who we are is more important than what we are or seem to be.

After that semester ended, I always received a friendly hello from my group. And I was always genuinely happy to see them.

Mrs. B gave us an A on that assignment. We should have handed it right back, for she was the one who truly deserved it.

Karina Snow

Kids Who Are Different

Here's to kids who are different,
Kids who don't always get As,
Kids who have ears
Twice the size of their peers,
And noses that go on for days.

Here's to the kids who are different,
Kids they call crazy or dumb,
Kids who don't fit,
With the guts and the grit,
Who dance to a different drum.

Here's to the kids who are different,
Kids with a mischievous streak.
For when they have grown,
As history has shown,
It's their difference that makes them unique.

Digby Wolfe
Submitted by Vania Macias

McDonald's

Most of my friends are what society would call "punks." We are the teenagers who hang out at the coffee shops or the movies for lack of anything better to do. But being punks doesn't mean much.

One evening, after a day of not doing much, we were sitting in McDonald's when a guy in our group whom I had just met that day walked in. Brian was the typical punk teenager, dressed in black with the dyed hair. Right before he stepped inside, he yelled something outside to a man walking down the street. I just hoped he wasn't trying to start trouble. He sat down and a minute later, a burly homeless man stuck his head in and looked at Brian.

"Did you say something to me?" the man demanded, and I thought I saw a mean glint in his eyes. I shrank back, thinking that if Brian had tried to pick a fight, this was the wrong guy to do it with. I had seen too many people and places kick teenagers like us out for pulling stuff.

While the rest of us were looking for a place to back into, Brian got up and walked up to him. "Yeah . . . would you like something to eat?"

The relief was almost audible, and the man smiled and walked in.

After a large meal of hamburgers, fries and dessert, the man left, and even the staff waved good-bye to him. When we asked Brian about it, he explained how he had money that he didn't need and the man had none, so it was only right.

Shelly Miller

A Valentine for Laura

Ann, a friend of mine, disliked Valentine's Day as a girl. She was plain—not ugly, but not beautiful. Valentine's Day is not kind to plain girls. It wasn't so bad in elementary school, when the obligatory thirty valentines arrived: one from each classmate. She overlooked the fact that her cards were not oversized like those of the popular girls, and did not contain the love notes like those of the pretty girls. But later, in middle school, the valentine exchange was no longer mandatory. Just when the yearning for romance budded, when the desire for admiration and flirtation became imperative, and a valentine was needed most, no card arrived. Not for Ann. Not for plain girls anywhere. Only for the pretty and the popular. At such a time, stories of ugly ducklings that will one day turn into beautiful swans do not assuage the hurt and rejection.

As fate would have it (and often does), in subsequent years Ann did become pretty and turned many a boy's head. As she received more attention and flirtations, she came to feel—and therefore to be—very beautiful. But even years later, grown and with a family of her own, she did not forget those long-ago days of rejection and dejection.

Today, Ann's family includes two boys in middle school. For a dollar, their Student Council will deliver a Valentine's Day carnation. Ann gives a dollar to each of her boys to buy flowers for their girlfriends. Then she adds another dollar apiece with this instruction: "Pick another girl, one who is nice, but plain—someone who probably won't get a flower. Send her a flower anonymously. That way she will know that someone cares, and she will feel special."

Ann has done this for several years, spreading Valentine's Day a little beyond her own world.

One year, Laura, who was plain to behold but beautiful to know, received one of these gifts. Ann's son reported that Laura was so happy and surprised, she cried. All day long, she carried the flower on her books and chattered with the other girls about who her admirer could be. As Ann heard the account, she too had to dry her eyes—for she remembered.

Don Caskey

A Simple Hello

I have always felt sympathy and compassion for the kids I see at school walking all alone, for the ones that sit in the back of the room while everyone snickers and makes fun of them. But I never did anything about it. I guess I figured that someone else would. I did not take the time to really think about the depth of their pain. Then one day I thought, what if I did take a moment out of my busy schedule to simply say hello to someone without a friend or stop and chat with someone eating by herself? And I did. It felt good to brighten up someone else's life. How did I know I did? Because I remembered the day a simple kind hello changed my life forever.

Katie E. Houston

Change for a Dollar

Make yourself a blessing to someone. Your kind smile or pat on the back just might pull someone back from the edge.

Carmelia Elliot

All he wanted was some juice. As tables full of high school students sat in Cafeteria B2 on that cloudy afternoon, he was thirsty. We sat near yet away from him, fixing our hair and worrying about the test next period we hadn't studied for. He was far away from our world, yet forced to be a part of it.

He stood at the drink machine with purpose, fumbling through his fake leather wallet for some change. He came up with a wrinkled dollar bill, and nervously glanced back at his table where other students in his special needs class were sitting. With the coordination of a six-year-old, he tried to make the machine accept his money. After a few unsuccessful attempts, the snickers and comments began. People were laughing. Some were even throwing things at him. He began to quiver, and his eyes misted with tears. I saw him turn to sit down, defeated. But for some reason, he decided against it. He wasn't leaving until he got a drink.

With a determined expression, he continued to aimlessly thrust the dollar bill in the machine. Then something terrific happened. A popular senior rose from her seat, and with a look of genuine compassion, went over to the boy. She explained how the machine had a hard time accepting dollars, then gave him some change and showed him where to place it. The boy gave her his dollar and chose a flavor of fruit juice. Then the two walked off in different directions.

Although it was clear that they were from very different worlds, for one moment, they'd shared a real understanding. As I walked away from my lunch table that day, I looked at the boy. I remember thinking how he and the dollar were very much alike. They both weren't accepted where the world said they were supposed to be. But just as the dollar had found a place in a caring girl's pocket, I was sure the boy would eventually find his, too.

Bonnie Maloney

My Friend Charley

As an insecure and scared freshman in college, my first year was filled with many new and strange experiences. I quickly learned the difficult lesson that things aren't always what they seem and love can be found in the most unexpected places.

My first introduction to the "real world" began at Camp Virginia Jaycee, a camp for people who are mentally retarded or handicapped. Twice a year, my college offered a volunteer opportunity to students who wished to donate a weekend of their time. At the last minute and after much deliberation, I made a decision that would soon change my life. I volunteered for camp.

I had no idea what to expect, and it was the complete and utter unknown that scared me the most. As the campers slowly arrived, the noises and sounds of the unfamiliar filled the air. I looked around the room at faces that expressed no clue just how different they really were.

Each student volunteer was assigned one camper for the weekend. As a counselor, I was expected to help "my" camper eat, bathe and walk. I was expected to be his friend.

My camper's name was Charley. He was forty years old, with a severe case of autism and no visible means of communication. I was scared. My hands shook with fear as I tried to introduce myself. His attention roamed everywhere except to me. He seemed completely uninterested in anything I had to say. We stood outside waiting to get into our cabin, when suddenly he went to the bathroom, right in front of everyone. I discovered that he was just as scared as I was; we just had very different ways of showing it.

Charley couldn't speak, but he could eat and walk. That night I showed him how to take a shower. As I stood in front of the shower and told him what to do, he did everything I said. I guess he did understand me, in some strange new way. By the next night when it was time for Charley to take his shower, he laughed and smiled like a young schoolboy. I proudly tucked him in that night, but as I started to walk away from his cot, he grabbed my arm. He placed my hand on his head wanting only comfort. It was so overwhelming that this complete stranger could need me to love him. For that instant, Charley made the world seem so simple.

As the weekend came to a close and the time to leave approached, Charley reached out to hold my hand. We were two scared human beings experiencing something so new that it was frightening. I forgot about facades and fake smiles, and instead felt a genuine love for another human being from the depths of my soul.

Robin Hyatt

My First Experience
at Tasting the Raindrops

My blue shirt blended in perfectly with the color of the concrete I leaned against. As my hands lightly brushed the bumpy surface, I considered staying in that spot forever. I thought about the past few days, and I started to cry. I felt lonely as I watched the other students. There were the "in" groups and the "dork" groups. All were laughing and talking, trying to catch the boys' eyes, and perfectly comfortable with their surroundings. I gazed down at my crumpled shirt and new Kmart brand jeans, and struggled to understand where I fit in the jigsaw puzzle of the seventh grade.

As the clock's hands slowly turned, the end of the day creeped in, and I stood in my hiding place. I could hear the groans of school buses arriving to take all the kids home. There were already students on the buses, and those were the ones I ached to join. They all looked the same in their navy blue skirts and matching white shirts. Stepping into the doors of a public school meant transforming my whole world from prayers and friends to brand names and gossip. Weeks passed by as I sank deeper and deeper into depression. Like my shirt and the concrete, I blended into the background of every situation, halfway wanting someone to notice me but at the same time longing to remain part of the masses. Then one day it all changed.

Every morning I dutifully filled the empty bus seat in the third row on the left side, and every morning I stared out the window and let my mind wander. There, I would imagine clouds and tons of friends and . . .

"Hey you." My thoughts were interrupted. "Yeah, you with the yellow shirt." I looked down at my yellow sleeve and slowly turned around. "Why do you always sit so close to the front?" I couldn't speak, and I got the feeling of comfort you get right before a huge storm when you can taste the raindrops in your mouth. Someone was talking to me. He stood at a height pretty average for his age and looked reasonably normal, so I quickly ruled out insanity as a reason for his sudden interest. The next day I sat in a seat farther back, the day after that one more, and another, and another. Finally, about a week later, I slowly made my way down the aisle of the bus, sat in the second seat to the back, turned around and said, "Hi." From that point on I had a friend.

At first I didn't say much, just sat back and listened, satisfied to be included. Each day I would say more and more. For the first time, when I spoke, someone really listened and remembered the conversation the next day. I'd found someone who cared, and I didn't feel so out of place anymore. My confidence and self-esteem soared and my hiding place started to collect dust. I still lurked in the shadows sometimes, but it was almost like they were pushing me away with their shady fingers and telling me to join the world.

Now I look forward to going to school, and gradually I am letting other people into my life. I owe it all to him. He acted like the big brother I never had. If something bothered me or made me mad, I'd tell him. We'd fight like cats and dogs until one of our stubborn minds finally gave up (I usually won). But perfection did not describe him. He had his bad sides as everyone does, but made up for it with his kind heart.

I shudder to think of what my life would have been like if I had never met him. Each day I grew stronger and more outgoing than the day before. Sometimes I would think that he was my guardian angel sent to help me with my problems and pick the best solutions. I knew I could make it and would be all right the day the bus driver glanced back in her mirror and screamed, "Christy, you're being too loud!" I laughed until the tears came because I finally realized I didn't have to be part of the concrete anymore.

Christy Clouse

So How Do You Boost an Ego?

If you treat an individual as he is, he will remain as he is. But if you treat him as if he were what he ought to be and could be, he will become what he ought to be and could be.

Goethe

Mr. Rickman, our psych teacher, doesn't give the kind of assignments other teachers do, such as read a thousand pages; answer the questions at the end of the chapter; work problems 47 through 856. He's more creative than that.

Mr. Rickman led up to last Thursday's assignment by saying that behavior is a means of communicating. "'Actions speak louder than words' isn't just an empty phrase," he told us. "What people do tells you something about what they are feeling."

He paused a minute for that to sink in before he gave the assignment. "Now see if you can build up somebody, boost his or her ego enough that you notice a change in the way the person acts. We'll report the results in class next week."

When I got home from school that afternoon, my mom was really feeling sorry for herself. I could tell the minute I came in. Her hair was straggling around her face, her voice was whiny and she kept sighing while she got dinner. She didn't even speak to me when I came in. Since she didn't speak, I didn't either.

Dinner was pretty dreary. Dad wasn't any more talkative than Mom and I were. I decided to try out my assignment. "Hey, Mom, you know that play the university drama club is putting on? Why don't you and Dad go tonight? I've heard it's really good."

"Can't make it tonight," Dad said. "Important meeting."

"Naturally," Mom said. Then I knew what was bugging her.

"Well then, how about going with me?" I asked. Right away, I wished I could take back the invitation. Imagine a high school kid being seen out in the evening with his mother!

Anyway, the invitation was hanging there in the air, and Mom said in an excited voice, "Really, Kirk?"

I swallowed a couple of times. "Sure. Why not?"

"But guys don't take their mothers out." Her voice was getting more pleasant all the time, and she pushed the straggles of hair up on top of her head.

"There's no law that says they can't," I told her. "You just go get ready. We're going out."

Mom started toward the sink with some dishes. Her steps were perky now instead of draggy.

"Kirk and I will take care of the dishes," Dad offered, and Mom even smiled at him.

"That was a nice thing for you to do," my dad said, after Mom left the kitchen. "You're a thoughtful son."

Thanks to psychology class, I thought gloomily.

Mom came back to the kitchen looking about five years younger than she had an hour earlier. "You're sure you don't have a date?" she asked, as if she still couldn't believe what was happening.

"I do now," I said. "C'mon, let's go."

That evening didn't turn out so badly after all. Most of my friends had more exciting things to do than watch a play. The ones who were there weren't at all startled to see me with my mom. By the end of the evening, she was genuinely happy, and I was feeling pretty good myself. Not only had I aced a psych assignment, I had also learned a lot about boosting an ego.

Kirk Hill

Losing an Enemy

If your enemy is hungry, feed him; if he is thirsty, give him something to drink.

Romans 12:20

Last year, my brothers were enrolled in Pioneer Clubs, a weekly kids program at our church. Daniel was nine, and Timothy was seven. My sister, my dad and I were all teachers at the same church program. At one point during the year, my brothers began to complain that a boy named John was picking on them.

John, an eleven-year-old foster boy, was in my dad's class. He was the type of kid who always seemed to be in trouble. Worse, he didn't consider that it was his behavior that was the problem, but instead decided my dad was picking on him. He often took it out on my brothers by knocking off their hats, calling them names, kicking them and running away. Even I received the occasional rude remark from John. We all thought he was a real pain.

When my mom heard about the problem, she came home from town a few days later with a bag of wrapped butterscotch candies.

"These are for John," she told Daniel and Timothy.

"For *who?*"

"For John." Mom went on to explain how an enemy could be conquered by kindness.

It was hard for any of us to imagine being kind to John; he was so annoying. But the next week the boys went to Pioneer Clubs with butterscotch candies in their pockets—one for themselves and one for John.

As I was heading to my class, I overheard Timothy saying, "Here John, this is for you." When we got home, I asked Timothy what John's response had been.

Timothy shrugged. "He just looked surprised, then he said thank you and ate it."

The next week when John came running over, Tim held on to his hat and braced himself for an attack. But John didn't touch him. He only asked, "Hey, Tim, do you have any more candy?"

"Yep." A relieved Timothy reached into his pocket and handed John a candy. After that, John found him every week and asked for a candy, and most times Timothy remembered to bring them—one for himself, and one for John.

Meanwhile, I "conquered my enemy" in another way. One time as I passed John in the hall, I saw a sneer come over his face. He started to open his mouth, but I said, "Hi, John!" and gave him a big smile before he had a chance to speak.

Surprised, he shut his mouth, and I walked on. From then on, whenever I saw him I would greet him with a smile and say, "Hi, John!" before he had a chance to say anything rude. Instead, he started to simply return the greeting.

It's been a while since John picked on my brothers, and he's not rude to me anymore, either. Even my dad is impressed with the change in him. He's a nicer John now than he was a year ago—I guess because someone finally gave him a chance.

He wasn't the only one to change. My whole family learned what it meant to love an enemy. What's strange is that in the process, we lost that enemy—he was "conquered" by love.

Love: It never fails.

Patty Anne Sluys

Give Random Acts of Kindness a Try!

One dismal evening, just a few months ago,
When the sky was dark and the streets were covered with
    snow,
I had nothing specific in mind and wasn't sure what to do,
Since it was one of those chilly nights that leave you feel-
    ing a bit blue,
I shuffled through a few papers and picked up a book
And without giving it much thought, decided to take a look.
It was one those volumes filled with dozens of stories
That told tales of victories, failures, and special glories.
There was an account of a boy who went to school and
    learned,
And another of a girl who got the toy for which she yearned.
Then I came to a story about someone just like us
Who decided to spend a day doing random acts of
    kindness.
Every thoughtful gift and kind word said with grace,
Brightened someone's day and left a smile on their face.
I sat back to ponder the story and came up with a
    thought—

If everyone tried to share some happiness and kindness
sought,
Wouldn't our world be so much more pleasant than it is
now
When a few more smiles and time for others we'd allow?
I baked a batch of cookies today, and I know a lady down
the street
Who I'm sure would love a few moments' company and a
home-baked treat,
And her lonely neighbor who always seems a bit sad and
gray—
I think a nice visit from someone would just make her
day.
Well, it was starting to get late, so I decided to get some
sleep
After I made a list of things to do the next day and
appointments to keep.
When I got up in the morning I went to school with a goal
in mind—
I would try to cheer a few people up and find ways to be
kind.
I bid "Good morning" and smiled at everybody I met.
A few returned the greeting, then our separate ways we
went.
Someone dropped their books, so I helped gather them
willingly,
And I noticed the more I helped others, the more they
helped me!
After I went home I packaged some cookies to share,
Attaching a note that said, "Just because I care."
When they opened the doors, you should have seen their
faces light with glee
And watched their smiles as they exclaimed, "You mean
you came to visit lonely old me!"
Later in the evening, I sat down and wrote a few notes

Wishing the recipient a great week, before sealing them in
  envelopes.
Then I took a few moments to think about my day
And realized I received even more joy than I had given
  away;
Because every time you smile or with a cheerful word
  part,
The warmth of that kindness penetrates into your own
  heart.
We're only given a short time to spread some cheer before
  we die,
So why not give random acts of kindness a try?

Melissa Broeckelman

4

TOUGH STUFF

The human spirit is stronger than anything that happens to it.

C. C. Scott

Losing Hope

Wherever you go, there you are.

Buckaroo Bonzai

"Hope is the hat rack upon which I hang my dreams . . ."? Oh, please! I crumple up the paper and fling it across my bedroom. I can't believe I kept my hopeless seventh-grade attempts at poetry. I thought I was a poet that year. Obviously I wasn't, and never will be.

"Here they are," I mutter, pulling a stack of yearbooks from the depths of the drawer. They go all the way back to elementary school. *Lauren will like these. Best friends since first grade, she's not talking to me now, but I'm sure she'll want these . . . after . . .*

"You're hopeless, Carrie," she yelled at me over the phone Friday night. Because I don't see everything exactly her way, because I tell her things she doesn't want to hear. The way I think best friends should. Now I don't even have a best friend. And I can't stand losing her friendship.

I peer into the drawer, empty of yearbooks but still

containing the debris of my life. Now what would Josh want from me? According to him, nothing. "There's no hope, Carrie," he told me that night two weekends ago. The night he broke up with me, practically pushing me away as I begged him for another chance. No, he shook his head at me. No, it's over. No hope for us. He hasn't spoken to me since. I can't stand losing him, either.

I slip my hand into the pocket of my robe and finger the little container of pills. My stepfather takes these for his back, and I've heard his repeated warnings to my little brothers never to touch them, how dangerous pills like these can be. He never warned me, knowing that I'm old enough, knowing that I understand about things like dangerous pills.

A knock on my door makes my hand fly from the pocket. Of course, my mother barges right in before I can respond.

"Carrie," she says in her exasperated tone, "we're all waiting for you out by the tree. You know we can't open the presents until we're all together." The faint melody of a Christmas carol and the scent of hot cocoa waft into my room through the open door.

"Honestly, Carrie, can't you dress up a little for Christmas Eve? Or at least get that hair out of your eyes," she continues. "Sometimes I think you're hopeless." She sighs—loudly, dramatically, as if otherwise I wouldn't understand the depths of my hopelessness. "Well, hurry up."

With that, she closes the door and leaves me screaming silently after her: *Yes, Mom, I know I'm hopeless, like you always tell me. Every time I forget to empty the dishwasher, fold the laundry, get the hair out of my eyes, whatever.*

So they're all waiting for me. Mom, my stepfather, Dave, and Aaron and Mark. Waiting for me to join in the singing of carols and unwrapping of gifts. Sure, I'll go. I'll unwrap a few presents. Not that they'll mean a thing to me. But it's Christmas. I'm supposed to be happy. I can pretend. After all, I took drama class last semester.

Ah, school. Another one of the victorious arenas of my life.

"I'm sorry, Carrie, but it's hopeless," Ms. Boggio told me the last day before winter break. "You'd have to get an A on every test for the rest of the year to raise that D to a C." Then she left me alone in the biology lab, staring at my latest test, the latest record of my failures.

I tossed the test away. *I won't even have to show Mom,* I thought. *I won't have to hear that lecture again. The one about how I'm ruining my chances for college. That there will be no hope for my future if I keep going on this way. In fact, I'll never have to hear another lecture again. The problem will be solved before school starts in January.*

How about a note? Would they want one? I used to think I was some great writer. I'd spend hours filling notebook after notebook with my stories and poems, sometimes just my thoughts and ideas. That's when I felt most alive—writing and dreaming of being good at it, of having other people read my words. And having my words mean something to them. But that was before the hopelessness of being Carrie Brock swallowed me up.

"Just a lousy note," I remind myself. That's all I have to write now. Or ever. I've lost everything: my best friend and my boyfriend. Or I've messed it up: my grades, even my hair. I can't do anything right, and I can't stand facing the reminders of my failures anymore.

"Come on, Carrie," Aaron's voice cries through the door. "I want to open my presents."

Oh, all right. I'll do the note later. I drag myself up and tighten the belt on my robe. As I walk down the hall, the pills make a satisfying clicking noise in my pocket.

I sink into the couch and watch as Mark, my youngest brother, tears open his gifts, flinging wrapping paper everywhere. Then it's Aaron's turn. That's the tradition in our family. Youngest to oldest. Everyone oohs and aahs over Aaron's gifts.

"Your turn, Carrie," Mark informs me.

"Can you bring them?" I ask. "I'm tired."

Mark carries over a rectangular box. Clothes, of course. From Mom. I mumble the appropriate thanks. My gifts are few this year. Nothing from Lauren or Josh, of course. Trinkets from Aaron and Mark.

"Okay, I'm done," I say.

"No, wait, here's another one," Mark says, handing me a small package.

"Who's it from?"

"Me." My stepfather speaks up. Dave, the man who resides in the background of my life. A good guy, he treats me well. I've never regretted my mom marrying him.

I tear off the paper, revealing a book. But opening it, I find there are no words inside.

"It's blank," I say, looking up at Dave.

"Well, not quite. There's an inscription up front. But it's a journal, Carrie. For your words."

I flip to the front and find Dave's handwriting in one corner. I read the inscription silently.

> *To Carrie:*
>
> *Go for your dreams. I believe in you.*
>
> *Dave*

I look up at Dave again. He shrugs slightly, as if embarrassed. "Well, I know you want to be a writer, Carrie," he explains. "And I know you can do it."

His last words are almost lost in the noise my brothers are making, digging under the tree and coming up with my mother's presents. But Dave's words are not lost on me.

Somebody believes in me and in my dreams, even

when I've stopped believing in them myself. When I thought I was beyond all hope. I clutch the journal to my chest and a feeling I haven't felt for a long time returns. I do want to be a writer. But most of all, I want to just be.

I watch the rest of the presents being opened, thinking there's something I need to do, but I can't quite figure out what. I can slip the pills back into the cabinet later, so that's not it. Then I know.

I grab a pen from the coffee table and open my journal. On that first blank page I write my words: "Hope is the hat rack I hang my dreams upon."

H'mm, I think. *Kind of sounds like a country song. Maybe it's not that bad after all.* I look up and smile at Dave, even though he's not looking my way. He's just given me the best Christmas present ever. I've gotten my dreams back. Maybe there's hope for me, after all.

Heather Klassen
Submitted by Jordan Breal

A Call for Help

My dear friend Lindsay: she had been part of my life since kindergarten. We met over her ninety-six-pack of Crayolas, a big thing to a five-year-old. She was a constant fixture in my life. She was a born comedian, with more talent, creativity, laughter, love and curly red hair than she knew what to do with. The greatest thing about our friendship was that we completely understood each other. We always had a smile, a joke, a shoulder or an ear to lend one another. In fact, our favorite thing to do was to have our parents drop us off at a restaurant, where we would have these outrageously long talks over Mountain Dews, Diet Cokes and the most expensive dessert our baby sitting money would allow.

It was over one such talk in seventh grade where the subject of suicide came up. Little did I know that this would be a conversation that would forever change our relationship. We talked about how weird it would be if one of our friends ever committed suicide. We wondered how families could ever get over such a tragedy. We talked about what we thought our funerals would be like. This conversation was definitely the most morbid one we had ever had, but I did not think about it too much. I assumed that, at one time or another, everyone wonders who will cry and what will be said at their funeral. It never entered my mind that this talk was a cry for help from my beloved friend. Whenever this topic came up, I had the same frame of mind as my mother—we could never understand how one's life could get so desperate that the only alternative was death. However, we ended our talk with a laugh about how we were too "together" to ever do something so drastic, and we parted with a hug and a "Call me if you need anything."

I didn't think about our conversation until three weeks later, when I received a phone call from Lindsay. I immediately knew something was wrong when she did not begin the conversation with a bouncy hello and a good story. Today she came right out and asked me if she was important to my life and if she meant anything to this world. I answered with an energetic "Of course! I don't know what I'd do without you!" Lindsay then told me something that sent chills up my spine and neck. She told me that she felt lost, confused, worthless, and that she had a bottle of pills in her hand. She said that she was fully prepared to take them all, to end her life. *Was this the girl who sat next to me in English class and with whom I loved to get in trouble? Was this the girl who loved bright colors, laughing, and striking up conversations with anyone in the world? Was this my wonderful, funny friend who was so bubbly and light that she practically floated through life?*

My reality then came into check and I realized that this was my friend, and for that reason, I had to keep her on the phone. I then started the longest phone conversation in my life. Over the next three-and-a-half hours, Lindsay told me her troubles. And for three-and-a-half hours, I listened. She spoke of how she got lost in her large family (fifteen children, and she was the baby), how her self-confidence was low from her appearance (which I thought was beautiful and unique), how she was anorexic the summer before

(I was too busy playing softball to notice), how she was confused about her future—whether or not she would follow her dreams or her parents' wishes, and how she felt completely alone. I kept telling her over and over how original, beautiful and important her dreams and personality were to our lives. By this time, we were both crying: she was frustrated, I was pleading for her life.

My mind then reached out at what I assumed was my final chance at helping Lindsay; I told her three simple things. I first told her that everyone has problems. It's a part of life. That overcoming these problems and moving onto greater heights is what life is all about. The second thing I told her was that if life was as bad as she said, then things couldn't possibly get worse. There wasn't room for any more failure—things had to improve. The final simple thing I told her was that I, or someone else close to her, would always be there, no matter what trials may come into her life. I told her that the fact that we were having this conversation, that she wanted me to know what was going on, proved my theory that she really wanted to live. If she wanted to end her life, she would have just done it. But, since she took time to call, her mind was saying "Help! I want to keep my life!" After I finished that last statement, I heard the best sound in the world—Lindsay flushing the pills down the toilet.

I then went to her house, and we talked about how she could start putting her life back together. We got her some help, and eventually, Lindsay overcame her issues. I am proud to say that Lindsay and I will be starting the eleventh grade together in the fall, she is getting excellent grades, and is a happy teenager. The road there wasn't easy, and we both slipped a few times. But, the important thing is that we raised ourselves up and arrived.

Jill Maxbauer

Tomorrow Came Again

My sister was twelve. My parents were separated. As for myself, I was eight. I really did not have a clue what my family was going through until that horrible, cold January night. How could I have had a clue? I mean, I was only eight years old. All I cared about was my afterschool snack, the cartoons on television and trying to stay up later than eight-thirty on school nights.

I remember that night like it was only milliseconds ago. My mother had asked me to carry the towels upstairs to the linen closet. After I moaned, groaned and procrastinated for about ten minutes, I finally agreed. I remember trying to peer over the tower of towels to make my way up the steep stairs safely. When I got to the closet, which just happens to be next to my sister's room, I heard her crying. Being the most concerned third-grader I could be, I opened the door a little bit wider, and I asked, "Shelley, what's wrong?"

She just looked at my confused expression, and then asked me to give her a hug. I was pretty much into the charade of showing that you hated your siblings, so I refused her request. She persisted and asked me once more. My shaky response was, "Why?"

Shelley explained to me that she had just swallowed an entire bottle of over-the-counter pills. I was not exactly sure at that point in time if this was a dangerous move on her part. But, I realized it must have been pretty serious. I ran down the stairs to my mother, crying the whole way. I told her exactly, word for word, what Shelley had just explained to me.

My mother raced up the stairs, two at a time. She burst into my sister's room, and she begged Shelley to get out of bed to tell her what happened. Shelley refused to tell my mother anything. My mother forced her out of bed, told her to get dressed, and they hurried to the hospital. My neighbor came over, and I cried myself to sleep. All I remember after that is waking up, and my neighbor was still there.

I later learned that Shelley was going to be all right, after she had gotten her stomach pumped. And especially after she had spent three months of her seventh-grade year in a rehabilitation center for adolescents. I never knew exactly why she had attempted suicide, and I never want to ask her. But what I do know is that life is our most precious gift, and I will never again pretend that I do not love my sister.

Ashley Hiser

It Happened to Me

Cancer. It's a funny word. It has two meanings. One of those meanings is the life-threatening disease we all know about. The other meaning isn't as accurate. We take it to mean something that happens to someone else, something that happens to your friend's aunt or someone in the newspaper. It's not something that happens to us, and it's definitely not something that happens to our own sister. But it happened to mine.

When I was about eight, every once in a while my eyesight would become blurry. I'd blink a few times and my eyes would go back to normal. I was taken to the eye doctor, and then for a CAT scan and various testing, but no one could find anything wrong. Eventually, it went away.

When my sister, Naomi, was about eight, she claimed to go blind when I hit her in the eye with an old nightshirt. I got in trouble, but when she was taken to the eye doctor, he couldn't find anything either. Eventually, she stopped complaining.

But when my sister, Tali, was about eight, she too began to complain that it was getting harder and harder to see out of one eye. My parents made an appointment with the eye doctor for about a month later, but they weren't too concerned.

But when my sister's complaints began to worsen, my parents began to get worried and made the eye doctor appointment sooner. When the appointment came, my parents were informed that it was possible that Tali had a form of cancer called melanoma. One of the places that this can form is the eye, though there is no known reason why it forms in a particular person. To ensure that the disease is completely removed from the body, the part of the body infected with the disease must be removed. In this case, it would be her eye. If it was proven, for certain, that she had melanoma, the doctors would have to work fast, or the disease could travel from her eye to her brain.

It was not time to worry yet, though, because all that was the worst-case scenario, and melanoma is very rare among children anyway. Nevertheless, I remember my mom coming home from the eye doctor and crying, along with my grandmother and my aunt and trying not to let my sister see. I remember thinking, *This isn't really happening. She can't really die, this will all blow over.* Maybe I was in shock, but it didn't feel like it. It was more like I had never even heard it, never even tried to acknowledge it was happening. Maybe it was crazy to feel like that, but maybe it was better that way, because I, the "unshaken one," was able to be the shoulder to cry on for everyone else. It makes it sound as if I was the brave one, but sometimes if you don't show your feelings on the outside, it means you're the most scared inside.

Well, Tali went in for her tests, and her X rays, and it was confirmed that she had cancer. Her eye would have to be removed immediately. We knew that if even one cancerous cell was left, the disease could fully return.

The operation took place soon after. My mother waited in the hospital, while I stayed home and answered various phone calls. "No, we haven't heard anything yet," "Yes, she's still in surgery," "Yes, we'll notify you immediately." I still didn't believe it was happening. My sister was in surgery. . . . and I still thought I was dreaming.

We later got a call that she was out of surgery, and just awakening from the anesthesia. All had gone smoothly, and tests had shown that they probably got everything out. She would be fine.

Never during the entire experience did I acknowledge what was happening. People would stop to comfort me, and half the time it would take me a few seconds to realize why. Almost every day, I have people stop me in the halls and ask, "Hey, how's Tali doing?" and I answer, "She's fine, why do you ask?"

Even now, as I write this, she's jumping on the bed across the hall, screaming, "Hey Joanie, you done writing the wonderful story of my life yet?" And though it's a miracle, it seems quite normal that there is nothing wrong at all.

Joanie Twersky

Tell Me Why You Cry

It is such a secret place, the land of tears.

Antoine de Saint-Exupéry

They say that everyone has a story that will break your heart. My little brother Nicholas had cancer. His hair had fallen out, and he was so weak that it was hard for him to walk. I couldn't stand to see the pain in his eyes any longer. His childhood memories were not of Christmases, camping trips and toys; his memories were of hospital visits, I.V.s and blood transfusions.

I remember when it first started, when he was only three. At first, it was the way he was always getting awful, ugly bruises. We didn't think anything of it until they started showing up in places they didn't belong, like in his armpit or on his scalp. Then there were his nosebleeds, which were a constant occurrence. My mom would always have to remind us, "Don't horse around with Nicholas; his nose will start to bleed."

His form of cancer was acute lymphatic leukemia (ALL), which is very curable. Seventy percent of children with ALL achieve remission within one year, and out of those in remission, 50 percent never relapse. Nicky's odds were very good.

He started chemotherapy immediately, to stop the cancer from getting any worse. It went well but it was hard. He was at the hospital Monday, Tuesday and Wednesday receiving treatment, and then he would come home for the rest of the week, sick and completely powerless. He missed preschool that year, but he was in remission in nine months, and we were all happy.

Life was back to normal for a while, until one day during my freshman year. I came home from school to see my parents sitting on the couch, which was odd, because my parents were never home after school. But when I saw the tears, I knew that my worst fear had come true. The cancer was back.

He was five by then and had been in remission for about two years. We all thought he had beaten it, but then they had found a cancerous tumor inside his chest. The doctors were not sure how big it was, so they set a surgery date. They were going to make a small incision on his chest and evaluate the tumor. If it was possible, they would remove it that same day.

The day of the surgery, we all woke up early to accompany Nicholas to the hospital. We sat in the stark white waiting room of B-3, the "cancer hall." I had been there far more than I could handle. In the last two years, I had seen too much of this hall, of cribs occupied by babies whose mothers visit less and less, of children who know they will not make it. The sickening smell of death lines each room, telling past stories of children whose lives were cut short by a silent killer.

We sat and waited for what seemed like an eternity. Finally, after four hours Dr. McGuiness, Nicky's cancer physician specialist, came out of the door marked SURGERY. He was still wearing his operating garb as he motioned for us to follow him, which meant that we needed to talk. As we sat down, fear consumed us.

"Nicholas is out of surgery now, and the medicine will wear off soon," Dr. McGuiness began.

"I'm sorry, though," he continued. "The tumor has grown too large. It has consumed one entire lung, and it has grown all down one side of his heart. There is nothing we can do now."

As I heard those words, my eyes filled with tears. Those words meant that it was time to stop fighting because we would not win. I looked around and knew I wanted to leave. I wanted to run far, far away, but I knew I couldn't. It wouldn't make my problems any better, and it wouldn't make Nicky live.

The doctor left for ten minutes so we could regain composure. When he returned, he asked where we wanted Nicholas to spend his last days. We said we wanted Nicholas home.

The next few months were torture, having to watch Nicky get sicker and weaker. As the tumor grew, his heart stopped pumping regularly and he became short of breath.

The summer went by much quicker than it should have. Nicholas's health remained steady, although still very fragile. We were even able to take a trip to Disneyland, Nicky's One Last Wish. It was so hard, though, trying to be happy for him and knowing it was our last vacation together as a family.

As the year went by, the bustle and jumble of the holiday season kept us occupied. Halloween was fun and Thanksgiving dinner was delicious. Then, as we started preparing for Christmas, Nicky's health deteriorated.

One day as everyone was decorating the tree, I went in to see Nicholas, who was sitting in a chair. The Christmas lights beautifully illuminated his face and brought out an innocent sparkle we had not seen in a long time.

As I came closer, I realized he was crying. I sat down in the chair with him and held him in my arms the way I had when he was younger.

"Nicky, tell me why you cry," I said.

"Sissy, it's just not fair," he blubbered.

"What's not fair?" I asked.

"Why am I going to die?"

"Well, you know that everyone dies," I replied, obviously avoiding the subject. I didn't want him to know, and deep down inside I didn't want to know either.

"But not like me. Why do I have to die? Why so early?" And then he started to cry. He buried his head in my chest, and I started to cry, too. We sat like that for a long time. A very long, lonesome and scary time. Afterwards there was an understanding between us. He was ready, and so was I. We could handle anything now.

In January, he slipped into a coma and we knew we were losing him. One day we sat in his room, holding his hand, because we knew this was going to be his last time with us. Suddenly, a certain peacefulness filled the room, and I knew that Nicholas had breathed his last breath.

I looked outside. The freshly fallen snow somehow seemed brighter. I hated myself for it, but I suddenly felt better. All the pain and sorrow of the past few years were gone, and I knew that Nicholas was safe. He was no longer scared or hurt, and it was better this way.

Nicole Rose Patridge

Nintendo Master

When I first saw you, I thought—*Nintendo Master*. There was this intensity about you. Your piercing blue eyes and the way your hands moved rapidly along the control buttons were subtle hints of your expert skill.

You didn't appear too different from all of the other video-crazed teens out there, but you were. I guess the fact that it was summer, and we were both stuck in the oncology ward of the hospital cruelly betrayed the normality with which you tried to present yourself. Or maybe it was the fact that we were prematurely robbed of the innocence of childhood, and it comforted me to know that there was someone else out there just like me. I can only speculate, but all I know for sure is that I was drawn to your energy and zest for life.

That was the summer of my first post-cancer surgeries. The doctors were trying to fix my left hip joint, which had shattered under the intense bombardments of chemotherapy treatments. It wasn't the only thing that had shattered. I had misplaced my usual optimistic attitude about life and was surprised at how nasty I could be. This did not help to endear me to anyone in my presence.

My surgery had gone "well," the doctors said, but I was in excruciating pain.

I saw you again in physical therapy, realizing only then the extent of what cancer had done to you. I wanted to scream, "Let him go back upstairs and play his video games, you idiots!" But I just sat there in stunned silence. I watched you get up and start walking with the aid of the parallel bars. Prior to your entrance into the room, I had been sitting in my wheelchair, wallowing in self-pity—"Wasn't the cancer enough? Now my hip is screwed up, and I really don't care anymore. If I get up, it is going to kill."

You will never know me, but you are my hero, Nintendo Master. With such courage and poise, you got up on your one remaining leg. Some might have the audacity to call you disabled or even crippled, but you are more complete than many can ever wish to be. After you had your walk for the day, a walk that was perfectly executed on your part, and you were safely tucked into your bed and were enjoying your video games once again, I decided that it was about time that I get up and take a walk myself. You see, Nintendo Master, it dawned on me then that you had innately known what it takes most of us a lifetime to grasp—life is like a game, you can't win them all and yet the game goes on, forcing all to play it. Nintendo Master, you play it better than most!

Katie Gill

Already Perfect

Other people may be there to help us, teach us, guide us along our path. But the lesson to be learned is always ours.

Melody Beattie

Everyone can identify with the need to fit in. Each one of us struggles with self-esteem and self-worth to some degree. I spent much of my time striving to achieve perfection in every aspect of my life. What I did not realize was that in my desperate need to be perfect, I sacrificed the very body and mind that allowed me to live.

I was a happy kid with lots of friends and a supportive family. But growing up was really hard and even scary sometimes.

During my childhood, I was constantly involved in something that included an audience viewing my achievements or my failures. I was into acting by age seven, and progressed to training for and competing in gymnastics, horseback riding and dance—all of which required major commitment, discipline and strength. My personality thrived on the high energy required to keep up. I wanted everyone's praise and acceptance, but I was my own toughest critic.

After I graduated from high school and moved out on my own, my struggles with self-esteem and happiness increased. I began to put pressure on myself to succeed in the adult world. Meanwhile, I was feeling very inadequate and unsuccessful. I started to believe that my difficulties and what I perceived to be my "failures" in life were caused by my weight. I had always been a thin-to-average sized person. Suddenly, I was convinced that I was overweight. In my mind, I was FAT!

Slowly, my inability to be "thin" began to torture me. I found myself involved in competition again. But this time, I was competing against myself. I began to control my food by trying to diet, but nothing seemed to work. My mind became obsessed with beating my body at this game. I slowly cut back on what I ate each day. With every portion I didn't finish or meal I skipped, I told myself that I was succeeding, and in turn, I felt good about myself.

Thus began a downward spiral of my becoming what is known as anorexic. The dictionary defines it as "suppressing or causing loss of appetite, resulting in a state of anorexia." When taken to an extreme, anorexia can cause malnutrition and deprive the body of the important vitamins and minerals that it needs to be healthy.

In the beginning, I felt great—attractive, strong, successful, almost super-human. I could do something others couldn't: I could go without food. It made me feel special, and that I was better than everyone else. What I didn't see was that I was slowly killing myself.

People around me began to notice my weight loss. At first they weren't alarmed; maybe some were even envious. But then the comments held a tone of concern. "You're losing too much weight." "Elisa, you're so thin." "You look sick." "You'll die if you keep this up." All their words only reassured me that I was on the right path, getting closer to "perfection."

Sadly, I made my physical appearance the top priority in my life, believing that it was the way to become successful and accepted. As an actress, I am constantly being judged by my appearance. The camera automatically makes people appear heavier than they are. So I was getting mixed messages like, "Elisa, you are so skinny, but you look great on camera."

I cut back on my food more and more, until a typical day consisted of half a teaspoon of nonfat yogurt and coffee in the morning, and a cup of grapes at night. If I ate even a bite more than my allotted "crumbs" for the day, I hated myself and took laxatives to rid my body of whatever I had eaten.

It got to the point where I no longer went out with my friends. I couldn't—if I went to dinner, what would I eat? I avoided their phone calls. If they wanted to go to the movies or just hang out at home, I couldn't be there—what if food was around? I had to be home alone to eat my little cup of grapes. Otherwise, I thought I was failing. Everything revolved around my strict schedule of eating. I was embarrassed to eat in front of anyone, believing that they would think I was gluttonous and ugly.

My poor nutrition began to cause me to lose sleep. I found it hard to concentrate on my work or to focus on anything for any length of time. I was pushing myself harder and harder at the gym, struggling to burn the calories that I hadn't even eaten. My friends tried to help me but I denied that I had a problem. None of my clothes fit, and it was hard to buy any, since I had shrunk to smaller than a size zero!

Then one night, like so many nights before, I couldn't sleep, and my heart felt as though it might beat its way out of my chest. I tried to relax, but I couldn't.

The beating became so rapid and so strong that I could no longer breathe. The combination of starving myself and taking pills to get rid of anything that I did eat caused me to nearly have a heart attack. I stood up, and immediately fell down. I was really scared, and I knew I needed help. My roommate rushed me to the hospital, beginning the long road to my recovery. It took doctors, nurses, nutritionists, therapists, medications, food supplements . . . and most important, a new sense of what was really true about myself to get back on track with reality.

Recovering from what I did to my body and reprogramming the way I think about myself has been a very slow and extremely painful process. I still struggle with the effects of anorexia every day. Although it has been a couple of years since that hospital visit, it is by no means over for me. I must be honest with myself and stay committed to being healthy.

I had used my anorexia as a means of expression and control. I used it as my gauge for self-esteem and self-worth. It was my identity. Now I realize that the way to success lies in my heart, mind and soul, rather than in my physical appearance.

I now use my intelligence, my talents and acts of kindness to express myself. This is true beauty, and it has nothing to do with the size of my body. With my experience of trying to be "perfect" on the outside, I had sacrificed who I was on the inside. What I know now is, we are—each and every one of us—already perfect.

Elisa Donovan

My Toughest Decision

Mistakes, mistakes, mistakes. Everyone makes them. No one saw mine coming.

Overall, I was a really good kid. At fifteen, I was a sophomore at a Catholic high school and a member of the National Honor Society. I played softball and ran cross-country. I had, and still have, aspirations of becoming a doctor. If someone would have told me that at the age of fifteen I would become pregnant, I would have said they were crazy. Why would anyone do something so foolish? It's still hard for me to believe, but it happened.

October 11, 1997, was the day my daughter was born. I took one look at her, and it was love at first sight. It was so overwhelming—a flood of emotions that I have never experienced. I loved her in a way that could only be described as unconditional. I looked at her, and in my heart I knew that I could not give her all the things that she needed and deserved to have, no matter how badly I wanted to. Physically, emotionally and in every other way, I was not capable of being a mother. I knew what had to be done. Putting all my emotions aside and doing what I felt was best for my daughter, I decided to give her up for adoption.

Placing my baby in the arms of her mother was the hardest thing I've ever had to do. My very soul ached. Even though I still get to see my daughter because I am blessed with having an open adoption, the pain is still there. I can feel it burning inside me every day, when I think about Katelyn. I only hope that when she gets older, she realizes how much I love her. I love her more than anything in the world.

Today is my daughter's first Christmas. I won't be there to share with her the joy of this season, or to play Santa and open her presents for her (she's only two months old). In fact, I won't be there to see her first step, or hear her first word. I won't be there to take pictures on her first day of kindergarten. When she cries for her mommy, it won't be me that she wants. I know in my heart that I made the right choice. I just wish with all my heart that it was a choice I never had to make.

Kristina Dulcey

It's Tough to Be a Teenager

It's tough to be a teenager, no one really knows
What the pressure is like in school, this is how it goes.

I wake up every morning, and stare into this face
I wanna be good lookin', but I feel like a disgrace.

My friends they seem to like me, if I follow through with
   their dare,
But when I try to be myself, they never seem to care.

My mom, well she keeps saying, I gotta make the grade
While both my parents love me, it slowly seems to fade.

It seems like everyone I know is trying to be so cool
And every time I try, I end up just a fool.

I've thought about taking drugs, I really don't want to
   you know
But I just don't fit in, and it's really startin' to show.

Maybe if I could make the team, I'll stand out in the crowd
If they could see how hard I try, I know they would be
proud.

You see I'm still a virgin, my friends they can't find out
'Cause if they really knew the truth, I know they'd laugh
and shout.

Sometimes I really get so low, I want to cash it in
My problems really aren't so bad, if I think of how life's
been.

Sometimes I'm really lost, and wonder what to do
I wonder where to go, who can I talk to.

It's tough to be a teenager, sometimes life's not fair
I wish I had somewhere to go, and someone to CARE.

Tony Overman

Not Your Typical Prom Night

It's supposedly the happiest night of a girl's life (aside from her sixteenth birthday, that is). The night when every girl in the free world does her hair for far too long, spends much more time on her face than she ever will the rest of her life, and waits for Mr. Right to whisk her away to a night filled with excitement, music, friends and fun. Ah, prom night.

Strange how things always look good in the theory stage, but never in the execution. When I look back on my prom night, I see those wonderful things that other girls saw—the pretty dress, the date, the car. However, that night I also saw something that a teenage girl should never have to see—a brother slowly dying of cancer.

This isn't as morbid as it sounds. My brother was never the morbid type. Everything was always "fine," even though as prom night approached, he couldn't see more than five inches in front of his face, and had limited use of his arms and legs because the cancer pressed on nearly every nerve in his body. It caused him excruciating pain with every touch—every hug.

This is how I found him the night of my prom. As I

entered the room, my father was already there, being a
dad and sitting there with my brother, watching whatever
sports event was on the television. My brother made a
feeble attempt to watch; he could even try to convince
himself that he could see what was going on. Looking
back on it, he had us all (except for my mother who spent
twenty-four hours a day with him) convinced that he
would get better. That night I fully believed he saw me
walk in the room.

"Hi, my Dacy," he said, in the ever-so-cute baby talk
tone he always used with me. I greeted him with a smile,
which to this very day I am not sure he saw. I wanted to
give him a hug, but the pain for him would have been too
great. So instead I leaned over and gave him a slight kiss
on the cheek. He heard my dress rustling as I did this, and
I could see him strain to see it. He always tried to hide this
act from us, but you couldn't help but notice it. He had
this funny way of tilting his head downward, because to
quote him: "It's like the bottom part of my eye is cut off
and I can only see what is above this line." And he would
hold his large hand up and divide his eye in half horizon-
tally, to try to demonstrate.

As he tilted his head, desperately trying to see me in all
my prom-night splendor, I couldn't help but sob quietly.
A tear hit my red satin gown and I tried to brush it away,
absurdly believing that he could see me.

"This sucks, Mom," he said, frustrated. "I can't even see
my own sister's prom dress." I took his hand and let him
feel the satin of my dress. Being the protective sibling that
he was, he felt around the neckline, and noticing there
wasn't a neckline, began to chastise me.

"I don't know about this, Dacy," he said protectively.
He then tried to look around, and proceeded to call my
date over and lecture him on what a gentleman he was
going to be that night. I stood back and watched him, this

bigger-than-average boy, who couldn't see or even walk on his own at this point, telling my date EXACTLY how he was going to treat his sister. I began to cry. I cried not only for his feeble attempt at protection (actually, as I found out from my date much later, my brother was still able to strike some fear into his heart), but at the fact that God, fate or whatever was doing this to a boy who all his life just wanted to be normal—who just wanted to live.

I knew at this moment, as I watched him talking, that he would be gone from me soon. Maybe I didn't admit it to myself right then, but I knew—somehow I knew, and I cried even harder. My brother heard me from across the room, and called me over.

"Don't cry, Stace . . . don't cry." He had changed tones on me. This was the Serious Brother tone now, the you-better-listen-to-what-I'm-saying tone. "It will be okay. It will get better. I know it will." He started crying at this. My mom tried to reassure me that it was his medication that was making him depressed; I wasn't convinced. Those tears were real. He tried to hug me and let me know that it was okay; to let me know that I should go to my prom, and live my life. I gave my brother one last kiss and was gone.

Stacy Bennett
Submitted by Diana Chapman

No Matter What Happens

I remember a time when each day was long,
When the world was a playground and my life a song,
And I fluttered through years with barely a care,
Ignoring the future and what waited there.

School was intriguing and filled with delights.
I played away daytimes and dreamed away nights.
My parents assured me I had nothing to fear,
And that no matter what happened, they'd always be there.

Little I knew of a world outside home,
Where tragedy, sorrow and murder could roam.
All I saw were blue skies, rainbows and stars.
I looked past destruction of buildings and cars.

As a child, my biggest concern was just me;
I had to be happy, I had to be free.
And if I was content, I would not shed a tear,
And no matter what happened, I still would be here.

But as I grow up, darkness starts to set in;
My bright world has turned into concrete and tin.
I now see the violence I looked past before;
My friends start to die and my heart hits the floor.

Deadly diseases claim people I love,
There are landfills below me, pollution above.
I often think back to when life was a game.
But no matter what happens, it can't be the same.

There are days when I just want to break down and howl,
To give up completely, to throw in the towel,
But I hold my head high and I push my way through.
I have too much to give and so much to do.

And I make a vow that, though it'll be hard,
I'll go on with a smile and play every card.
I'll give all I can, help others and love.
No matter what happens, life will bloom again,
And the strength I don't have will come from above.

So come, take my hand, and through darkness we will
    sail—
If we all join together, we never can fail.
We'll remember to care, remember to feel,
And no matter what happens, our world we will heal.

Alison Mary Forbes
Submitted by Barry Weber

Hero of the 'Hood

When you have to cope with a lot of problems, you're either going to sink or you're going to swim.

Tom Cruise

By all odds, Mike Powell should never have survived. Addiction, drug pushing, prison or early death are the most likely cards dealt to street kids growing up in the "jungle" of South-Central Los Angeles—a violent combat zone of drug wars, gang slayings, prostitution and crime. But Mike's young life had a special purpose. For eight years, he braved terror and brutalization to keep his family of seven kids together. Incredibly, during that time, no one ever discovered that the only real parent the family had was just another kid.

When Mike was born, his father, Fonso, was in prison for drug dealing. Mike's fifteen-year-old-mother, Cheryl, dropped out of school to support the baby. "Without you, my life could have been different," she later told Mike over and over. It was the guilty glue that would make Mike stick with her through the coming years of horror.

Fonso was released from prison when Mike was four, but instead of security, the six-foot-five, 300-pound Vietnam vet brought a new kind of fear into Mike's life. Fonso had severe psychological problems, and his discipline was harrowing. For minor infractions, such as slamming a door, he forced Mike to do pushups for hours. If the little boy collapsed, his father beat him. So fanatical was Fonso's insistence on school attendance that Cheryl had to hide Mike in a closet when he was sick.

Perhaps it was some dark premonition that drove Fonso to toughen up his young son and teach him self-reliance far beyond his years. Mike was barely eight when his father was murdered in a run-in with drug dealers.

Overnight, the protection and income Fonso had provided were gone. It was back to the streets for twenty-four-year-old Cheryl, who now had three kids: Mike; Raf, age four; and Amber, one year. Life was bitterly hard, and another baby was on the way.

It wasn't long before Cheryl brought home Marcel, a cocaine addict who terrorized the family even more than Fonso had. When Mike innocently questioned what Marcel had done with Cheryl's wages as a transit worker, Marcel broke the little boy's jaw so badly it had to be wired in place.

Marcel soon got Cheryl hooked on cocaine, and the two would disappear on drug binges, at first leaving the children locked in a closet but eventually just leaving them alone for weeks at a time. Cheryl had convinced Mike that if anyone found out what was happening, the children would be separated and sent to foster homes. Remembering his father's fierce admonitions to "be a man," the eight-year-old became consumed by the need to keep his family together, no matter what.

To make sure no one suspected anything, Mike began cleaning the apartment himself, doing laundry by hand

and keeping his sisters fed, diapered and immaculate. He scavenged junk shops for hairbrushes, bottles and clothes, whatever they could afford, and covered up for his mother's absences with an endless litany of excuses. Cheryl and Marcel were soon burning through everything the family had in order to buy crack—even money for rent and the children's food. When their money situation became desperate, Mike quietly quit elementary school at nine to support the family himself. He cleaned yards, unloaded trucks and stocked liquor stores, always working before dawn or late at night so the smaller children wouldn't be alone while awake.

As Cheryl and Marcel's drug binges and absences became longer and more frequent, their brief returns became more violent. Sinking deeper into addiction, Cheryl would simply abandon Marcel when his drugs ran out and hook up with someone who was better supplied. A crazed Marcel would then rampage through the slum apartment, torturing and terrorizing the children for information about where more money was hidden or where he could find their mother.

One night, Marcel put Mike's two-year-old sister in a plastic bag and held it closed. Without air, the toddler's eyes were bulging and she was turning blue. "Where's your mother?" the addict screamed. Sobbing, Mike and little five-year-old Raf threw themselves at Marcel again and again, beating on his back with small, ineffectual fists. In desperation, Mike finally sank his teeth into Marcel's neck, praying the savage tormentor would drop the plastic bag and pick on him instead. It worked. Marcel wheeled and threw Mike through the window, cutting him with shattered glass and breaking his arm.

Cheryl's parents, Mabel and Otis Bradley, loved their grandchildren deeply, but they worked long hours and lived a difficult multiple-bus commute away, and could see them only rarely. Sensing the family was struggling, Mabel sent toys, clothes and diapers, never dreaming that even the diapers were being sold by Cheryl for drug money. Although Mabel's constant phone calls and unconditional love became Mike's only anchor of support, he didn't dare tell her that anything was wrong. He feared his gentle grandmother would have a heart attack if she learned the truth—or worse, a violent confrontation with Marcel.

The family was forced to move constantly, sleeping in movie theaters, abandoned cars and even fresh crime scenes at times. Mike washed their clothes in public restrooms and cooked on a single-burner hot plate. Eventually, Cheryl and Marcel always caught up with them.

Despite the moves, Mike insisted the younger kids attend school, get good grades and be model citizens. To classmates, teachers and even their grandmother, the children always seemed normal, well-groomed and happy. No one could have imagined how they lived or that they were being raised by another child. Somehow Mike had managed to sort through the good intentions but brutal methods of his father, and blend them with the loving example of his grandmother, to form a unique value system. He loved his family deeply, and in return, the children loved, trusted and believed in him. "You don't have to end up on the street," he told them. "See what Mamma is like? Stay off drugs!" Secretly he was terrified that his mother would one day O.D. in front of them.

Over the next few years, Cheryl was jailed repeatedly for possession and sale of narcotics and other crimes, and was sometimes gone for up to a year at a time. Out of jail, she continued to have more children, making the family's financial situation increasingly critical. Hard as Mike tried, it was becoming impossible for him to care for three new babies and support a family of seven kids at the same time. One Christmas there was only a can of corn and a box of macaroni and cheese for all of them to share. Their only toys for the past year had been a single McDonald's Happy Meal figurine for each child. For presents, Mike had the children wrap the figurines in newspaper and exchange them. It was one of their better Christmases.

The young teenager now lived in constant anxiety, but still refused to fall into the easier world of drug dealing and crime. Instead, he braved the dangerous streets late at night selling doctored macadamia nuts, which, to half-crazed addicts, looked like thirty-dollar crack-cocaine "rocks." He knew he risked his life every time he took such chances, but he felt he had few choices. In the nightly siege of gang and drug warfare, the odds were against him, though. By age fifteen, Mike had been shot eight times.

Worse, his reserves of strength and hope were running dangerously low. For as long as he could remember, he had lived with relentless daily fears: *Will we be able to eat today? Will we all be on the street tonight? Will Marcel show up tomorrow?*

And after more than forty moves, it seemed they had finally hit rock bottom. "Home" was now the Frontier Hotel, a filthy dive on Skid Row where pimps and prostitutes stalked the halls and drug deals went down on the stairways. The kids had watched a murder in the lobby, and Mike was now afraid to leave them alone or to sleep. For the few nights they had been there, he had stayed up with a baseball bat to kill rats as they crawled under the door.

Sleep-deprived and overwhelmed by stress, Mike felt crushed by the responsibilities of his life. It was 2:00 A.M. His brother and sisters were huddled under a single blanket on the floor. Michelle, the youngest baby, was crying, but he had no food for her. The boy who had shouldered his secret burden for so many years suddenly lost hope.

Stumbling to the window in despair, Mike stood at the edge, steeling himself to jump. Silently asking his family to forgive him, he closed his eyes and took a last deep breath. Just then, a woman across the street spotted him and began screaming. Mike reeled back from the edge and fell into a corner, sobbing. For the rest of the night, he rocked the hungry baby and prayed for help.

It came a few days later on the eve of Thanksgiving 1993, shortly before Mike's sixteenth birthday. A church outreach group had set up a sidewalk kitchen nearby to feed the hungry, and Mike took the children there for free sandwiches. So impressed were the volunteers with him and the polite youngsters that they began asking gentle questions. A dam deep inside Mike finally broke, and his story spilled out.

Within days, the church group was at work trying to find the family permanent shelter, but no single foster home could take all seven children. Advised that the family would have to be separated "for their own good," Mike adamantly refused, threatening to disappear back into the jungle with the kids. The only person he trusted to keep the family together was his grandmother. Reluctantly, he finally told her of their life for the past eight years.

Stunned and horrified, Mabel Bradley immediately agreed to take the children, but the Los Angeles County social welfare system balked. Mabel was sixty-six, retired, and the children's grandfather was diabetic. How could the Bradleys possibly cope with seven youngsters? But Mike knew better. He hid the children and refused to negotiate any alternative except his grandparents. Finally the social workers and courts agreed, and an ecstatic Mabel and Otis Bradley were granted permanent legal custody of the children. Somehow every child had survived unscathed. Nothing short of miracles, it

seemed—and Mike's unfathomable strength and love—
had kept them together.

Mabel has since returned to work and now willingly
commutes more than one hundred miles a day, while Otis
cares for the children. Mike works as many jobs as he can
to help support the family, but smart, willing and honest
as he is, only minimum-wage jobs are available. More
than anyone, he realizes the value of an education and is
working on his GED.

His dream is to someday start a small company that
can simultaneously employ and counsel street kids like
himself who are without the traditional education and
skills to make it in the normal work world, but who don't
want to be forced back to street life because they can't
find work.

Mike is also dedicated to reaching other inner-city kids
through his music. A talented singer and songwriter, he
writes inspirational rap with his own unique message of
hope. Having seen so many kids die in his young life, he
wants desperately to reach those who might live.
"Surviving is against the odds, but it happens, and we
have to get that message out. If a thousand people hear
me and two kids don't get shot, don't deal, don't die, then
we've done something."

There is little time to sing right now, though, for Mike
and his family are still struggling themselves. But Raf,
Amber and Chloe are now stepping proudly into Mike's
big shoes to do their part at home. They are the three oldest street babies he raised—and taught to live with
courage and hope.

They remember well all of Mike's words, whispered
fiercely to them over and over during the bad times, during the many moves when, each time, they had to leave
everything behind: "Whatever you have, be grateful for
it! Even if you have nothing, be grateful you're alive!

Believe in yourself. Nobody is stopping you. Have a goal. Survive!"

Mike Powell will have his company for street kids some day. And there will be time, later, for the rest of his dreams, too. Mike is, after all, only nineteen.

Paula McDonald

Visionary

When I was fifteen, I stood in front of my English class and read an essay I had written. I talked about how excited all my friends were to be taking driver's education and getting driver's licenses. I was jealous. I knew that I'd always be walking everywhere I went or else dependent on others to drive me. I am legally blind.

Since I was four years old, I have had a condition called dry-eye syndrome. While I do have some sight, I never know when I wake up in the morning exactly how much vision I will have that day. The reason for this is that my eyes do not produce enough tears to lubricate my corneas. As a result, my corneas are scarred. Glasses cannot help me.

There are many things I cannot do. I can't drive, read the blackboard in school or read a book comfortably. But there are far more things I can do.

In high school, I played varsity basketball. My teammates gave me oral signals and I learned to gauge where the ball was by the sound of their voices. As a result, I learned to focus extremely well. I earned the sportsmanship award my senior year.

In addition to basketball, I was a representative to the student council. I also participated in a Model United Nations program, traveling to Washington, D.C., with my class to see our legislators in action. I graduated from high school with a dual curriculum in Jewish and general studies.

After graduation, I studied in Israel for two years. Today, I am a sophomore at Yeshiva University. I plan to go to law school and maybe rabbinical school.

Do I wish I could see like other people? Of course. But being blind hasn't limited me in any of the ways I consider really important. I'm still me. If I've had to be more dependent on my friends, at least I've learned who my friends really are.

Because I've had to struggle to find ways to learn that didn't include sight, I've made superior use of my other senses.

I don't know why God chose to give me only a little vision. Maybe he did it so that I would appreciate what I do have even more. Maybe he did it so that I would have to develop my other capabilities and talents to compensate. Or maybe he gave me this special "gift" because I am, in every other respect, so normal that he wanted to push me to excel. It worked.

There are many different ways to look at life. This is how I see it.

Jason Leib

The Mom I Never Had

I still remember the first time I heard that my mom had been admitted to the hospital for drug-related problems. I was angry, scared, sad and confused, and I felt betrayed. Questions ran through my mind. How could she do this to me? How could she do this to her family? Was it my fault? I felt that it was; that I had done something wrong. As if I had fought with her too much the day before. As if I had rebelled enough to drive her over the edge.

I think back to when I was younger, and I don't really remember my mom being there when I needed her. I never talked to her about the guys I liked, or shared my feelings if I was upset. In turn, she never confided in me when she was sad or needed someone to talk to. My life was never "normal" like all the other girls in my class. Why didn't my mom take me shopping? Why didn't my mom ever come to basketball games, teacher conferences or orthodontist appointments? Then it hit me. My mother, an R.N. who worked in the emergency room for numerous years—a great nurse, and friend to all—was a drug addict. My dad tried to convince me that everything would be okay, that if she moved away for a while, we would all be fine. But I knew deep in my heart that I needed my mother.

The next few days while my mother was in de-tox were hell. It still hadn't sunk in. I had no one to talk to, and there were so many unanswered questions. I watched home videos of when I was a little girl and wished everything would be "normal." I know now that it was never normal.

Then my mom called from the hospital. I remember her voice so soft and weak. She said she was sorry for everything. I wanted to tell her to come home, that I loved her and everything would be okay from now on. Instead, I kept telling her that it wasn't her fault, and between my sobs I said good-bye. You see, I wasn't supposed to cry. I was supposed to be the strong one.

The next day, we went to visit her. I didn't want to be alone with her. I didn't want to talk to her because I was afraid of what she might say. It was weird having those feelings toward my own mother. I felt like she was a stranger, someone I didn't know.

She came home on a Tuesday. We talked for a while and she said she wanted me to come to meetings with her. I said that I would, not knowing what kind of people I would meet or what they would be like. So I went, and the meetings really helped me understand that what my mom was dealing with was a disease, and that no one was at fault. I also met some great people who helped me understand things even further.

I was still unsure, though. At meetings, I heard all this talk about relapse and how to prevent it. What if my mom relapsed? How would I deal with this a second time? I remember when my mom was using drugs, she would stay in her bedroom for long periods of time. One day, after noticing that my mom hadn't come downstairs for a while, I got frightened. I tried to tell myself that even if she slipped, we would get through it, but I didn't really believe we could. I forced myself to go upstairs and see what she was doing. I was scared as I opened the door to her bedroom, afraid of what I might see. But I wasn't disappointed. I found her in her bed, reading a prayer book. I knew then that my mom was going to make it!

She had pulled through, and because of it, we were able to begin the mother-daughter relationship that we never had. I finally had my mom.

Becka Allen

Good Night, Dad

"You afraid of heights?" my dad asked, as I climbed up the seemingly unstable ladder to the second-story rooftop. I was up there to help him fix our TV antenna.

"Not yet," I replied, as he climbed up after me with tools in hand.

I didn't have much to do up there on the roof—mostly I just held the antenna still and handed my dad tools—so I began to talk to him as he worked. I could always talk to my dad. He was more like a big kid than an actual adult. In fact, he looked much younger than his forty-one years. He had straight black hair and a mustache, with no signs of graying or balding. He stood at a strong six feet and had dark green eyes that seemed to always be laughing at some secret joke. Even my friends, whom he'd make fun of without mercy, loved him. Most of my peers would be embarrassed to have their dad hang around with them, but not me; in fact, I took great pride in him. No one else had a dad as cool as mine.

After he finished working on the antenna, we went inside, and I began to get ready for bed. As I entered my room, I looked over and saw my dad working intently at his computer in his office, which was adjacent to my bedroom. As I watched him, I had the most incredible urge to just poke my head in and tell him that I loved him. I quickly brushed that urge away and continued on into my room. I couldn't possibly say to him "I love you"; I hadn't said that to him or anyone else since I was seven, when my mom and dad would come and tuck me in and kiss me good night. It just wasn't something a man said to another man. Still, as I walked in and closed my bedroom door behind me, the feeling continued to grow inside of me. I turned around, opened my door and poked my head into my dad's office.

"Dad," I said softly.

"Yes?"

"Um . . ." I could feel my heartbeat rising. "Uh . . . I just wanted to say . . . good night."

"Good night," he said, and I went back to my room and shut the door.

Why didn't I say it? What was I afraid of? I consoled myself by saying that maybe I'd have the courage to say it later; but even as I told myself that, I knew it might never happen. For some reason I felt that was going to be the closest I'd ever come to telling my dad I loved him, and it made me frustrated and angry with myself. Deep within me, I began to hope he'd know that when I said "Good night," I really meant to say "I love you."

The next day seemed like any other. After school, I began to walk with my best friend to his house, as I frequently do; however, his mom surprised us by picking us up in the parking lot. She asked me whose house I was going to, and when I said "Yours," she paused and said, "No, I have this feeling that your mom probably wants you home right now." I didn't suspect anything; I figured she had something she wanted to do with her own family, and so I shouldn't butt in.

As we pulled up to my house, I noticed a lot of cars in front and quite a few people I knew walking up our front steps.

My mom greeted me at the front door. Her face was streaming with tears. She then told me, in the calmest voice she could manage, the worst news of my life. "Dad's dead."

At first, I just stood there as she hugged me, unable to move or react. In my mind, I kept repeating *Oh God, no; this can't be true! Please . . .* But I knew I wasn't being lied to. I felt the tears begin to run down my face as I quickly hugged some of the people who had come over, and then I went upstairs to my bedroom.

As I got to my bedroom, I looked over into my dad's office. *Why didn't I say it?!* That was when I heard my little three-year-old brother ask, "Mommy, why is my brother crying?"

"He's just feeling a bit tired, honey," I heard my mom tell him as I closed my bedroom door behind me. She hadn't told him yet that Daddy wouldn't be coming home from work again.

Once in my room, I hurt so badly that my body went numb and I collapsed on the floor, sobbing. A few moments later, I heard a scream from downstairs and then my baby brother's voice crying out, "Why, Mommy?!" My mom had just told him what had happened. A few seconds later, she came into my room and handed my crying baby brother to me. She told me to answer his questions while she stayed downstairs to greet people who came over. For the next half hour I tried to explain to him why Heavenly Father wanted our dad back with him, while I simultaneously tried to pull myself back together.

I was told that my father had died in an accident at work. He worked in construction and somehow, he had

been knocked off the crane he was inspecting. Some workers nearby said they didn't hear him shout or anything,
but had run over to him when they heard him land. He
was pronounced dead on arrival around eleven o'clock
that morning, April 21, 1993.

I never really told my dad I loved him. I wish I had. I
miss him very much. When I see him again after this life,
I know that the first thing I'm going to say to him is "I love
you." Until then, "Good night, Dad."

Luken Grace

5

ON FAMILY

Family . . . a group experience of love and support.

Marianne Williamson

Beautiful, She Said

I never thought that I understood her. She always seemed so far away from me. I loved her, of course. We shared mutual love from the day I was born.

I came into this world with a bashed head and deformed features because of the hard labor my mother had gone through. Family members and friends wrinkled their noses at the disfigured baby I was. They all commented on how much I looked like a beat-up football player. But no, not her. Nana thought I was beautiful. Her eyes twinkled with splendor and happiness at the ugly baby in her arms. Her first granddaughter. Beautiful, she said.

Before final exams in my junior year of high school, she died.

Seven years earlier, her doctors had diagnosed Nana with Alzheimer's disease. Our family became experts on this disease as, slowly, we lost her.

She always spoke in fragmented sentences. As the years passed, the words she spoke became fewer and fewer, until finally she said nothing at all. We were lucky to get one occasional word out of her. It was then that our family knew she was near the end.

About a week or so before she died, her body lost the ability to function at all, and the doctors decided to move her to a hospice. A hospice: where those who enter never come out.

I told my parents I wanted to see her. I had to see her. My uncontrollable curiosity had taken a step above my gut-wrenching fear.

My mother brought me to the hospice two days later. My grandfather and two of my aunts were there as well, but they hung back in the hallway as I entered Nana's room. She was sitting in a big, fluffy chair next to her bed, slouched over, eyes shut, mouth numbly hanging open. The morphine was keeping her asleep. My eyes darted around the room at the windows, the flowers and the way Nana looked. I was struggling very hard to take it all in, knowing that this would be the last time I ever saw her alive.

I slowly sat down across from her. I took her left hand and held it in mine, brushing a stray lock of golden hair away from her face. I just sat and stared, motionless, in front of her, unable to feel anything. I opened my mouth to speak but nothing came out. I could not get over how awful she looked, sitting there helpless.

Then it happened. Her little hand wrapped around mine tighter and tighter. Her voice began what sounded like a soft howl. She seemed to be crying in pain. And then she spoke.

"Jessica." Plain as day. My name. Mine. Out of four children, two sons-in-law, one daughter-in-law and six grandchildren, she knew it was me.

At that moment, it was as though someone were showing a family filmstrip in my head. I saw Nana at my baptizing. I saw her at my fourteen dance recitals. I saw her bringing me roses and beaming with pride. I saw her tap-dancing on our kitchen floor. I saw her pointing at her own wrinkled cheeks and telling me that it was from her that I inherited my big dimples. I saw her playing games with us grandkids while the other adults ate Thanksgiving dinner. I saw her sitting with me in my living room at Christmas time, admiring our brightly decorated tree.

I then looked at her as she was . . . and I cried.

I knew she would never see my final senior dance recital or watch me cheer for another football game. She would never sit with me and admire our Christmas tree again. I knew she would never see me go off to my senior prom, graduate from high school and college, or get married. And I knew she would never be there the day my first child was born. Tear after tear rolled down my face.

But above all, I cried because I finally knew how she had felt the day I had been born. She had looked through what she saw on the outside and looked instead to the inside, and she had seen a life.

I slowly released her hand from mine and brushed away the tears staining her cheeks, and mine. I stood, leaned over, and kissed her and said, *"You look beautiful."*

And with one long last look, I turned and left the hospice.

Jessica Gardner

Steeped with Meaning

My mom and I sat in the small college café with our large mugs of something that smelled like lemon and tasted like home. We were catching up on the past four months of our lives and the hours just weren't long enough. Sure, we had talked on the phone and occasionally written. But the calls were long distance, and it was rare to find a moment when my roommate wasn't waiting for the phone, or my younger brother or sister wasn't waiting for my mom. So while we knew of each other's experiences, we had not yet dissected them. As we discussed her new job, my latest paper, my new love and her latest interview, I leaned back into my cushion and thought: *I always knew when she became my mother, but when had she become my friend?*

As far back as I can remember my mom was always the first person that I came to with every tear and every laugh. When I lost a tooth and when I found a friend, when I fell from my bike and when I got back on it, she was there. She never judged me; she let me set my own expectations. She was proud when I succeeded and supportive when I didn't. She always listened; she seemed to know when I was asking for advice and when I just needed a good cry. She multiplied my excitement with her own and divided my frustrations with her empathy and understanding. When she picked me up from school, she always asked about my day. I remember that one day when I asked about hers. I think I was a little surprised that she had so much to say. We rarely had late-night talks (because she was already asleep), nor early-morning ones (because I was not yet up), but in between the busy hours of our filled days, we found the time to fill each other's ears with stories and hearts with love. She slowly shared more and more of her own life with me, and that made me feel more open with her. We shared experiences and hopes, frustrations and fears. Learning that she still had blocks to build and to tumble made me more comfortable with my own. She made me feel that my opinions were never immature and my thoughts never silly. What surprises me now is not that she always remembered to tell me "sweet dreams," but that she never forgot to tell me that she believed in me. When she started going through some changes in her life, I had the opportunity to tell her that I believed in her, too.

My mother had always been a friend. She had given me her heart in its entirety; but her soul, she divulged in pieces, when she knew that I was ready.

I sat across from the woman who had given me my life and then shared hers with me. Our mugs were empty, but our hearts were full. We both knew that tomorrow she'd return to the bustle of Los Angeles and I'd remain in the hustle of New Haven. I know that we are both growing and learning. Yet, we continue to learn about each other and grow closer. Our relationship was like the tea that we had sipped: the longer it steeped, the better it tasted.

Daphna Renan

There Is an Oz

They arrive exactly at 8:00 A.M. to take her home, but she has been ready since before seven. She has taken a shower—not an easy task lying down on a shower stretcher. She isn't allowed to sit up yet without her body brace, but regardless, here she is, clean and freshly scrubbed and ever so anxious to go home. It has been two-and-a-half months since she has seen her home—two-and-a-half months since the car accident. It doesn't matter that she is going home in a wheelchair or that her legs don't work. All she knows is that she is going home, and home will make everything okay. Even Dorothy says so: "Oh, Auntie Em, there's no place like home!" It's her favorite movie.

As they put her in the car, she thinks now of how much her father reminds her of the scarecrow in *The Wizard of Oz*. Like the scarecrow, he is built in pieces of many different things—strength, courage and love. Especially love.

He isn't an elegant man. Her father is tall and lanky and has dirt under his fingernails from working outside. He is strictly blue collar—a laborer. He never went to college, didn't even go to high school. By the world's standards he isn't "educated." An awful lot like the scarecrow—but she knows differently. He doesn't speak much, but when he does, she knows it is worth remembering. Even worth writing down. But she never has to write down anything that her father says because she knows she'll never forget.

It is hard for her to sit comfortably while wearing the body brace and so she sits, stiff and unnatural, staring out the window. Her face is tense and tired and older somehow, much older than her seventeen years. She doesn't even remember the world of a seventeen-year-old girl—it's as if that world never was. And she thinks she knows what Dorothy must have meant when she said, "Oh, Toto, I don't think we're in Kansas anymore." It is more than an issue of geography, she is quite certain.

They pull out onto the road to begin their journey and approach the stop sign at the corner. The stop sign is just a formality; no one ever stops here. Today, however, is different. As he goes to coast through the intersection, she is instantly alert, the face alive and the eyes flashing. She grips the sides of the seat. "Stop! That's a stop sign! You could get us killed! Don't you know that?" And then, more quietly and with even more intensity, "You don't know what it's like—you have never been there." He looks at her and says nothing. The scarecrow and Dorothy journey onward.

As they continue to drive, her mind is constantly at work. She still hasn't loosened her grip on the seat. She thinks of the eyes, the eyes that once belonged to her—big, brown, soulful eyes that would sparkle with laughter at the slightest thought of happiness. Only the happiness is gone now and she doesn't know where she left it or how to get it back. She only knows that it is gone and, in its absence, the sparkle has gone as well.

The eyes are not the same. They no longer reflect the soul of the person because that person no longer exists. The eyes now are deep and cold and empty—pools of color that have been filled with something reaching far beyond the happiness that once was there. Like the yellow brick road it stretches endlessly, maddeningly, winding through valleys and woodlands, obscuring her vision until she has somehow lost sight of the Emerald City.

She lightly touches the tiny gold bracelet that she wears. It was a present from her mother and father, and she refuses to remove it from her wrist. It is engraved with her name on the side that is visible to others, but as in everything there are two sides, and only she knows the other is there. It is a single word engraved on the side of the bracelet that touches her skin and touches her heart: "Hope." One small word that says so much about her life and what is now missing from it. She vaguely remembers hope—what it felt like to hope for a college basketball scholarship or maybe a chance to dance professionally. Only now, she's not sure she remembers hope as it was then—a driving force, a fundamental part of her life. Now, hope is something that haunts her.

The dreams come nightly. Dreams of turning cartwheels in the yard or hitting a tennis ball against a brick wall. But there is one, the most vivid and recurring, and the most haunting of all. . . . There is a lake and trees, a soft breeze and a perfect sky. It is a scene so beautiful it is almost beyond imagining. And in the midst of it all, she is walking. She has never felt more at peace.

But then she awakens and remembers. And remembering, she knows. She instinctively fingers the bracelet, the word. And the fear is almost overwhelming—the fear of not knowing how to hope.

She thinks of her father's God and how she now feels that God abandoned her. All at once, a single tear makes a trail down her thin, drawn face. Then another and another, and she is crying. "Oh Daddy, they say I'll never walk again! They're the best and they say I'll never walk. Daddy, what will I do?"

He looks at her now and he stops the car. This is the man who has been with her down every road, every trail and every path—so very like the scarecrow. And he speaks. "I know that they can put you back together. They can put steel rods in your back and sew you up. But look around you. Not one of your doctors can make a blade of grass."

Suddenly she knows. He has taught her the most valuable lesson in her life and in all her journey: that she is never alone. There is an Oz; there is a wizard; there is a God. And there . . . is . . . hope. She releases her grip on the seat, looks out the window and smiles. And in that instant she loves her father more than she has ever loved him before.

Terri Cecil

A Father's Wish

It's a wonderful feeling when your father becomes not a god but a man to you—when he comes down from the mountain and you see he's this man with weaknesses. And you love him as this whole being, not as a figurehead.

Robin Williams

I write this . . . as a father. Until you have a son of your own, you will never know what that means. You will never know the joy beyond joy, the love beyond feeling that resonates in the heart of a father as he looks upon his son. You will never know the sense of honor that makes a man want to be more than he is and to pass on something good and hopeful into the hands of his son. And you will never know the heartbreak of the fathers who are haunted by the personal demons that keep them from being the men they want their sons to see.

You will only see the man that stands before you, or who has left your life, who exerts a power over you—for good or for ill—that will never let go.

It is a great privilege and a great burden to be that man. There is something that must be passed from father to son, or it is never passed as clearly. It is a sense of manhood, of self-worth, of responsibility to the world around us.

And yet, how to put it in words? We live in a time when it is hard to speak from the heart. Our lives are smothered by a thousand trivialities, and the poetry of our spirits is silenced by the thoughts and cares of daily affairs. The song that lives in our hearts, the song that we have waited to share, the song of being a man, is silent. We find ourselves full of advice but devoid of belief.

And so, I want to speak to you honestly. I do not have answers. But I do understand the questions. I see you struggling and discovering and striving upward, and I see myself reflected in your eyes and in your days. In some deep and fundamental way, I have been there and I want to share.

I, too, have learned to walk, to run, to fall. I have had a first love. I have known fear and anger and sadness. My heart has been broken and I have known moments when the hand of God seemed to be on my shoulder. I have wept tears of sorrow and tears of joy.

There have been times of darkness when I thought I would never again see light, and there have been times when I wanted to dance and sing and hug every person I met.

I have felt myself emptied into the mystery of the universe, and I have had moments when the smallest slight threw me into a rage.

I have carried others when I barely had the strength to walk myself, and I have left others standing by the side of the road with their hands outstretched for help.

Sometimes I feel I have done more than anyone can ask; other times I feel I am a charlatan and a failure. I carry within me the spark of greatness and the darkness of heartless crimes.

In short, I am a man, as are you.

Although you will walk your own earth and move through your own time, the same sun will rise on you that rose on me, and the same seasons will course across your life as moved across mine. We will always be different, but we will always be the same.

This is my attempt to give you the lessons of my life, so that you can use them in yours. They are not meant to make you into me. It is my greatest joy to watch you become yourself. But time reveals truths, and these truths are greater than either of us. If I can give them a voice in a way that allows me to walk beside you during your days, then I will have done well.

To be your father is the greatest honor I have ever received. It allowed me to touch mystery for a moment, and to see my love made flesh. If I could have but one wish, it would be for you to pass that love along. After all, there is not much more to life than that.

Kent Nerburn

Heartwood

One autumn evening I sat on the third-base line in Miami's Pro-Player Stadium watching a critical game between the Florida Marlins and the New York Mets. My attention was distracted off and on by a teenage boy and his father who sat one row in front of me. The father was a Mets fan by the look of his cap; his son's had the Marlins' logo.

Something the boy said provoked his father, who began to tease his son about the Marlins. When it became clear the Marlins might lose this game, the boy's responses to his father's jibes became sharp and petulant. Near game's end, the boy—now in a mean sulk—said something harsh that spun the man's head around to face his son. In a full-bore adolescent snarl, he stared at his father. His eyes narrowed, his troubled skin flushed. Anger overwhelmed him, "I hate you, you know that!" He spat the words as though they tasted as bad in his mouth as they sounded once spoken. Then he ran for the shelter of the grandstand. In a moment the man stood and followed the boy.

As I watched them, I sympathized with both father and

son because I, too, had once turned on the man whose child I was. It was a time when I thought I would never grow up, never be at ease in my own skin, never get it right. It is a time not to be forgotten.

* * * *

On a June day, during the summer of my freshman year in high school, I got into an ugly argument with my father. He was a country doctor who had a farm in southern Indiana where he raised Hereford cattle and kept a few horses. That summer he decided to extend the pasture fence along the south field. That's what started the trouble.

We were sitting under a sycamore at the edge of the pasture. My father was thoughtfully whittling at a piece of wood. He pointed to a stand of hemlocks about three hundred yards away and said, "From here to there—that's where we want our fence. Figure 'bout 110 holes. Three feet deep. Won't take forever."

I said in a tight voice, "Why don't we get a power augur?"

"Because power augurs don't learn anything from work. And we want our fence to teach us a thing or two."

What made me mad was the way he said *"we* want *our* fence . . ." *We* had nothing to do with it. The project was *his.* I was just forced labor and I thought that was unfair.

I admired a lot about my dad and I tried to remember those things when I felt mad at him but I got angry easily that summer. One evening as we checked out the cattle, my father's attention fixed on a river birch that grew on the east bank of the farm pond. The tree forked at ground level and was my retreat. I'd get my back up against the dark bark of one trunk and my feet against the other so that I was wedged solid. Then I could look at the sky or read or pretend.

"I remember you scrunchin' into that tree when you were a little kid," my father said. "You don't do that much anymore."

Amazed, I heard myself say, "What the hell do you care!" And ran to the barn, let myself into the tack room, sat on a nail keg and tried very hard not to cry. It wasn't long before he opened the door. He sat opposite me on the old stool he always used. Although I was staring at my tightly folded hands, I could feel him looking at me. Finally, I met his gaze.

"It's not a good idea to doctor your own family," he said, "but I guess I need to do that for you right now." He focused on me. "Let's see. You feel strange in your own body. Like it doesn't work just like it always has. You're a little slow. You think no one else is like you. And you think that I live in dim-wit land. You think I'm too hard on you, and you wonder how you got into a family dull as we are."

I was astonished. I didn't understand how he knew my most treacherous night thoughts.

"The thing of it is, your body is changing. You've got a lot more male hormone in your blood. And, Son, let me tell you, there is not a grown man in this world who could handle what that does to you when you're fourteen. But you have to learn to deal with it. It's what's making your muscles grow and your hair, and it's making your voice change. It will make you a grown man before you know it. At least you'll *look* like one. *Being* one is a different thing. Right now you think you can't. Right now you think you're a very misunderstood guy."

He was right. For the past few months I had begun to think no one really knew a thing about me. I felt irritable and restless and sad for no reason. So because I couldn't talk about it, I began to feel really isolated. I wasn't a boy anymore and I wasn't a man. I was nowhere.

"So," my dad said after awhile, "One of the things that'll help you is work. Hard work."

As soon as he said it I suspected this help-me thing was

a ploy to get me to spend my summer doing things around the place. But there was no way around my father. When he said something, he meant it. That was that.

I began that summer by digging post holes by hand across the north meadow where a new fence was going to go. I did that all morning, every day. I slammed that digger into the ground until I had tough calluses on my hands. But I noticed one day as I was coming out of the shower that my shoulders looked bigger somehow. I hated the work, but still the anger I felt went slamming into the earth and somehow made me feel better.

One Saturday morning I helped my father patch the barn roof. We worked in silence for a long time. Then he suddenly looked directly at me and almost reading my thoughts, said, "You *aren't* alone, you know."

I looked up at him, squatting near me with the handle of the tar bucket in his hand. "Think about this. If you drew a line from your feet down the side of our barn to the earth and followed it along any which way you pleased, it would touch every living thing there is in the world. That's what the earth does. It connects us all. Every living thing. So you're never alone. No one is."

I started to argue with that idea in my mind, but the notion of being connected to all the life there was in the world made me feel so good that I let my thoughts quiet down and said nothing.

That summer I gradually began to pay attention to doing chores well. I began to take a more serious interest in the farm and ever so slowly I began to feel I could somehow get through this rotten time. My body got bigger, I got hair on my face and elsewhere, and my feet grew a whole size. Maybe there was hope.

Near the end of that summer, I went down to the pond to sit in my tree. It was kind of a last visit to the world of my boyhood.

But I no longer fit in the fork of the tree and had to scuttle up almost eight feet high in order to get space enough for my body. As I stretched out I could feel the trunk that my feet pressed against was weak. I could push it away easily with my legs. I began to push at it harder until, at last, the trunk gave and slowly fell to the ground, raising dust from the weeds. Then I walked back to the barn, got the chain saw and cut up my tree for firewood.

The day I finished the work on my father's fence, I saw him sitting on an outcropping of granite in the south pasture. His elbows were on his knees, his hands clasped between them. His ruin of a Stetson was pushed back on his head. As I walked toward him, I knew he was thinking.

I sat down beside him on the flat rock. "You thinking about how long this grass is going to hold out without some rain?"

"Yep," he said. "How long you think we got?"

"Another week. Easy."

He turned and looked me deep in the eyes, the way he did when he wanted to be sure he'd gotten the real gist of what you were asking him. Of course, I wasn't really talking about the state of the pasture as much as I was trying to find out if my opinion mattered to him. After what seemed to me a very long time he said, "Could be. You could be right." Then he said, "You did a fine job on our fence. Custom work. Custom."

"Thanks," I said. I felt almost overwhelmed by the force of his approval. I smiled what I am sure was the biggest smile of my life.

"You know," he said, "you're going to turn out to be one hell of a man. But just because you're getting all grown up doesn't mean you have to leave behind everything you liked when you were a boy."

I knew he was thinking about why I had cut down my tree. I looked at his lined face. He seemed much older to me now. He reached into his jacket pocket and pulled out a piece of wood. It was about the size of a deck of cards. "I made this for you," he said. He handed me a piece of the heartwood of the river birch. He had shaped and carved the face of it so that the tree from which it came appeared again on the surface, tall and strong and all leafed out. And beneath were carved the words, "Our Tree." And for the first time I felt really good about those words.

* * * *

When I was leaving the field that September day, after the Marlins missed their bid to win a play-off spot in front of the home-town fans, I saw the man and boy who had been sitting in front of me in the stands. They were walking toward the parking lot with the noisy crowd. The man's arm rested on his son's shoulder for a moment. They looked relaxed, comfortable with each other, their immediate problem resolved.

I wondered how their peace had been made that day. But whatever they'd done was on the right road, it seemed to me, and was worth acknowledging. So as I passed I tipped my cap to them in a small, personal tribute to both their present moment and to my own memories.

W. W. Meade

The Cheerleader

Everyone wants to be a cheerleader. Every girl wants the chance to shine, to have all eyes on her, to be the one to wear the uniform, be part of the "squad," be in the "in" group—everything that cheerleading connotes. Any girl who says differently is either the exception to the rule or fooling herself. Everyone wants to be a cheerleader—but not everyone gets the chance.

In the fall of my senior year in high school, I was faced with more pressure than I knew how to handle. My friends and I were applying to college, taking the college admissions tests and writing essays. Each essay, it seemed, asked a variation of the question, "What makes you different from the other thousands of high school seniors who are seeking admission to our school?" It was in the midst of these other pressures that cheerleading tryouts for the varsity team took place every year.

Varsity tryouts were different from trying out for the freshman, sophomore and junior teams. Pretty much every girl who tried out for those teams got to be a cheerleader because there were two squads for each grade—one for football season and one for basketball. But the varsity cheerleaders were ten senior girls who got to cheer for the whole year. Out of the many who tried out, each having had some experience as an underclassman, only that very special ten made it.

Those ten girls knew, without a doubt, the answer to that essay question that the colleges asked. They knew the moment they put on that uniform what made them unique. They felt it the minute they ran out onto the field at the first game. They reveled in it the first time they walked down the halls of the school, all eyes on them.

I knew I had to be one of them.

As I listed all the other things I had done in school and extracurricular—all the clubs and sports I had enjoyed, the awards I had won, the jobs I had held—I knew instinctively that none of them was special enough to set me apart. None of them meant what being a senior cheerleader meant. At least to me. At seventeen, I was sure that the college admissions departments felt the same way.

My younger sister, Molly, started high school that year. I thought she would have it especially easy since I had already told her everything to expect—which teachers to fear, which courses were easy. From my experiences, she already knew which activities were offered and when, and how much time each one required. She even knew many upperclassmen, which was a real plus for a freshman.

The first few weeks of school were fraught with tension for me. With everything going on, I admit I wasn't too attentive to Molly. Still, I waited for her every afternoon in the parking lot to drive her home. I thought that was enough for her, getting a ride instead of having to take the bus, like many of the other freshmen.

Cheerleading practice was held after school and sometimes ran long during those weeks before the tryouts. Molly had to either wait for me or take the bus. Most of the time she waited, watching me from the bleachers.

I could see the tension mounting in my friends as tryouts approached. We got into a lot more fights, sniping at
one another. One of my friends confided that she thought
she stood a better chance of making the team if she lost a
few pounds. So she stopped eating—I mean completely!
Another girl began skipping other activities to practice
after school. She was a really talented dancer and had
always loved her dance classes. But she stopped going so
she could practice for the tryouts. When I asked her if she
was going to give up dance altogether if she made the
team, she said yes.

But the worst was when I saw one of my friends crying
in the bathroom. When I asked her what was wrong, she
told me her parents were getting a divorce. Then she said
that if she made the cheerleading team, they would both
have to come see her at the games. She thought that
might get them back together.

Making that team meant a lot more than it should have
to so many of us. But like my friends, I didn't think about
whether or not it was worth it.

The day of tryouts came. I gave it everything I had. I
screamed the loudest, smiled the widest, jumped the
highest. I was perfect. At least I thought so.

The list of the ten girls selected was to be posted that
Friday at the end of the day, outside the principal's office.
My last class was just down the hall, so I would be one of
the first to see the list.

Friday morning, I drove Molly to school as usual. But I
hadn't slept well the night before and was so on edge that
I thought I'd scream if anyone even talked to me. Molly
must have sensed that because she didn't say anything
the whole ride to school. But when she got out of the car
she handed me a note. I was in a hurry so I stuffed it into
one of my books and headed for class.

Friday was the longest day of my life. The last period was English, and as I took out my copy of *Tess of the D'Urbervilles*, Molly's note fell out. It said,

Dear Sis,

No matter what happens today, whether you make the team or not, I think you are the best sister in the world. I was so scared to start high school—you know how lowly freshmen are treated. But having a sister who's a senior makes me special. All of my friends are jealous. I just wanted to tell you.

Love,
Molly

The bell rang, but I didn't run to see if my name was on that list. For just a minute I stayed where I was, rereading my sister's letter, rereading it until the words blurred. Then I stood up, gathered my books and headed for the door.

At the end of the hall I could see Molly leaning against the door, patiently waiting for me to drive her home. Between us, on the bulletin board outside the principal's office, was the list. There was a huge crowd around it already. I knew I would have to wait a long time to get to the front of the line. I looked at Molly and gripped the note in my hand. Suddenly, I knew what I would write for my college essay. I knew what made me different, unique. And it didn't depend on whether or not I had made the squad.

I made my way down the hall, without stopping, my eyes glued to the form of my very own personal cheerleader, waiting patiently there for someone she thought was very special.

Marsha Arons

The Bridge Between Verses

Things do not change. We change.

Henry David Thoreau

My brother is the boy with the big black eyes. He has an aura about him that feels strange and nervous. My brother is different. He doesn't understand when jokes are made. He takes a long time to learn basic things. He often laughs for no reason.

He was pretty average until the first grade. That year, his teacher complained of him laughing in class. As a punishment, she made him sit in the hall. He spent all his time on the fake mosaic tile outside the room. The next year, he took a test that showed he needed to be placed in a special-education class.

As I grew older, I began to resent my brother. When I walked with him, people stared. Not that anything was physically wrong with him; it's just something that radiated from him that attracted attention. I would clench my teeth in anger sometimes, wishing he were like other people, wishing he were normal.

I would glare at him to make him uncomfortable. Every time my eyes met his, stark and too-bright, I would say loudly, "What?" He'd turn his head quickly and mutter, "Nothing." I rarely called him by his name.

My friends would tell me I was being mean to him. I brushed it off, thinking that they were also horrible to their siblings. I did not consider the fact that their brothers and sisters could retaliate. Sometimes I would be nice to my brother just because they were around, but return to being mean the minute they left.

My cruelty and embarrassment continued until one day last summer. It was a holiday, but both my parents were working. I had an orthodontist appointment and was supposed to take my brother with me. The weather was warm, being a July afternoon. As spring was over, there was no fresh scent or taste of moisture in the air, only the empty feeling of summer. As we walked down the sidewalk, on impulse I began to talk to him.

I asked him how his summer was going, what his favorite kind of car was, what he planned to do in the future. His answers were rather boring, but I wasn't bored. It turns out I have a brother who loves Cadillacs, wants to be an engineer or a business person, and loves listening to what he calls "rap" music (the example he gave was Aerosmith). I also have a brother with an innocent grin that can light up a room or an already sunny day. I have a brother who is ambitious, kind, friendly, open and talkative.

The conversation we had that day was special. It was a new beginning for me.

A week later, we were on a family trip to Boston, and I was in the back seat of our van. I was reading a Stephen King novel, *Rage*, while my dad and my brother sat up front talking. A few of their words caught my attention, and I found myself listening to their conversation while pretending to be engrossed in my book. My brother said, "Last week, we were walking to the bus stop. We had a good conversation and she was nice to me."

That's all he said. As simple as his words were, they were heartfelt. He held no dislike toward me. He just accepted that I'd finally become the sister I should have been from the beginning. I closed the book and stared at the back cover. The author's face blurred as I realized I was crying.

I will not pretend everything is fine and dandy now. Like changes in a *Wonder Years* episode, nothing's perfect, and nothing's permanent. What I will say is that I do not glare at my brother any more. I walk with him in public. I help him use the computer. I call him by his name. Best of all, I continue to have conversations with him. Conversations that are boring in the nicest possible way.

Shashi Bhat

The Ones in Front of Me

At some point in my childhood, I realized that my parents were never going to get along; the lines had been drawn and the die had been cast. So when my parents announced that they were filing for a divorce, it wasn't a huge shock. I never thought it was my fault. I also never had the illusion that they would miraculously fall back in love. So, I guess I accepted their decision.

For most of my childhood it didn't bother me that they weren't together. In fact, I had the best of both worlds. I got to live in Hawaii with my mom and travel to Los Angeles to see my dad. Somewhere during the process, however, I began to feel the effects of our "broken home." Although they tried not to make it too obvious, my parents' disdain for each other was becoming apparent.

When I was twelve, I wanted to live with my dad, so I moved to Los Angeles. It's not that I didn't love my mom; it's that I had spent most of my childhood with her and started to feel as if I didn't know much about my dad.

After the move, I started to realize how much my parents' divorce really affected me. My dad would tell me to tell my mom to send me money, and my mom would tell me to tell my dad that she shouldn't have to. I felt caught in the middle. My mom would try to pull information out of me about how it "really" was at my dad's. It was a constant struggle to duck out of the line of fire.

My parents tried to respect each other, for my sake I guess, but it was obvious that a lot of hurt lay underneath their actions. It had been ten years since they divorced, but it felt as if the struggle had just begun. They constantly argued over money and parenting styles. As much as they both promised that it didn't involve me, it always did. I felt they were fighting over me, and that it was somehow my fault—feelings I didn't have when I was five.

Growing up with divorced parents today seems to be a regular occurrence. It's actually rare to find two parents who are still together, but that doesn't make going through it hurt any less. Although I may not have felt it at the time, eventually, it was something that I had to work through—whether I was five or fifteen.

I wish I could say that my parents have worked out all their problems, and that we now work as a perfect team. It is never that simple. But, they try. They love me, and while it took all of us a while to realize it, now we know that their love for me will always keep them together in some way—they have learned to work together in order to raise me.

The other day, the three of us got together to talk about my upcoming trip to visit colleges. I think they are both sad about the idea of me leaving—and that is what keeps them together: the joy and sadness of watching me grow.

As we sat there the thought crossed my mind, *What if my family were still together?* Then, as I watched my parents intently looking through my college brochures, I smiled to myself, *This is my family, and we are "together."*

Lia Gay

Role Reversal

It was a Friday night, and I had just returned from climbing one of the Red Rocks of Sedona. The night was chilly, the moon was high and I was looking forward to crawling into my warm bed. My faculty adviser, Bunny, approached me as I walked through the arches to my dorm room. She took me to her home where she told me that my mother had been in a terrible car crash and had been taken to the intensive care unit of a nearby hospital in critical condition.

When I got to the hospital my grandmother pulled me aside and said whatever I did, I mustn't cry in front of my mother.

A nurse unlocked the door that led down a wide hallway with machines all around. A strong smell of medicine brought a nauseous feeling to my already turning stomach. My mother's room was right next to the nurses' station. As I turned into the room, I saw her lying on her side, with her tiny back to me and a fluffed pillow between her bandaged legs. She struggled to turn around but couldn't. I slowly crept to the other side of the bed and said "hi" in a calm voice, stifling my urge to cry out.

The cadaverous condition of her body stunned me. Her

swollen face looked like it had been inflated and kicked around like a soccer ball, her eyes had huge dark bruised rings around them, and she had tubes down her throat and in her arms.

Gently holding my mother's cold swollen hands, I tried to keep my composure. She kept looking at me and rolling her eyes into the back of her head as she pounded her hand against the bed. She was trying to tell me how much pain she was in. I turned my face away from her, trying to hide the tears that were rolling down my face. Eventually I had to leave her for a moment because I couldn't hold my anguish in any longer. That was when it struck me that I really might lose my mother.

I kept her company all day long; in time the doctors took the respirator out of her throat for a short while. She was able to whisper a few words, but I didn't know what to say in return. I felt like screaming but knew I mustn't. I went home and cried myself to sleep.

From that night on, my life completely changed. Up to that point, I'd had the luxury of just being a kid, having to deal with only the exaggerated melodramas of teenage life. My concept of crisis was now forever altered. As my mother struggled first to stay alive and then to relearn to walk, my sense of priorities in life changed drastically. My mother needed me. The trials and tribulations of my daily life at school, which had seemed so important before, now appeared insignificant. My mother and I had faced death together, and life took on new meaning for both of us.

After a week of clinging to life in intensive care, my mother's condition improved enough to be taken off the respirator and moved to a regular hospital room. She was finally out of danger but, because her legs had been crushed, there was doubt that she would be able to walk again. I was just grateful that she was alive. I visited my mother in the hospital as often as I could for the next two months. Finally, a sort-of hospital suite was set up in our family room, and to my relief and joy, she was allowed to come home.

My mother's return home was a blessing for us all, but it meant some unaccustomed responsibilities for me. She had a visiting nurse, but much of the time I took care of her. I would feed her, bathe her, and when she was eventually able to use a toilet, would help her to the bathroom. It struck me that I was pretty much playing the role of mother to my own mother. It wasn't always much fun, but it felt good to be there when my mother really needed me. The difficult part for me was trying to always be upbeat, and to keep my mother's spirits up when she became frustrated with the pain and her inability to do simple things for herself. I always had a smile on my face when, really, I was suppressing tears in my heart.

My mother's reliance on me changed our relationship. In the past, we had more than our share of the strains of mother-daughter relationships. The accident threw us into a relationship of interdependence. To get my mother back, I had to help her regain her strength and ability to resume an independent life. She had to learn to accept my help as well as the fact that I was no longer a child. We have become the closest of friends. We genuinely listen to one another, and truly enjoy each other's company.

It has been over two years since my mother's crash. Although it was devastating to see my mother go through the physical pain and emotions that she still continues to experience, I have grown more in that time than in all the years before. Being a mother figure to my own mother taught me a lot about parenthood: the worries, the protectiveness and, most of all, the sweetness of unconditional devotion and love.

Adi Amar

"I'm grounded for two weeks or until my dad
learns that 'funk' is not a bad word."

Snowdrops

"Are they up yet?" Grandmother asks hopefully.

"No, not yet," Mother answers patiently, as if addressing an eager child. From her position on the edge of my grandmother's bed, I see her smile silently as she continues knitting. She is smiling because of the familiarity of the question. For the last few weeks of her illness, my grandmother has been living to see the snowdrops bloom in her garden. Sometimes I think the only reason she doesn't succumb to her cancer is so she will live to see the tiny, white flowers she so adores, one last time. I don't understand her strong feelings for the snowdrops, as they are, by far, not the most beautiful flowers growing in Grandmother's garden. I wish to ask why she is so drawn to them but Mother's presence stops me. For some reason, I feel the need to ask the question in private. I realize then that Grandmother's eagerness for such a simple thing is almost childlike, and this causes me to reflect. We come into this world as children, and exit in almost the same way.

"Grandmother, why do you like snowdrops so much?" I ask during a visit one day, once Mother has gone downstairs.

She looks so fragile lying in her bed, I almost regret asking the question. Answering may prove to be too much exertion for her weak lungs to handle. However, she takes a breath and begins to talk, slowly and quietly.

"When your grandfather and I were married, around this time of year, the snowdrops were in bloom. I wore them in my hair at our wedding. Your grandfather adored them. Every year we planted them in our garden, and through some bizarre miracle, they always bloomed on our anniversary.

"After your grandfather died, I missed him terribly. All I had to do, though, was look at the snowdrops, and I felt close to him, as if he were with me again. Our snowdrops were what saved me on days I missed him so much I wanted to die." Grandmother finishes her story and stares silently into space, thinking. I don't want to interrupt her thoughts, so when she closes her eyes and drifts off to sleep, I still don't speak.

We visit Grandmother again, but on this day Mother asks me to stay downstairs. Grandmother's condition is worsening and she can't cope with any visitors except Mother. She no longer has the strength to talk, and I remember my most recent talk with Mother. She was in need of someone to confide in, and I was the only ear available; otherwise, I'm sure she wouldn't have burdened me with her pain. She told me of her visits alone with Grandmother, and how she wished Grandmother would just give up and allow herself to go, to end her own suffering. I could see Mother's pain, and how much she longed to cry; but for my sake, she would not. I imagine what my mother is doing upstairs right now—sitting on Grandmother's bed, holding her hand and encouraging her not to fight anymore.

My thoughts are interrupted as I notice a glossy, white album on a shelf across from where I am seated. On the binding there is a date printed in gold ink: April 13, 1937. I pull the large book from the shelf and gingerly open it. I am mesmerized by the black-and-white photo that greets my eyes. I recognize Grandmother and Grandfather, posing together happily, and I know this must be their wedding album. Grandmother's beautiful white gown draws my attention. Then my eye is attracted by the tiny white flowers perched in Grandmother's hair. They are her snowdrops, and for the first time, I can see just how beautiful they really are.

The telephone rings on the most gorgeous day of spring so far. When Mother answers it, I know right away what has happened. My first question is, "What day is it?" Through her tears, Mother answers, confirming my suspicions. She doesn't want me to come with her today, but I insist. There is something I need to see.

When we arrive at Grandmother's house I immediately run to the backyard. While the image of the snowdrops is blurred by my tears, they have bloomed just the same. I am upset that Grandmother didn't get to see them, but then I realize that this year she didn't need to. For the first time in many years, she won't miss Grandfather on their anniversary. Despite my sadness I smile, for I know they are celebrating together in heaven.

Sarah McCann

My Most
Memorable Christmas

The fall of 1978, our daughter Carol, age thirteen, was thrown from a motorcycle on which she had been a passenger. She sailed eighty-nine feet through the air and landed in a ditch, where she almost died. My wife and I were on a mission in Korea when we got the news that the doctors were in the process of amputating her left leg.

Our flight home took twenty-two hours. I suppose I did more crying on that flight than I ever have in my entire life. When my wife and I arrived at our daughter's side, unable to think of adequate words of comfort, surprisingly enough, Carol began the conversation.

"Dad," she said, "I think God has a special ministry for my life to help people who have been hurt as I have." She saw possibilities—positive ones—in tragedy! What a lift those words gave me. But we were just beginning what would prove to be a long, exhausting battle.

Carol's femur had broken in four places and plunged through the thigh bone into the ditch of an Iowa farm, next to a slaughterhouse. There it picked up a form of bacteria that had previously been resistant to any known antibiotics.

In November, Carol went back into the hospital for surgery that would, hopefully, release muscles in her knee that might make her leg more usable. The doctor was delighted when he opened her thigh and knee and discovered no pus pockets. But the hidden bacteria, which until that time had remained dormant, erupted like a prairie fire when exposed to the open air. Three days after surgery, she was the sickest little girl I've ever seen.

Each passing day, the bacteria multiplied with increasing impatience. Carol's fever soared to 104 degrees and lingered there day after day, night after night. Her leg continued to swell and the infection raged out of control.

About that time, we were blessed with a minor miracle. With no knowledge of my daughter's need, the Federal Drug Administration released, for the first time, an antibiotic that was declared significantly effective against the specific strain of bacteria that Carol contracted while lying in that Iowa ditch. She was the first human being in Children's Hospital, Orange County, California, to receive it. In a matter of hours after the first dosage, her temperature went down. Each successive culture reading showed fewer and fewer bacteria. Finally, about three weeks before Christmas, a culture came back that showed no bacteria growth.

Lying in her hospital bed with the intravenous tubes still in her hands, Carol asked the visiting doctor, who was standing in for her own surgeon, when she would be released. "Will I be home for Christmas, Doctor?" she asked.

"I don't know," he replied cautiously.

"Will I be able to get my new prosthesis?" she asked.

"Well," the doctor cautioned, "I don't believe you can get it yet."

But when her own doctor returned, he checked her over. That same day Carol called me at my office. "Daddy,

I have good news," she announced.

"What is it?" I asked.

"Doctor Masters is an angel," she exclaimed. "He said I can come home for Christmas!"

On December 16, a Saturday night, Carol was released from the hospital. I was told to stay home and await a surprise. My wife went to pick her up. I saw the lights of the car as it rolled up the driveway, and I ran to the front door. My wife barred my way and said, "Bob, you have to go back in and wait. Carol wants you to wait by the Christmas tree."

So I waited nervously by the Christmas tree, counting the seemingly interminable seconds. Then I heard the front door open and the squeak of rubber on the wooden floor. I knew the sound came from the rubber tips of Carol's crutches. She stepped into the open door, ten feet away from my seat by the Christmas tree. She had gone straight from the hospital to the beauty parlor, where her hair stylist gave her a beautiful permanent. There she stood with lovely curls framing her face. Then I looked down and saw two shoes, two ankles, two legs and a beautiful girl.

She had come home and, because of it, made that Christmas my most memorable.

Reverend Robert Schuller

My Real Father

I came across a quotation the other day: "He who raises a child is to be called its father, not the man who only gave it birth." How true this is! I only wish I had realized it sooner, for my failure to do so caused every person in my family a lot of unnecessary grief, including me.

My mom married the man I knew as Dad when I was four years old, and even then I felt this animosity toward him that was incredible, especially for a child so young. My dad tried so hard to be a good father to me, and I responded with spite and anger. He showered me with love, and I spit in his eye. Oh, he legally adopted me, and I called him Dad, but in my heart, I was a fatherless child. This incredible anger only grew when we moved from Ohio, where I had relatives on every street corner, to South Dakota, where I knew nobody. When I reflect now on my terrible behavior, I feel such shame. Just because he loved my mother, he was stuck with a little brat whose every move was calculated to bring him grief. But he didn't give up on me as a lesser man might have.

The strange thing is, I had come to love this man, but I didn't know how to stop my hateful behavior. I can only be glad that eventually, I grew out of it.

When people find out I'm adopted, their first question is always, "Who's your real father? Do you know him?" My answer is, "Yes, I know him. I live with him."

My dad is the man who refused to spank me, even though I deserved it. He's fed me and clothed me and loved me for thirteen years. He's there when I cry, and when I feel sick. Dad can always fix it with something out of his magical medicine collection. He worries about me if I'm out late. He bought me my first car, my first prom dress. He's the one who is proud of me when I get a good report card or win an honor or just handle a difficult situation in a mature way. He's my father, my dad and my daddy in every way except the one that doesn't count.

And as soon as my daddy gets home, I'm going to tell him, for the first time, how much I love him and how much I appreciate that he didn't give up on me . . . even when I had given up on myself.

Anonymous

"You mean Dad started out as a date?"

Making Dad Proud

It was about 7:30 as I pulled into the driveway on that hot July evening. I shut the door of my Jeep and packed my stuff into the house. I passed the ancient, brick-red Chevrolet with the cancerous case of rust. That meant Dad was home.

I opened the front door, dropped my bag on the floor and started to fix myself something to drink. As I thumbed through the mail on the kitchen counter, a faint rumbling from the backyard grew louder, then dissipated into near obscurity again. Dad was mowing the lawn.

From the paperwork on the couch, it was evident that he had not been home from work long. Sometimes I just don't understand how he does it. As if being a father and husband weren't enough, he manages a full-time job, church activities and carpentry jobs for friends and family. On most nights, he stays up later than I do and wakes up at the crack of dawn to leave for work. Nevertheless, he can tap his energy reserve when challenged to a game of Nintendo or the rare pickup basketball contest. Gray temples and a slight paunch season his thirty-five-year-old frame with traces of sagacity. If he is old before his time, it is because he has had so little time to be young.

Dad's premature journey into the adult world was, in a way, my fault. There's not much a high school senior with a pregnant wife can do but grow up. Sacrificing the things and life to which he was accustomed, he took on a full-time job bagging groceries and stocking shelves at Sureway during the night. School took up his days. This might explain his tendency toward late-night television viewing. I mention all this so that you may better understand, or at least attempt to understand, May 22, 1994.

On that Sunday evening, I sat between my parents in a pew at First Assembly of God. We patiently waited as my youth pastor explained to the congregation the meaning of True Love Waits, a nationwide and nondenominational campaign for sexual abstinence until marriage. I had gone through about six weeks of sermons, videos and presentations about love, sex, dating and marriage. I was here to make a commitment to God, myself and my future spouse. The participants of the program were brought forward and presented with rings, symbols of our commitment that were to be presented to our husbands/wives on our wedding nights.

As I returned to my pew, hands folded and head bowed in prayer, I felt a weathered and callused hand close over mine. I looked at my father. This man, who had always remained stoic during emotional moments, had eyes that were glazed over with tears. A single tear fell, and then another, as he wrapped his arms around me. Without a single word, he communicated volumes. That moment told me that he was proud. I think it told him that he had not sacrificed all those things for nothing. That maybe it was a chance for him to start over. A chance, for a while, to be young.

Josh Nally

"I already know about sex, but could you explain
where Beanie Babies come from?"

The Perfect Family

Divorce. That's a word I dreaded more than any other word in the English dictionary.

All my life, I thought I had the perfect family. Perfect parents, two great sisters and a younger brother. We all got along well. But during the last several years, my parents had started to fight more and more.

My dad came home less and less, working more hours than ever in Vermont. And now here we all were, sitting in the television room as a family, with my parents saying they had an announcement to make. I began to cringe.

There it was: that nightmare word, the one that made me sick to my stomach. They were, they announced, getting a divorce. The big D word. My sisters and brother and I gaped at each other. How many times had I asked my mom and dad: "Are you getting a divorce?" How many times had they assured me that would never happen and given me hugs and kisses?

"This is some sort of April Fool's joke, right?" I said.

My mom's eyes welled with tears and she held me in her arms.

"No, Marc, I'm sorry," she whispered.

I felt betrayed. How could they do this to us? Most of all, I wanted to know what we had done wrong. What had *I* done wrong?

My mother could see the dread in my eyes, the fear, the hurt and the pain. It all welled within my belly and I felt sick. She promised she would take care of me, of us. All of us.

But how could I believe her now? My family had collapsed before my eyes. We were splintered. Shattered. There would be no more perfect family. And of course, things would get worse rather than better. They'd get a lot worse.

My mom told me that we would have to leave our home. The home I'd lived in all my life.

I felt like I was losing everything. My family. My home. My dad. The good news: My mother would have custody of all of us and my father wouldn't dispute it.

We moved into a tiny home with my mom's parents. At first, I wasn't very happy. The house was small. We were all squished in together. Sometimes I felt there wasn't enough room to breathe. There was one thing, however: We loved each other. My grandparents, Mom, sisters, brother and visiting aunts and uncles tried to do everything to fill the house with warmth and caring. My grandparents paid special attention to all us kids. I'd never felt so close to them in my life.

They asked me about school and were actually interested. They asked me about my friends, my grades. We sat at the kitchen table and talked often. They could never replace my father, but they spread their warmth to all of us.

Still, I carried a lot of guilt. I couldn't understand what bad thing happened to split up my parents. At times, I agonized over it, lying in bed, wondering in a cloud-like state what possibly could have been the reason that my parents quit loving each other. Was it something I had done?

And then more unexpected news: We learned my father was gay.

I was sure as word got around that the other kids would laugh and make fun of me. Some did. But, there were a lot of kids, however, who didn't say a word. They still hung around me and could care less what my dad did. They liked me before and they liked me still. I had learned who my real friends were, and the ones I lost were not the kind of people I wanted in my life anyway.

I also learned that I was really loved by my family. They supported me. They cared about me. My grandparents adored me. Eventually, we were able to move out from their home and get a condominium. I started junior high school and started doing well.

I have since learned to redefine that funny concept I had about a perfect family.

Maybe a perfect family really means a lot of love and a lot of support. Maybe it really means giving, sharing and caring. Maybe I still have a perfect family after all.

Marc St. Pierre

$\overline{6}$

LEARNING LESSONS

I am always ready to learn; but I do not always like being taught.

Winston Churchill

Making Sarah Cry

He stood among his friends from school,
He joined their childhood games
Laughing as they played kickball
And when they called poor Sarah names.
Sarah was unlike the rest;
She was slow and not as smart,
And it would seem to all his friends
She was born without a heart.
And so he gladly joined their fun
Of making Sarah cry.
But somewhere deep within his heart,
He never knew just why.
For he could hear his mother's voice,
Her lessons of right and wrong
Playing over and over inside his head
Just like a favorite song.
"Treat others with respect, son,
The way you'd want them treating you.
And remember, when you hurt others,
Someday, someone might hurt you."
He knew his mother wouldn't understand

The purpose of their game
Of teasing Sarah, who made them laugh
As her own tears fell like rain.
The funny faces that she made
And the way she'd stomp her feet
Whenever they mocked the way she walked
Or the stutter when she'd speak.
To him she must deserve it
Because she never tried to hide.
And if she truly wanted to be left alone,
Then she should stay inside.
But every day she'd do the same:
She'd come outside to play,
And stand there, tears upon her face,
Too upset to run away.
The game would soon be over
As tears dropped from her eyes,
For the purpose of their fun
Was making Sarah cry.
It was nearly two whole months
He hadn't seen his friends.
He was certain they all must wonder
What happened and where he'd been
So he felt a little nervous
As he limped his way to class.
He hoped no one would notice,
He prayed no one would ask
About that awful day:
The day his bike met with a car,
Leaving him with a dreadful limp
And a jagged-looking scar.
So he held his breath a little
As he hobbled into the room,
Where inside he saw a "Welcome Back" banner
And lots of red balloons.

He felt a smile cross his face
As his friends all smiled, too
And he couldn't wait to play outside—
His favorite thing to do.
So the second that he stepped outdoors
And saw his friends all waiting there,
He expected a few pats on the back—
Instead, they all stood back and stared.
He felt his face grow hotter
As he limped to join their side
To play a game of kickball
And of making Sarah cry.
An awkward smile crossed his face
When he heard somebody laugh
And heard the words, "Hey freak,
Where'd you get the ugly mask?"
He turned, expecting Sarah,
But Sarah could not be seen.
It was the scar upon his own face
That caused such words so mean.
He joined in their growing laughter,
Trying hard to not give in
To the awful urge inside to cry
Or the quivering of his chin.
They are only teasing,
He made himself believe.
They are still my friends;
They'd never think of hurting me.
But the cruel remarks continued
About the scar and then his limp.
And he knew if he shed a single tear
They'd label him a wimp.
And so the hurtful words went on,
And in his heart he wondered why.
But he knew without a doubt

The game would never end, until they made him cry.
And just when a tear had formed,
He heard a voice speak out from behind.
"Leave him alone you bullies,
Because he's a friend of mine."
He turned to see poor Sarah,
Determination on her face,
Sticking up for one of her own tormentors
And willing to take his place.
And when his friends did just that,
Trying their best to make poor Sarah cry,
This time he didn't join in,
And at last understood exactly why.
"Treat others with respect, son,
The way you'd want them treating you.
And remember, when you hurt others,
Someday, someone might hurt you."
It took a lot of courage
But he knew he must be strong,
For at last he saw the difference
Between what's right and wrong.
And Sarah didn't seem so weird
Through his understanding eyes.
Now he knew he'd never play again
The game of making Sarah cry.
It took several days of teasing
And razzing from his friends,
But when they saw his strength,
They chose to be like him.
And now out on the playground,
A group of kids meets every day
For a game of kickball and laughter
And teaching their new friend, Sarah, how to play.

Cheryl L. Costello-Forshey

The Wedding Ring

In the high school creative writing class I teach, I try hard to give assignments designed to make my students think about the details of life. In describing these details, I've found, they produce some of their best writing. They make good use of each of their senses as well as their creativity to get to the heart of things. This is how, if they and I are lucky, they find their own best creative writing voices. For some of my students, those voices express certain sentiments that desperately need an outlet.

Recently, I asked the students to describe an object and its particular significance to them personally. They had a week to complete the assignment. But one of my students, Kerry Steward, approached me the next day and told me she wouldn't do it.

I knew Kerry fairly well. She had been in my class for two years, her sophomore and junior years. She was a good writer and very cooperative. So this statement of hers surprised me. I looked at her for a minute as she stood by my desk. Her attitude of defiance was completely uncharacteristic, so I asked her to come in after school to discuss this further.

When I saw her again later that day, she wasn't defiant anymore, but she still said she wouldn't do the assignment. She asked if she could have a different one. Something in her voice made me ask her what this was all about.

"Are you having trouble thinking of some object?" I asked.

She was quiet for a minute. Then she said, "No. Last night, when I told my mom about the assignment, she said she had an idea of something special for me to write about. She took me into her room. She opened this big jewelry box she has. I thought she was going to show me a pair of earrings or something that had belonged to her mother. I was already thinking about lots of terrific things she had told me about my grandmother to write about. That would have been an easy essay to write."

She stopped for a moment. I could see that she was having a hard time with her next thoughts.

"But, she didn't give me a piece of my grandmother's jewelry. She took out the wedding ring my father had given her and handed it to me."

I thought for a minute. I remembered from conferences that Kerry's parents had a different last name. But her stepfather had always been as interested in Kerry's progress and as proud of her achievements as her mother. So I had just assumed that even though they were a blended family, they were a happy one. And Kerry always seemed so well-adjusted that I never had any reason to assume differently.

But, the teenager in front of me was miserable. "How could she have kept that ring? How could she want me to have it?" Kerry began to cry. "They got divorced when I was a baby. I don't even know what he looks like. He's never wanted to see me or hear from me. I hate him! Why would I want to have that stupid wedding ring?"

Kerry's anger was acute. I let her cry for a minute. Then I asked, gently, "What did you do then?"

"I threw the ring as hard as I could against the wall. It made a mark and fell behind the oak dresser. Then I ran into my room and slammed the door." Kerry took a tissue from my desk and blew her nose. "My mom didn't yell at me or anything. She didn't even make me move the dresser and get the ring."

Wise woman, I thought.

"You don't have to write about that ring," I said. "You know you can choose anything you want, don't you?" Even as I said it, I knew that Kerry had, in fact, wanted to at least talk if not write about that ring. I knew that all the rage and frustration of an abandoned child were symbolized in that ring. But I'm an English teacher, not a psychologist and certainly not Kerry's mother. It wasn't my place to force her to express painful feelings. I told her she was excused from the assignment.

That night, I called Kerry's mother. I thought she should know about Kerry's and my conversation. She thanked me for letting her know. Then she said, "I didn't realize how angry she is—not just at her father, but at me also. But, I kept that ring to remind me of the good times in my marriage—there were good times." She paused. Then she said softly, "If I hadn't married him, I wouldn't have Kerry."

"Tell her," I said.

The next day, I waited anxiously for Kerry's class to begin. I had spent a sleepless night. Kerry's feelings were so understandable. But, I hoped that the obvious love between mother and daughter and the secure family they had now would help Kerry deal with those feelings.

Kerry smiled at me when she came in. She said, "I'm a little sore today. I moved some heavy furniture last night."

I smiled back. For just a minute, I was tempted to make

some comment about weights being lifted, but then Kerry stepped forward and put a composition on my desk. "Read it later," she whispered.

Her essay about the wedding ring was short. Kerry wrote: "Things are just things—they have no power to hurt or to heal. Only people can do that. And we can all choose whether to be hurt or healed by the people who love us."

That was all.

And that was everything.

Marsha Arons

Andrea's Fresh Start

Down the hall I could hear buzzing, then a click, then "Can I help you?" as a night nurse responded to a patient's call.

But it wasn't the noise that was keeping me awake. In the morning, I was having surgery. And I was scared. I got up to splash water on my face. *If I get past this, I'm going to make a fresh start,* I said to my reflection. I was only seventeen. . . .

It's still hard to know exactly why I grew to feel so angry and isolated. I think it started with how I felt about the girl in the mirror.

"You *are* pretty," my mother would say, but I felt ugly, different from the smiling girls at school.

"They're phonies," I'd tell my sisters Loren and Melissa. So I made friends with kids like me who felt they didn't belong, and reacted with anger.

By high school, I wore black clothes and makeup, daring others to say something. At least once during the day, the door to the school bathroom would swing open behind me as girls in the clique came in, pushing their way to the mirror.

"Going to the dance?" they'd ask each other. A few times I'd catch them gawking at me, but usually I was invisible to them. I told myself it didn't matter. But I ached with loneliness.

"How was school?" Mom would ask. I'd snap, "Why do you care?" I'd mope around. I'd pull away from hugs. And when she said, "I love you, Andrea," I never said, "I love you, too, Mom."

My dad tried, too. "Why don't you join a club?" he'd ask. "We want you to have a bright future." *I don't fit in,* I'd rage. *What kind of future does someone like me have? And how on earth can anyone love me?*

So I couldn't believe it when a boy I thought was nice liked me too. We went out for over a year before we broke up. If I'd been angry before, now I became wild—and dangerous. To myself. As the weeks passed, I'd reach at night for my favorite poetry—somber, depressing verses by Edgar Allen Poe. I'd write my own: *Maybe the angels would accept me as I am.* I'd make lists of people I wanted to come to my funeral—kids who had never looked at me twice. Maybe they'd feel bad. I thought of suicide. Was I strong enough? But then one night, watching a movie about someone fighting a terminal disease, I thought, *That could be my way out. I could get sick and die.*

It was a dark teenage dream that came back to haunt me. First, I thought the pain was menstrual cramps. But then it felt like a knife. Then Mom took me to the doctor, who said it was nerves. After all, I *was* "emotional," a word they used instead of "troubled." But the pain got worse and my stomach bloated.

The doctor did an ultrasound. "The sonar's picking up a mass. You have to go for tests."

Mom's mouth dropped open and my heart stopped. "Am I dying?" I whispered. "Don't worry," Mom assured me. Tears sprang to my eyes as I looked into her terrified face. I hated seeing someone I *loved* look so scared.

"The best scenario is a benign ovarian cyst," the surgeon said. "The worst? Ovarian cancer, but that's very rare for a girl your age. For that, we'll have to do a hysterectomy."

Cancer! People die of cancer. A hysterectomy meant never having children. My head swam. This couldn't be happening! Had I tempted fate?

I thought of all the years I'd been angry. Why? Because I didn't have dimples or wasn't captain of the field hockey team?

Is it too late for second chances? I worried. Suddenly it struck me. I'd fantasized about dying. Now I knew I wanted to live more than anything. *If I get the chance,* I promised, *I won't waste it.*

"We'll be here," Mom and Dad said, holding back tears as I was taken to surgery. Loren held my hand, and she was holding my hand when I woke up from anesthesia.

"Is it . . . ?" I managed to ask, my mouth dry and slow. The news was scary: along with a cancerous tumor, my reproductive organs and part of my stomach had been removed. I'd need nine weeks of chemotherapy.

"We love you," Dad said tearfully. The words had been hard for me for so long, but full of tears too, I cried, "I love you!" back.

I told my parents "I love you" a lot as the months passed. As Mom took days off to sit with me during chemo. As Dad brought me bandannas to wear when my hair fell out. As Loren and her friends wore bandannas so I wouldn't feel out of place. As the kids at school—*all* of them—wished me luck. And I thought, *Had they ever really shunned me? Or had I imagined that?*

When I finished my chemo, the cancer was gone. So was my depression. I figured it had all happened for a reason: so I could help other people who felt alone. After graduation, I joined City Year, a Boston youth group, volunteering at a women's shelter. "You have to fight to live," I'd tell them, "whether it's against disease or circumstance."

But my heart broke for the children, living in a strange place. It's hard feeling like you don't fit in. That's why I'm studying child psychology now. And that's why even though Loren has offered to carry a child for me when the time comes, I think I'll adopt, because I know what it's like for a child to feel unwanted.

Those dark days are behind me. I've made new friends in college. And although I've been in remission for just two years, I know I've been cured . . . of a lot of things.

Peg Verone
Excerpted from Woman's World Magazine

A Lesson for Life

The turning point in the process of growing up is when you discover the core strength within you that survives all hurt.

Max Lerner

"Look at fatso!"

Freshmen in high school can be cruel and we certainly were to a young man named Matt who was in my class. We mimicked him, teased him and taunted him about his size. He was at least fifty pounds overweight. He felt the pain of being the last one picked to play basketball, baseball or football. Matt will always remember the endless pranks that were played on him—trashing his hall locker, piling library books on his desk at lunchtime and spraying him with icy streams of water in the shower after gym class.

One day he sat near me in gym class. Someone pushed him and he fell on me and banged my foot quite badly. The kid who pushed him said Matt did it. With the whole class watching, I was put on the spot to either shrug it off or pick a fight with Matt. I chose to fight in order to keep my image intact.

I shouted, "C'mon, Matt, let's fight!" He said he didn't want to. But peer pressure forced him into the conflict whether he liked it or not. He came toward me with his fists in the air. He was no George Foreman. With one punch I bloodied his nose and the class went wild. Just then the gym teacher walked into the room. He saw that we were fighting and he sent us out to the oval running track.

He followed us with a smile on his face and said, "I want you two guys to go out there and run that mile holding each other's hands." The room erupted into a roar of laughter. The two of us were embarrassed beyond belief, but Matt and I went out to the track and ran our mile—hand-in-hand.

At some point during the course of our run, I remember looking over at him, with blood still trickling from his nose and his weight slowing him down. It struck me that here was a person, not all that different from myself. We both looked at each other and began to laugh. In time we became good friends.

Going around that track, hand-in-hand, I no longer saw Matt as fat or dumb. He was a human being who had intrinsic value and worth far beyond any externals. It was amazing what I learned when I was forced to go hand-in-hand with someone for only one mile.

For the rest of my life I have never so much as raised a hand against another person.

Medard Laz

Remember Me?

My name is Gossip.

I have no respect for justice.

I maim without killing. I break hearts and ruin lives.

I am cunning, malicious and gather strength with age.

The more I am quoted, the more I am believed.

I flourish at every level of society.

My victims are helpless. They cannot protect themselves against me because I have no name and no face.

To track me down is impossible. The harder you try, the more elusive I become.

I am nobody's friend.

Once I tarnish a reputation, it is never the same.

I topple governments and wreck marriages. I ruin careers and cause sleepless nights, heartaches and indigestion. I spawn suspicion and generate grief. I make innocent people cry in their pillows. Even my name hisses.

I am called GOSSIP. Office gossip—Shop gossip—Party gossip—Telephone gossip. I make headlines and headaches. REMEMBER, before you repeat a story, ask yourself: is it true? Is it fair? Is it necessary?? If not, do not repeat it. KEEP QUIET.

GREAT minds discuss ideas. . . . Average minds discuss events. . . . Shallow minds discuss people. . . . Which are you?

Ann Landers
Submitted by Amanda Kurlan

A Wider Classroom

Our white van meandered its way through the broken West Virginia landscape and pulled up alongside Jim's avocado-colored house. As the doors opened, we poured out with hammers in hand. We were eight teenagers on a week-long service project to repair the homes of the less fortunate residing in the Appalachian mountains. The area seemed to contradict itself, for it held so much beauty yet housed so much poverty. Maybe we hailed ourselves as being able to serve those people in need; I do not think we ever imagined that what they could give us would perhaps be more valuable then any services we could render.

We rotated jobs as we basked in the southern sun; some of us scraped and painted windows, while others stained the deck or worked on the roof. All the while Jim sat in a lawn chair observing us: the kindest of old men, only too sorry that he could not labor alongside us on the ladders. We passed the time with inside jokes and songs, truly enjoying ourselves regardless of the tedium of treating window after window as Jim just silently observed.

As the clock neared noon, we took our lunch break

in the shade of a small tree in Jim's front yard. Sam, our moderator, planted Jim's chair beside us and announced that since he was eager to help in any way possible, Jim would lead us in a before-meal prayer. He kept it succinct and we all began to eat.

"Let me tell you a story. . . ." he then began. And from the pit of his humble heart he began to unravel his eighty-some-odd years for us. He was a school teacher and a baseball coach who had a loyal dog named Pretty-Face. He told of old hunting expeditions in the mountains where his life was almost lost to a bear, and he talked of conquering a rattlesnake, even showing us the rattles.

Then his cavernous eyes just wandered off as if he was no longer talking solely for our benefit, but more for his own. He described that day his dog died, as fat tears rolled down his weathered cheeks and he gripped the end of his cane. He recalled her loyalty to the end as with one last thump of the tail, looking up at him, Pretty-Face passed on. He remembered his wife gazing up at him much the same way seconds before her death.

He always affectionately called his wife "Mama," and he told of how she'd always stayed up until the small hours of the morning to bake the bread for the next day, while he, often tired from a long day of teaching or hunting, would retire to bed.

"Why didn't I just stay up with her?" he said in a distant voice as his eyes gazed beyond us. "Why couldn't I have just taken that extra time? Why?"

I remember how profoundly those words rang inside of me. Here was a man brimming with wisdom and reflections on his life, telling me to make the most of mine, to take that extra time with those I love. I was inspired; I was mesmerized by this extraordinary old man that I had thought I was helping. Jim's house was not a job at all, it was a classroom.

Kate McMahon
Submitted by Olive O'Sullivan

The Bat

The best part about running, for me, is the finish. The moment when, flushed and out of breath, I reach my destination: my backyard. Ironically, I have run full circle, ending up where I began. Yet, I have also taken a positive step forward in my life, determined and acted out by no one other than myself. My decision, my action.

As I sit and wait for my breathing to slow and the rush to subside, I wish upon a star. "Star light, star bright . . ." A bat flits across my path of vision and my eyes follow it. Without any warning, the bat suddenly swerves and changes direction. It has changed its path forever.

And now, having been interrupted, my wish seems futile and absurd. I am filled with a rushing understanding of the part I play in my own life.

I am not just a bystander. My life is not to be controlled by the stars, but by me, and me alone. Like the bat, I am free to choose my own path, however haphazard and illogical it might appear to be.

Bryony Blackwood

The Player

It was his attitude that got me. That self-assured smile and those cocky mannerisms gave me the irresistible urge to challenge such conceit. I had never met a person so sure of himself. He assumed that when you first met him, you had no choice but to like him. It made me want to prove him wrong. I would show him that I could not only resist his charms, but that I could beat him at his own game.

So our relationship began as a battle, each trying to gain a foothold, trying to pull ahead of the other and prove our dominance. We waged an unrelenting war of mind games, insults and tests.

But somewhere in the middle of our warfare, the teasing became playful and we became friends. We found in each other not just a challenge, but someone to turn to when we didn't feel like fighting anymore. Josh loved to "communicate." He often talked for hours as I listened, covering every topic that affected him and his life. I soon realized that he was more concerned about himself than anything else. But because I didn't always have a lot to say, it didn't seem that it would be a conflict in our relationship.

It was several months after our friendship started that

Josh began a discussion about love. "It takes a lot for me to love someone," he told me, in a tone more serious than I had ever heard from him. "What I need is trust. I could never fall in love with someone who I didn't feel I could tell everything to. Like you. You're my favorite person in the entire world. I could tell you anything," he said, looking straight at me.

I blushed, unsure of what response I should give in return, afraid that whatever I said would betray the new emotions I had begun to feel for Josh over the past few weeks. The look in my eyes must have given me away, because from that moment on, it seemed that he began to do everything in his power to make me fall deeper and deeper into the way I felt about him. Was it love? He seemed to glow in the attention that I paid him. And I enjoyed adoring him. Yet it didn't take me very long to figure out that Josh had no intention of returning my devotion.

When we were alone, he would kiss me and hold me and tell me how special our relationship was to him, and that he didn't know anyone else who made him so happy. But a few weeks into our relationship, I found out that he was involved with another girl and had been for some time. The pain I felt at his betrayal was overwhelming, but I found I couldn't be angry with him. I felt sure inside that he really did care, and that it was his friendship that was important to me.

At school one day, I saw him standing with a group of girls, and by the flirtatious smile on his face, I could tell he had again been working his magic. "Josh!" I yelled down the hallway to him. He looked up at me, then back at the girls, and with a groupie under each arm, he turned and made his way in the opposite direction. I stood completely deflated, not wanting to acknowledge what had just happened. But I couldn't avoid the truth any longer. My "best friend" had ignored me so I wouldn't hurt the reputation he was working on.

After that, I began to watch Josh, not as someone who had a crush on him, but as an outside observer. I began to see the darker side of his personality. It was only when I moved away from him that my cloudy vision cleared. It was as if the shadow my adoration had thrown over the situation grew smaller, and I finally saw what I had not been able to see before.

Josh spent day after day making new acquaintances that he thought might adore him. He flirted with girls, knowing how to make them feel pretty. He knew how to play the game just right—to make sure that everyone felt they had his complete attention. When you were with him, you felt he was interested only in you. He hung out, telling jokes and acting cool, giving off an aura that made people want to be around him. But now I could see that he did it all for himself because he needed to be surrounded by people who thought he was great.

And while he acted as though he really cared about these people, I heard him belittle them behind their backs, saw him ignore them in the process of making new friends. I saw the pain on their faces that I understood only too well.

I talked to Josh once more after that day. Even though I understood his nature and was opposed to everything he stood for, there was still a part of me that wanted him to care, and still wanted things the way they used to be.

"What happened?" I asked him. I cringe when I think how pitiful I must have sounded. "I mean, I thought we were best friends. How can you just give up all the time we spent together? All the things we talked about? The . . . the love that you always told me was there?"

He shrugged and replied coldly, "Hey, these things happen," before he turned and walked away.

I stood, watching him go, with tears running down my

face. I cried not for him, but for the friendship I thought we had, for the love I thought we had felt. I had lost the game in a big way.

Now, even though it was one of the most painful experiences I've ever endured, I am grateful for my "friendship" with Josh because it made me stronger. Now I know the kind of person and the kind of friend I never want to be.

Perhaps I won the game after all.

Kelly Garnett

"I want the prime rib with a baked potato.
My boyfriend isn't sure what he wants.
He can't commit to anything."

The Porcelain Bride Doll

When I was a little girl, I was given a porcelain bride doll as a gift from my father. The doll was gowned in layers of lace. The material was shot through with strands of shiny silver so that if I turned her slowly in the sunlight, she sparkled. Her soft blond hair, partially covered by her mantilla-like veil and train, curled gently around her face. It was her face that was made of porcelain, and whoever painted her features was truly an artist.

Her small rosebud mouth, a soft rosy pink, was curved in a perpetual shy smile, and her cheeks blushed gently with the merest suggestion of color. And oh, her eyes! They were the most wonderful clear shade of blue, like clean lake water reflecting the summer sky. Her irises had been painted with a small fleck of white so that there appeared always to be a light in them. She wore tiny pearl-drop earrings and white high heels, and I thought she was the most beautiful, serene-looking doll in the world. My own dark hair and eyes and olive skin notwithstanding, I knew that when I became a bride, I would look just like her.

Every day after school, I would come home and take

the doll down from its stand on my dresser and carefully hold her, fingering her dress, her shoes, the little earrings. My enjoyment of her was not diminished by the fact that she was a "doll for looking at" and not for playing with, as my father had explained. It was enough for me just to have her in my room, where I could see her and gently touch her.

My best friend, Katy, was as delighted by the doll as I was. She often begged me to allow her to hold it. Sometimes I did. Often, we'd play "wedding," holding sheets on our heads and letting them drape the floor in back of us, like the train on my doll. We'd practice the exaggerated slow steps we'd seen brides in movies take, then collapse in giggles as we fantasized about who our grooms would be.

Katy wanted a doll like mine and told me that she had asked for one for Christmas. But Christmas came and went, and Katy did not get a doll. I knew she was disappointed. She stopped asking to hold my doll when she came over and didn't want to play "pretend wedding" anymore. But one day, while we were coloring on the floor in my room, under the gaze of my bride doll, Katy said, "You know, someday I'm going to be a bride and look just like that doll!"

"Me, too," I said happily, thinking that Katy was beginning our old game again.

But then she said, "Don't be silly. You'll never look like her. You look too Jewish."

It was the way she said it that shocked me. Her words stung, flung as they were, like so many sharp stones. Without thinking, I shoved my friend backward. She fell against my dresser, shaking it. My lovely bride doll toppled over face forward, stand and all. Her head hit the wood floor and broke. But it didn't shatter as I would have expected. Instead, it just kind of popped open cleanly, revealing the black empty space between the two halves.

For just a moment neither of us moved. We were too stunned by the appearance of the doll's head. To a young child, there is something frightening about that black hole inside. It's a place that children aren't supposed to see. But the next moment, Katy was screaming that I had hurt her, and my mother was running into the room.

My mother picked up the two pieces of the doll's head and asked for an explanation. Katy was crying and would only say that I had pushed her and she wanted to go home. I was confined to my room.

After Katy had gone, my mother asked me why I had pushed my friend. I repeated Katy's remark. Just then, I didn't know if I was angry at Katy because her comment was so obviously meant to insult me, or if I was sad that what she said was true. My mother just stared at the doll in her hands.

That night, Katy and her mother appeared at our door. Katy's mother apologized for the incident and offered to buy me a new doll. My mother just said no. She did not say "thank you."

After they had gone, my mother gave me the doll back. She had glued the head back together. The break had been on a seam, and she was able to fix it so that you couldn't even tell it had come apart. My mother looked at me a long time before she finally spoke. Then she said, "Your doll is better now than when she was new." She explained that the original glue wasn't of very good quality. As a result, the doll was too delicate to be enjoyed. So my mother had fixed it; she made that doll's head stronger, less fragile. Now it wouldn't fall apart when it was bumped. There was something substantial holding it together, and it could withstand whatever childish insult it might encounter. "Do you understand?" she asked. I did.

I held the bride doll in my arms, fingering the thin, barely visible line across her head. I realized that I had looked into a gaping black hole—the type of place where ugly things like mean-spirited ethnic slurs might be allowed to exist. But my mother had repaired the damage to the doll, making it stronger. And she showed me that the special type of "glue" was in me, as well. I didn't ever need to be afraid.

Katy and I continued to play together after that, but more often at my house than at hers. Children learn from their parents. Katy's parents had taught her an effective way to hurt someone. My mother taught me that even though I was a child, I was entitled to respect and I had the power to take it when I needed to. She taught me that some things you'd ordinarily think are delicate—like porcelain, or a child's ego—are really quite resilient.

I kept that doll for many years and gave her to my first daughter when she was about six. But my daughter put the doll on a shelf and rarely took the time to play with it. The doll's blue-eyed, blond, lacy perfection didn't seem to hold the same charm for my child as it had for me.

The last time I looked at that bride doll, the lace had faded and she was missing an earring and a shoe. She didn't seem quite as wonderful as she had when my father gave her to me years ago.

But that glue that my mother used was still holding fast.

Marsha Arons

Myself

A human being's first responsibility is to shake hands with himself.

Henry Winkler

I have to live with myself, and so
I want to be fit for myself to know
I want to be able as days go by
Always to look myself straight in the eye;
I don't want to stand, with the setting sun,
And hate myself for things I have done.
I don't want to keep on a closet shelf
A lot of secrets about myself,
And fool myself, as I come and go,
Into thinking that nobody else will know
The kind of man I really am;
I don't want to dress myself up in sham.
I want to go out with my head erect,
I want to deserve all man's respect;
And here in the struggle for fame and wealth,
I want to be able to like myself.
I don't want to look at myself and know

That I am a bluffer, an empty show.
I can never hide myself from me:
I see what others may never see,
I know what others may never know;
I never can fool myself, and so,
Whatever happens, I want to be
Self-respecting and guilt-free.

Peer Counsellor Workbook

Firmer Ground

I'd had a crush on him for as long as I could remember. His sandy blond hair was to his shoulders. His eyes were brown, his skin pale. He was quiet, mild-mannered. Most of all, I was drawn to his smile—when I could coax it out of him. I was in junior high. He was in high school.

He was my friend's brother and, for some reason, I believed he was taboo. Maybe because I knew instinctively my friend would be angry if I ever started to see him. Or maybe I knew the age gap of three years would not sit well with my parents. Or maybe, more than anything, I was terrified he'd reject me.

So I kept my feelings as quiet as a cat hiding from a pack of dogs. But every time I saw him at my friend Tina's house, my heart beat hard and I could barely breathe. When I saw him walking up the street alone, I'd rush over to him and glow in his warmth. He'd wave, smile a weak hello and ask me how I was doing.

He was an artist and a good one, and the day he gave me a pen drawing of a seagull soaring through the sky, I was in my glory. I saw it as a symbol, a sign perhaps, of affection shown by an older boy who felt it wise to keep his love for me inside. Of course, it was more likely that he just felt sorry for such a gangly kid.

It didn't matter. I cherished his artwork and truly believed that he would be a great artist someday. If only I had such talent, I'd moan. He'd always tell me that I probably did have a lot of talent. I just hadn't found it yet.

Somewhere as we were growing older and suffering the pangs of adolescence, Mike lost his ground. I'm not sure if he knew where to put his feet anymore. His family life was a disaster: a mentally ill mother, a father with a wicked second wife (at least that's how the children saw her) and a new baby who took all the interest away from three other kids.

Whenever I walked by his home, there was always a man—often a different man—parked in a car across the street from Mike's house. It happened so often that I began to wonder what was going on. I began to ask questions of my friends. I learned that my sweet, reserved Mike had turned into a high school drug dealer. Not the small kind of drug dealer. He was a big fish and according to my friends, he was in trouble. Someone was closing in on him—the police or the creeps who got him involved in the first place.

I knew that a lot of kids dabbled in drugs—mostly marijuana. But no one, and I mean no one, took the risk of dealing. The odds of getting hurt or busted were far too great in this middle-class neighborhood. I often wondered what led Mike there. Did he hate his parents? Did he feel lost? Did he want payback time for his dad remarrying and leaving his mom? Who knows what went on in his brain. I just wished he had talked to me because I really cared about him. The problem was that he didn't care. And I was too afraid to go to Mike and confront him about whether he was selling drugs.

When the knock on the door came, I looked out the

balcony of my house and saw one of my neighbors standing there. "I thought you and your family should know I
found Mike in the canyon this morning. My sons and I
were walking there and I saw Mike bowing as though he
were praying. It didn't look too good."

Our neighbor had held his young boys back as he
investigated. Mike was dead. He had hung himself from a
tree, and had died in a kneeling position on the ground,
his head slumped forward. The news pounded my face as
if a block of cement had struck. I thought I would pass
out, but instead, I was sobbing. Within the hour, I raced
up to Mike's to see how Tina was.

She was sitting on her bed, just staring out at empty
space. I would learn later that she was in shock. In a dull
voice, she explained that she and her older brother, Gary,
had known that Mike was dealing drugs. After Mike's body
was discovered, Gary went into Mike's room and cleaned
out Mike's top drawer before the police came. There,
tucked underneath a few shirts, was every drug imag-
inable: LSD, cocaine, pot and an abundance of colorful pills.
Soon after, Tina ran away. It took us hours to find her.

My parents tried to explain why Mike died. But they
couldn't. They didn't even know he was a dealer. They
didn't know the ugly things we kids faced going to school
every day. It was a trying time not only because Mike
died, but because I was shocked to peel away the layers
and find a Mike I had never known. Or maybe he was that
kind, sweet boy who let his difficult life suck him into a
world of deceit, fast bucks and danger.

To this day, I always wonder if he really killed himself
or if some other drug dealers helped him along the way.
It was just too odd that he had supposedly hung himself
from a thin tree limb but was kneeling, his weight
supported by the earth.

I will never know the answer. But I do know this: He

was a good artist. I kept that drawing he gave me for years after, always looking at it with wonder and admiration, wishing I could sketch that way.

I also know that along the way Mike lost his ground, but he gave me a lot to think about, and what I thought about gave me strength. My family moved to the East Coast my first year of high school. My new friends were just beginning to experiment with drugs, and there was tremendous peer pressure for me to go along.

But by now, I felt old and weary when it came to drugs. Been there, done that, seen what they can do. I decided I wanted the chance to know what I was going to be in the future. Mike had given me some firm ground to stand on.

Diana Chapman

Love and Belonging

Walking down the steps of the psychology building, I spot my buddy Walter and his girlfriend, Anna. Walt and I have known each other almost all our lives. We grew up next door to each other, and fought and played our way through elementary school, adolescence, junior high and high school. Our parents had been best friends, and life even as recently as a year ago seemed so simple, so secure.

But now, while I'm struggling with my parents' divorce, Walter's world is intact—his parents are still together and living in the same house where he grew up. My mom is alone now in our house, while Dad is living the life of a newlywed with his second wife, in an apartment across town. I feel my stomach churn as I think of that, and mild irritation as Walter puts his arm around Anna.

"Hey, Jesse," he says as he sees me. I notice a sudden, self-conscious grin wash over his face. "How was the exam?"

"Oh, okay, I guess." I wish Anna would disappear. Walter's apparent happiness irritates me, and I suddenly feel very tired. "What are you up to?" I don't care if I seem rude in ignoring Anna.

"Well," Walter begins, and his grip around Anna's shoulder tightens, "we're on our way to check out some CDs at that new sound shop down the street. Want to come along?"

"Nah, I think I'll take a nap before my next class."

Anna speaks up. "How are you doing these days, Jesse?" I can see the sympathy in her eyes, and I hate her.

"I'm fine—just great. Life couldn't be better."

"Well . . ." she struggles with what to say next. I find myself enjoying her obvious discomfort. "Sorry you can't go with us." But I hear relief in her voice even as she says it. Walter takes Anna's hand, and together they cross the street.

Why should they seem so happy and look so secure? They don't have a clue as to what's going on in the real world.

I turn and walk down the sidewalk and across the Commons. Maybe it's true, what my Coach Carter said, that I have my antennae out these days. It seems as if every couple reminds me of the failure in my family.

"How can this have happened to my family, Carter? Why didn't I realize what was happening? Maybe I could have done something!"

Just then Carter picked up a crystal paperweight from his desk and tossed it to me. I caught it purely from reflex.

"Why did you do that?" I asked, half mad–half serious.

Looking around the room, he said, "You knew you had to be careful with that paperweight, didn't you, Jesse?"

"Sure. It might break." I put it back on his desk.

"People take care of things that seem obviously fragile. Think about it. When you buy a house, you don't expect it to maintain itself. Or a car; you make sure you do things like change the oil every few thousand miles and buy tires when they are worn.

"With so many things in life, Jesse, you expect to have to care for them, keep a close eye on them, nurture them.

We're more careful with an insignificant paperweight than we are with our closest relationships."

"You're telling me that my mom and dad were careless with their marriage?" I heard my voice rise unnaturally, my fingers clenched in my palms.

"Not necessarily careless, Jesse. Perhaps they just expected it to flourish on its own. But marriage, like anything else, won't flourish in an environment of neglect. No one should take a good relationship for granted."

"But what do I do? You're telling me to accept all this—Mom and Dad splitting up; Dad marrying someone I don't even know. She can't take Mom's place. No way!"

"I'm suggesting that you try to accept it," Carter said gently, "because for you, that's all you can do. You can't change your parents, and you can't change what happened. You don't have to love your stepmother as you do your mother, and probably no one expects you to. But to get beyond this and to be able to handle your parents' new, more complex relationships—and your future relationships with women—then you do need to learn to accept what has happened."

"Well, I just don't see how you can ask me to do that. I can't stand seeing them apart!"

As I stood up to leave his study he said, "I know you're feeling pretty alone right now. But believe me, you'd be surprised at how many young people have sat in this office and asked me why divorce had to happen in their family. Maybe it will help if you remember that there are a lot of people who are hurting just like you. And remember—this divorce is not your fault. Don't ever forget that."

Walking down the street, I see a city bus slow down and then stop at the corner. On impulse, I get on.

I pay the driver and begin to look for a seat.

An elderly couple is seated at the back of the bus. I sit beside them.

We ride in silence toward town. I glance over at the couple and notice that they are holding hands. The wedding ring on the old woman's finger is a dull gold, and there is a tiny diamond in the center of the band.

I watch as the old man rests his left hand on top of hers, and I see that his wedding ring matches hers. His, too, is scratched and dull with age.

As they sit in companionable silence, I notice the resemblance of their features. Both wear glasses, and both have short, pure white, wiry hair. They even wear the same style of shirt—simple white cotton, short-sleeved.

Occasionally the woman points at something as we pass by, and the man nods in agreement. I am mystified, and yet I feel a sense of peace sitting next to them.

Before too long we reach their stop. A row of neat, white frame houses lines the quiet side street.

The old man gets up slowly and pulls his walking stick from the seat next to him. He waits patiently for his wife to get up before he starts to walk to the front of the bus. The woman rises just as slowly and pulls a blue cardigan over her thin arms. He takes her hand, and as they turn to walk to the front of the bus, I catch his eye. I can't let them leave without asking, "How long have you two been married?"

He looks inquisitively at her. She smiles and gently shrugs her shoulders. It doesn't matter. It hasn't mattered for some time.

Finally he says in a raspy voice, "I don't know exactly—many years." Then he adds, "Most of our lives."

They walk down the aisle of the bus and are gone.

I lean back in my seat. It takes me a few moments to realize that the cold, hard knot in my stomach doesn't seem so tight now. And the face reflected back at me from the glass of the bus window looks a little less tense.

Watching the colors of the trees slide by, my mind wanders back to the old couple and finally comes to rest on my parents. The realization quietly dawns on me that I have been looking for answers when maybe I don't have to know at all. I don't have to hurt for them and me, too. I don't have to have all the answers about love and life and why things work out the way they do sometimes. Maybe no one has the answers.

"Hey, buddy," the bus driver says to me. I look up and realize I'm alone on the bus. We're downtown at the square. "This is the end of the line. You can get off here or go back."

I think for a minute. "Do you go by that new sound shop close to campus?"

"Yeah, sure."

"Well, drop me off there," I say. "There's someone there. A friend. And I need to talk to him."

T. J. Lacey

What I Wish I'd Known Sooner

For the past year or two, I have devoted a section of my home page on the Internet to a list entitled "What I Wish I'd Known Sooner." Since I am seventeen, there are a lot of stupid things I do that make me wish I had already known not to do them! Anyone can add to this list—I have received additions from all over the world, by people of all ages. I often add to it myself (after the fact)!

Some are lighthearted, some are serious, all are very true. Here are a few of the gems:

- Don't drink grape juice while wearing a white shirt and driving to school.
- Don't let your life wait for other people.
- Dropping a cellular phone into a bathtub of water kinda kills the phone.
- Your mother will find out if you dye your hair purple.
- You haven't really lived until you've gotten a 48 on an Advanced Placement U.S. History test.
- Don't ever fall in love with someone who is more than one thousand miles away from you. It usually doesn't work.
- Milk crates make boring pets.

- If it hurts, DON'T DO IT AGAIN!
- That which does not kill you will ultimately make you stronger.
- Speaking in public gets easier with practice.
- Don't sprint around a pool if you're trying to impersonate Jim from Huck Finn.
- Ten years from now most of what we freak out about won't make any difference.
- All that's gold doesn't glisten.
- Zits always pop up when you really can't afford for them to pop up.
- Always stay after class because that's where connections are made.
- When in doubt, duck. When certain, don't bother, 'cause you're already screwed.
- While driving a car through a gate, always, ALWAYS make sure the gate is open! The consequences might be fatal to your car.
- If you're not living (I mean really living), you're dead already.
- Never pierce your belly button in the dark.
- Just because someone flirts with you incessantly doesn't necessarily mean he or she likes you.
- If your calculus teacher tells you to quit talking after a test or he'll give you a zero for your test grade, he means it. Really.
- Sometimes smart people can do very, very stupid things.
- Being nice to people will get you far.
- The one person you can truly love is often right in front of you.
- Never, ever, EVER let a member of the opposite sex make you compromise your standards. Never.
- Nothing is ever too good to be true (said by Michael Faraday).
- If you start to like a girl, her roommate will immediately start liking you.

- Parents aren't around forever, and you need to treasure them while they are.
- Don't take the SAT twice if you already have a good score in the first place.
- Never do something if the risk is greater than the reward.
- Think carefully before you act.
- Dreaming and doing go hand in hand.
- Life moves fast, but not so fast that you can't slow down to enjoy it.
- Instead of waiting for life to get better, do something about it.
- You REALLY should do what needs to be done NOW, and not later. Procrastination is the easiest way, but not the most profitable.
- If your intuition is telling you not to do something, then don't. Your intuition is not stupid!
- Cereal is a vital staple food for all college students. Who cares how ridiculous you look eating it at 7:30 P.M.?
- If he doesn't respect you, then he's not worth any of your time.
- Learn to play an electric guitar: young women really dig it.
- Don't juggle knives unless you're really, really good at it.
- If at first you don't succeed, try again. Then give up. No sense being ridiculous about it.
- Sticking things up your nose isn't the smartest idea in the world.
- You can't light fireworks in the basement and not get caught.
- Hair is flammable. *Very* flammable.
- Never ever trust your friend with a pair of scissors against your hair.
- Dyeing hair strawberry blond that is already strawberry blond makes it turn strawberry pink.
- White dogs and black pants don't mix.
- God doesn't make junk!

- Someday you will look back on this and it will all seem funny.
- You never know when you're making a memory.
- The heart does heal and you will love like this again— except that when you do, you'll deny that you ever loved like this before.
- Nothing matters if you don't have loved ones to share it with. Your siblings are incredibly precious. If you don't know this now, you will—trust me!
- If you can laugh at yourself, you are going to be fine.
- If you allow others to laugh with you, you'll be great!
- Kissing is the most fun thing. Dancing is almost as fun.

Meredith Rowe

"Yes, I'm wearing my birthday suit!
This is a birthday party, isn't it?"

"No, the BMWs, Saabs, and Jaguars are the pupils'.
The Fords, Chevys and Dodges
belong to the teachers."

Reprinted by permission of Harley Schwadron.

My Most
Embarrassing Moment

[AUTHOR'S NOTE TO HER MOM AND DAD: *I'm sorry you have to find out about this at the same time all of America does. I never told anyone.*]

Honor student, tennis team player, Spanish Club president. Sunday school teacher assistant, Swing Choir piano accompanist. Although these publicly recognized accomplishments of my teenage years went on to influence my life in many ways, there was one particular group activity I participated in that had an even greater impact on me: Mustard Gang Member.

The fall of 1977 found me enrolled as a freshman in the school system I had attended since kindergarten. My student file over the last ten years could be summed up with positive comments such as "consistently above average," "enjoys extracurricular activities" and "cooperates with teachers and fellow classmates." No suspensions. No detentions. Basically, a model student. However, within a total time period of approximately one hour, this trademark behavior would fly right out the window (at the speed of sound).

Three of my lifelong girlfriends—who would fall under a fairly close ditto description of that above—caught up to me after school on a Friday afternoon. One of them had just received her driver's license and was going cruising in a nearby town to celebrate. She asked if I would like to come along. (Rhetorical question.) The final bell was sounding as we piled into an older model Dodge Charger on its last leg of life. Regardless of its condition, it had a full tank of gas and the ability to get us from Point A to Point B.

Within minutes of leaving the school parking lot, we were on the open highway. As I look back now, that highway was pretty significant. It not only separated two towns, it separated those of us in the car from the people who knew us and the people who didn't. We became daring.

When the novelty of just driving around wore off, someone suggested it might be fun to squirt mustard on parked cars as we drove past them. *(Author's sensible reaction twenty years later: WHAT?!)* A unanimous agreement must have followed, because all four of us stood beside each other in the checkout line where the bottle of mustard was ultimately purchased.

Loading back into the car, each of our faces looked as though we couldn't believe what we were doing. We couldn't. Four kids, four clean records. *Lost time was about to be made up for.*

We decided that the person sitting by the passenger's side window would be the Designated Squirter, while the others in the car would be responsible for choosing the target ahead. Since I was cowardly, trying to hide in a corner of the backseat, I thought this sounded swell. Feeling my guilt would be somewhat lessened if I didn't actually *touch* the mustard bottle, I thought. I was off the hook. A nervous sigh of relief was escaping me until the words "and we'll pull over every other block and switch seats so it will be fair." Hook re-inserted.

The "talk" in the car proved to be more productive than the "action" as the first and second girls took their turn in the passenger seat, both chickening out at the last second, squealing, "I can't!" Before I knew it, the car had stalled and it was me who was climbing in beside the driver. Sliding my sweaty palms up and down the bottle's sides, the target was being pointed out to me, loudly and with demanding encouragement. The attack was to be launched on a little red Volkswagen up ahead, fast approaching. "Do it! Do it! Do it!" my friends chanted. . . . *And I almost did.* But, as was the case with the girls before, feathers grew from within me and we soon sped past the car, leaving it as solid red as it had been when first spotted.

Since the driver couldn't take a respective turn as the shooter, we headed for home, the mischief supposedly ended. Just when we were nearing the highway, we passed two girls jogging, their hands moving up and down in front of them. Still looking for trouble, we interpreted their innocent actions. "Hey! They just gave us the finger!" And of course, if we had been needlessly insulted, they certainly would have to pay. Simple as that.

Within seconds, they were jogging into a Kmart parking lot. . . . And we were right behind them. Jumping out of the car, we ran toward our unsuspecting prey yelling, "Get 'em!" We did. Well, *I* did. After all, there was only one bottle, and it was my turn. Silently, they just stood there.

My hearing must have been the last of my senses to fail, for the car door did not slam shut behind me without the words from one of these mustard-covered strangers ringing in my ears: "That wasn't very funny, Rochelle." Clear words. Echoing words. Rochelle. Rochelle. Rochelle. Not only had I just left two people covered with mustard back in a parking lot, but at least one of them wasn't a stranger.

Although no one in the car physically recognized either victim, there was no doubt among any of us that the voice that just spoke was a familiar one. But whose? The longest minute of my life followed until I figured it out: *Miss Greatens, MY TYPING TEACHER!*

Miss Greatens, fresh out of college, was committed to making a strong professional impression on the business class students she taught. Her hair was always gathered on top of her head, large glasses covered her eyes and crisp business suits were her chosen attire. And yet outside of her work environment, she suddenly changed. Drastically. Her hair looked as though it grew a foot or so (since just this afternoon), she shrank a solid two inches (heels removed), contact lenses replaced glasses and her business suit was traded in for a sweatsuit. She no longer looked like Miss Greatens; she looked more like . . . well, *us!*

Situation assessment: WE HAD A PROBLEM. The Dodge Charger immediately went chasing back to the parking lot, but the joggers were nowhere in sight. Plan B was implemented. A telephone booth directory could provide her home address. Success. She lived right across from Kmart in an apartment complex.

Little did we know that Miss Greatens was doing some of her own phone referencing while we were trying to find her. First she called the school principal at home, then she called my parents. *(My life, as I knew it, was about to end.)* However, she hung up after the first two rings before anyone answered either call. She had decided to speak to us first.

And here we were.

Miss Greatens answered the door graciously, standing before us with mustard-stained clothes and tear-stained cheeks, wanting to hear what possible explanation warranted her pain. There was none. Absolutely none. What we had done was uncalled for. Our consciences made that perfectly clear as we poured out a flood of genuine remorse and tears to equal her own.

Then something extraordinary happened: *She forgave us.*
Fully. Right there on the spot. She could have spoken to
all of our parents about what happened, but didn't. She
could have contacted school officials and sought stern
reprimands for each of us, but didn't. And she could have
held the incident over our heads for a very long time and
reminded us of what we had done at will, but didn't.

Will we ever do anything like that again? NO WAY. You
see, that is the power of forgiveness.

Rochelle M. Pennington

Call Me

"I know it's here somewhere." Cheryl drops her book bag at her feet so she can dig through her coat pockets. When she dumps her purse out onto the table, everyone waiting in line behind her groans.

Cheryl glances up at the lunch room clock. Only three minutes until the bell and this is the last day to order a yearbook, if you want your name imprinted in gold on the front. And Cheryl did, if only she could find her wallet. The line begins to move around her.

"Come on, Cheryl." Darcy might as well stamp her foot, she sounds so impatient. "We'll be late for class."

"Darcy, please!" Cheryl snaps back. Best friends or not, Darcy and Cheryl often frustrate each other. They are just so different. Today is a good example. Darcy had "budgeted" for her yearbook and ordered it the first day of school while Cheryl had almost forgotten . . . again.

"Darcy, my wallet's gone." Cheryl throws her things back into her purse. "My yearbook money was in it." The bell interrupts her search.

"Someone took it!" Darcy, as usual, is quick to point away from the bright side of things.

"Oh, I'm sure I just misplaced it," Cheryl hopes.

They rush into class just before the second bell rings. Darcy takes center stage to Cheryl's problem and happily spreads the news about the theft.

By gym the last hour, Cheryl is tired of being stopped and having to say over and over again, "I'm sure I just left it at home." Rushing into the locker room, she changes quickly and checks the list posted by the field door to see where her group is playing soccer, then hurries out to catch up with them.

The game was a close one, and Cheryl's team is the last one back to the locker room.

Darcy stands waiting for Cheryl by her locker. Cheryl brushes passed Juanita, the new girl. It's the shocked look on Darcy's face and the startled gasps of those around her that stop Cheryl.

There, at her feet, is her wallet.

"It fell out of her locker!" Darcy points at Juanita. "She stole it."

Everyone speaks at once.

"The new girl stole it."

"Darcy caught her red-handed."

"I knew there was something about her."

"Report her."

Cheryl turns and looks at Juanita. She's never really noticed her before, beyond her "new girl" label.

Juanita picks up the wallet and holds it out to Cheryl. Her hands are trembling. "I found it in the parking lot. I was going to give it to you before gym, but you were late."

Darcy's words spit anger. "I'm so sure!"

"Really. It's true." Juanita's voice is high and pleading.

Cheryl hesitates. Juanita's eyes begin to fill with tears.

Cheryl reaches for her wallet.

"I'm so glad you found it." Cheryl smiles. "Thanks, Juanita."

The tension around them breaks. "Good thing she found it." Everyone but Darcy agrees.

Cheryl does another quick change and then bangs her locker closed. "Hurry, Darcy. There's just enough time to order a yearbook."

"*If* there is any money left in your wallet."

"Not now, Darcy!"

"You are so naive!"

It isn't until they are standing in line that Cheryl opens her wallet.

"It's all here." Cheryl can't help feeling relieved. A small piece of paper flutters down from her wallet.

"She just didn't have time to empty it yet." Darcy bends down to pick up the note. "I know her type. I had her pegged the first day she came." She hands the note to Cheryl.

Cheryl reads it and then looks up at Darcy. "You had her pegged, all right. Maybe that's the problem. Maybe you spend too much time pegging people."

Darcy grabs the note, reads it and throws it back at Cheryl. "Whatever!" she says and stomps off.

Cheryl reads the note again.

Cheryl,

I found your wallet in the parking lot. Hope nothing is missing.

Juanita

P.S. My number is 555-3218. Maybe you could call me.

And Cheryl did.

Cindy Hamond

$\overline{\underline{7}}$
MAKING A
DIFFERENCE

It's important to be involved and stand up for what you believe in.

Ione Skye

For You, Dad

"Here we go!" Dad would say, and I'd climb on his back. "There! Look! See London Bridge?"

Lying on the floor with his arms outstretched, he was my Superman and together we were weaving our way around make-believe clouds. But like those clouds, my moments with Dad always vanished too quickly—because there was something stronger than love in Daddy's life, something that was stealing him away. It was an enemy I would end up fighting when he no longer could. . . .

"He's sick," my mother would say when Dad passed out. "It doesn't mean that he doesn't love you."

I knew he did. He could make us laugh with his funny faces and cartoon drawings. I loved him, and I wanted to believe Mom still did, too. As my little brothers and I grew, she explained that Dad hadn't always been "this way." He was just a little wild when they'd met in high school. And with his wavy hair and wide smile, I could understand how he'd captured Mom's heart.

But soon he must have been breaking it. Sometimes we didn't see him for weeks. One day, he called to say he wasn't coming home again. "I'm not far. We'll see each other on weekends," he said after he'd moved out. "I'll swing by and get you Saturday."

"Mom," I called out. "Can we go with Daddy?"

Grabbing the phone, Mom said, "No, John, you have to visit them at the house. You know I won't let them get into a car with you."

I thought of the commercials I saw on TV—the ones with the twisted metal and chalk outlines. And the words *Drunk driving kills.* Could that happen to Daddy? *Please God,* I'd pray at night, *help Daddy get well.* But too often, when he pulled into the driveway, we could smell the booze.

"Daddy, don't drive like that," I'd plead. Usually, he tried to shrug off my worries, but once he pulled me close, his eyes heavy with sadness. "I wish I wasn't like this," he said. "I wish I was a good dad."

I wished that, too. I hated alcohol for what it had done—to all of us.

At first, I was too embarrassed to tell my friends the truth about my dad. But as I started to see kids drinking, I couldn't hold back. "That's why my dad isn't around," I'd say, pointing to the bottles.

All Dad's visits were brief. In between hugs and kisses, he drew pictures for us, and we crammed in stories about school and friends. "I'm getting help," he'd say. Maybe my brothers, Justin and Jordan, believed it—but I didn't. And yet with all my heart, I wanted to believe. I can still feel the rocking of the porch swing and my father's arm around my shoulder.

"The day you turn sixteen," he once said, "I'm going to buy you a car." I nuzzled closer to him. I knew he'd give me the world if he could. But I understood that no matter how much he wanted to, he couldn't.

Then one night during my senior year of high school,

I got a call at the store where I worked part-time. "Heather?" Mom's voice was strained. I knew what was coming. "There's been an accident."

I raced to the hospital; Dad's motorcycle had hit a minivan. Blood tests showed he'd been drinking and doing drugs that night. The other driver was fine, thank God.

"I love you, Daddy," I sobbed, sitting by his bed. Though he was unconscious, his heart monitor quickened at the sound of my voice. He had found a way to let me know he'd heard me, and that he loved me. But there was something I had to make sure that he knew.

"I forgive you," I choked. "I know you did your best."

Moments later, he was gone. An accident killed my father, but his death was not sudden.

Everyone told me I needed to grieve, and for a while, I did. But in a sense, I'd been grieving for Dad all my life. Now I needed to do something that would help me feel less powerless against the enemy that had stolen him.

I went to the library to find what I could on substance abuse. *Almost every family is affected. . . . Children may repeat the patterns*, I read. My heart broke even more. My father's life hadn't amounted to very much. Maybe his death could.

That afternoon, I picked up the phone and called the area schools. "I'd like to talk about substance abuse," I began. "I've lived with it in my own family, so I think I can help."

Before I knew it, I was standing before a sea of young faces ready to speak, in a presentation called "Drug-Free Me."

"People who do drugs and alcohol aren't bad," I began. "They've just made the wrong choice." Then I asked the kids to draw pictures of what they wanted to be. They drew firemen and doctors and astronauts.

"See all those pretty dreams? They can never come true if you turn to drugs and alcohol." Their eyes grew wide.

I'm reaching them, I thought. But I knew it wasn't that simple—I'd have to keep trying every day if I really wanted to make a difference.

Since then, I've used cartoon characters to get the message to younger kids. I've organized a tuxedo-stuffing program, sticking statistics on drunk driving into pockets of prom-goers. And I've joined Mothers Against Drunk Driving and the National Commission on Drunk Driving.

Today, as a college junior, I do presentations at middle and high schools. I also speak at victim-impact panels, sharing stories of loss with people convicted of driving under the influence. Most people on the panel have lost loved ones to people like my father. But I was a victim, too, and maybe my story hits harder.

"It's hard to think of a faceless stranger out there you may kill," I tell the offenders. "So think about the people you are hurting now—like a child at home who will miss you forever if you die."

I'd been missing my father long before he was taken for good. I remember once he said that we, his children, were the only things he'd ever done right in his life. Daddy, because of you, I'm doing something very right in mine.

Heather Metzger
As told to Bill Holton
Woman's World Magazine

Somebody Loves You

Don't forget to be kind to strangers. For some who have done this have entertained angels without realizing it.

Hebrews 13:2

One miserable rainy night, a man named Mark decided to end his life. In his mid-fifties, Mark had never been married, had never experienced the joy of having children or spending holidays with his family. Both his parents had been dead for seven years. He had a sister but had lost contact with her. He held a menial job that left him unfulfilled. Wet and unhappy, he walked the streets, feeling as if there was nobody in the entire world that cared if he lived or died.

On that same soggy night, I was sitting in my room watching the rain hit my window. I was six years old, and my life revolved around my Star Wars action figure collection. I was dreaming of the day when I'd have earned enough money to add Darth Vader to my new collector's case. To help me make money, my father paid me to jog with him. Every day, at seven o'clock, we jogged together.

And every day, I was fifty cents closer to getting Darth Vader.

When I heard the doorbell ring, I jumped from my chair and raced out of my room to the top of the steps. My mother was already at the door.

Opening it, she found herself face-to-face with a very disheveled-looking man with tears streaming down his face. My mother, overcome by pity, invited the man inside, and he sat with my parents in our living room.

Curious, I snuck downstairs so that I could get a better look. I couldn't understand what they were saying, but the sight of the rumpled man, holding his head in his hands and crying, made my chest ache. I raced back upstairs to my room and stuck my hand into my money jar. Pulling out the Kennedy half-dollar I had earned that day, I ran back downstairs.

When I reached the door of the living room, I walked right in. The three adults looked at me in surprise as I quickly made my way over to the stranger. I put the half-dollar in his hand and told him that I wanted him to have it. Then I gave him a hug and turned and ran as fast as I could out of the room and back up the stairs. I felt embarrassed but happy.

Downstairs, Mark sat quietly with his head bowed. Tears streamed down his face as he tightly clutched that coin. Finally looking up at my parents, he said, "It's just that I thought nobody cared. For the last twenty years, I have been so alone. That was the first hug I have gotten in—I don't know how long. It's hard to believe that somebody cares."

Mark's life changed that night. When he left our house, he was ready to live instead of die. Although my family never saw Mark again, we received letters from him every once in a while, letting us know that he was doing fine.

Being a six-year-old kid, I hadn't thought about what I

was doing that night. I had just reacted to the sight of someone else's pain. On our morning jogs, my dad and I had talked about the importance of giving, but I hadn't had any idea of what it really meant. My life changed that night, too, as I witnessed the true healing power of giving. Even if it's only a gift of fifty cents.

Before Mark left, my parents asked him why he had knocked on our door. Mark said that as he'd walked the streets that rainy night, hopeless and ready to die, he had noticed a bumper sticker on a car. He'd stood in the driveway and wondered about the people who lived in the house where the car was parked. Then, in a fog of unhappiness, he had made his way to the front door. It's hard to imagine that a bumper sticker and fifty cents could change two people's lives, but somehow they did.

The bumper sticker on our car read: SOMEBODY LOVES YOU.

Wil Horneff

"Thanks anyway, Dad, but I'll walk.
I wouldn't be caught dead driving around
with your bumper stickers."

The Power of a Smile

There is so much in the world to care about.

Laura Dern

Waiting tensely in the small, single room of the Portland Blanchet House, I could hardly control the knot of nervous excitement forming in my gut. It was my first time here with the church youth group to help feed the homeless, and I'd been given the hardest job of all. Nineteen tables in careful rows crowded the room, and it was my job to stand in the center, where I could see every table, telling new people to come in and fill the seats as they emptied.

I was thrilled and eager to be actively doing something directly to help people in the community, but I was also very nervous and curious. What would these people be like? I knew I was doing good and that I could learn a lot from hands-on work, but along with that zealous enthusiasm to broaden my perspective there tugged the urgent voice of a sheltered little suburban girl, whispering for me to hide.

There was no turning back now; it was time. People trudged in, a huddled line of bundles and packs. Red or blue patches of near frozen skin showed here and there beneath ragged scarves and overcoats, muffled eyes peered around the room with an air of bewilderment.

The seniors, who were always the first to be served, quickly occupied the seats farthest from the draft coming from the open door. They immediately started filling the complimentary plastic bags with portable food items such as cookies and rolls. I watched with a kind of naive awe, searching their faces, wondering what were their reasons for living this way, imagining what it would be like to live on the city streets twenty-four hours a day.

I was fidgety, having little to do at this point except wait for the first round of people to finish their meal, so I focused on the advice of the house director: "Lots of 'em come here as much to see a friendly face as to eat the food, so don't be afraid to smile."

This I could handle. Smiling the warmest, most sincere smile I could muster, I caught the eyes of every person I could, and though few smiled back, I felt good about it.

One old man with flyaway tufts of white hair kept looking at me with an expression of far-off wonderment. Vague gray-blue eyes shone amidst the wrinkled sandpaper of his face, and a not-quite-all-there smile beamed out with childlike simplicity. I was greatly touched by his evident pleasure at alternately swallowing a spoonful of ice cream and staring at my face. When he motioned me to come over closer to him, I was only a little alarmed. His speech was slurred and gentle, and he appeared mildly senile. As he reached out one thick-skinned hand to take mine, I felt no threat in his grandfatherly presence.

"I just wanted to ask you," he murmured sweetly, "how much do I owe you for your smile?"

In a laughing rush, I told him, "nothing," and that aged

smile grew even more wide and amazed.

"Well, in that case, may I have another?"

I complied with a helpless blush. He told me that as long as he remembered that smile, he'd be doing just fine.

I thought, *Me, too.* Sometimes that's all it takes.

Susan Record
Submitted by Mac Markstaller

Pay Attention

Jason came from a good family with two loving parents, two brothers and a sister. They were all successful academically and socially. They lived in a posh neighborhood. Jason had everything a boy could desire. But he was always into some kind of mischief. He wasn't a bad kid who caused trouble, but he always wound up in the thick of things.

In first grade, Jason was labeled Special Ed. They tried to keep him out of the regular classes. In middle school, he was the "misfit troublemaker." In high school, although never officially tested, Jason was tagged with having attention deficit disorder (ADD). More often than not, his teachers kicked him out of class. His first report card had one C and the rest Ds.

One Sunday the family was enjoying brunch at the country club when a teacher stopped and said, "Jason is doing so well these days. We're pleased and delighted."

"You must be mixing us up with another family," said the father. "Our Jason is worthless. He is always in trouble. We are so embarrassed and just can't figure out why."

As the teacher walked away, the mother remarked,

"You know, honey, come to think of it, Jason hasn't been in trouble for a month. He's even been going to school early and staying late. I wonder what's up?"

The second nine-week grading period was finally up. As usual, Jason's mom and dad expected low grades and unsatisfactory marks in behavior. Instead, he achieved four As and three Bs and honors in citizenship. His parents were baffled.

"Who did you sit by to get these grades?" the dad asked sarcastically.

"I did it all myself," Jason humbly answered.

Perplexed and still not satisfied, the parents took Jason back to school to meet with the principal. He assured them that Jason was doing very well.

"We have a new guidance counselor and she seems to have touched your son in a special way," he said. "His self-esteem is much better and he's doing great this term. I think you should meet her."

When the trio approached, the woman had her head down. It took a moment for her to notice she had visitors. When she did, she leaped to her feet and began gesturing with her hands.

"What's this?" asked Jason's father indignantly. "Sign language? Why, she can't even hear."

"That's why she's so great," said Jason, jumping in between them. "She does more than hear, Dad. She listens!"

Dan Clark

Joe Camel

"I don't believe it. They are actually taking it down!"

"We really do make a difference!"

As we sit in the bleachers of our high school stadium, we're feeling elated as the huge Joe Camel billboard, positioned directly in sight of our school, is being disassembled—and we did it!

Have you ever raised your hand simply to be part of something, and then have it turn into a life-altering event? That's exactly what happened to Eddie, Marisol and me. We belong to a school club called Friday Night Live, which promotes alcohol- and drug-free friendships and activities. It's not easy resisting the temptation to drink and smoke when, wherever you turn, advertising companies are using big money trying to hook us into using their products. The message is loud and clear: Use this stuff and you are cool, beautiful and popular.

During one of our FNL meetings, Eddie said, "It really makes me mad that everywhere I go on this campus, I can see the Joe Camel billboard, and yet the big tobacco companies tell everyone they are not targeting teens. Yeah, right!"

There are other billboards, but this is the only one you

can see from our school. Our counselor, Ms. Bambus, asked if anyone would be interested in writing to the billboard company and asking them to take it down. What followed was an amazing process that landed us on the *Today* show, CNN and many local TV shows.

We did some research and found out that there was a group called Human Health Services. We asked them if there were any other groups that had done this before and what they did. They gave us a few examples and recommended writing a polite letter to the billboard company. It seemed like it would be more fun if we just marched over and ripped up the billboard, but logic won out and we contacted the company and simply explained our concerns. We also cited the code that does not permit tobacco and alcohol advertisements within sight of a school. The vice president of the company said he couldn't see that the billboard was doing any harm.

Eddie wrote an article about it for the school newspaper, which was picked up by the local city paper. From then on, we had national media coming to our campus. One day, when I was on my way to lunch, Channel 10 came up to me and said, "Irene, we've been looking for you. We heard you and your friends are taking on Joe Camel." They asked for permission to film us talking about how we got started and what we hoped to accomplish.

Five months after all the excitement, the billboard came down. It was replaced by an ice cream advertisement. We were glad that it was all over and were looking forward to getting on with just being teens.

During the time we were involved with this, my grandfather—a smoker who started in his teens—was diagnosed with cancer. Maybe there was a higher power calling me to raise my hand to help write the letter that day. I believe if we help people not to start smoking, that's one family that won't have to watch a loved one die from it. That's a big deal!

Meladee McCarty

Anything Is Possible

It's funny how life works out. One day I was a regular high school student worried about landing the right career, and a year later, I was the owner of a company committed to changing the world, one teenager at a time. You see, my whole life I have been driven, to do something, to be something. I've always wanted to succeed, and I've never let anything come in the way of my goals.

It all started when I was eight years old. I felt like my life was over. My dad had just told me that he was no longer going to live with us; he and my mom were getting a divorce. That night, my loneliest night ever, my whole life changed. I became the man of the house. Although I felt a lot of pain when he left us, my new, important role in the family left me no choice but to move on and assume new responsibilities. Because my dad's leaving left us broke, I knew that my first job would be to earn some money for the family. As an eight-year-old, making money was not such an easy task. But I was a determined kid and not easily dismayed. I partnered with my best friend to start a lawn mowing company. I was director of marketing and he was director of labor. Our instant success gave me newfound confidence.

My ambitions to be successful did not end with the grass-cutting business in my childhood years. My drive to achieve my goals carried with me into my teenage years, where I first began exploring various career possibilities, confident that my explorations would unleash a hidden passion and begin the path to my future career. I attacked each possibility with intensity and determination. But neither medicine nor archaeology left me satisfied, so I continued to search for my passion.

During the time that I spent devoted to discovering my career, I also took some time to help a friend, five years older than I, learn to read. While my career searches left me unsatisfied, I felt an extreme sense of accomplishment in helping my friend. For the first time in my life, I became consciously aware of the power of helping others, and it was an experience that changed my life forever, although I didn't realize it at the time.

Still frustrated by the lack of career direction in my life, I decided that the stock market held my future and once again jumped head first into exploring this profession. Luckily, this one stuck. Before I knew it, I had landed myself an internship at a successful stock brokerage and eventually, after a great deal of hard work and commitment, I was offered many positions throughout the country.

Excited about my offers, but not wanting to ignore my education, I put my job offers on hold to attend classes at the University of Texas. It was during one of my classes that I was forced to reexamine my money-driven career choice. A successful young entrepreneur, Brad Armstrong, asked me what I wanted to do when I "grew up," a question many teenagers are asked and never want to answer. Feeling confident I replied, "I'll graduate when I'm nineteen or twenty, work in New York or Chicago, and retire young—like you." My teenage American dream.

Then he said, "Fantastic! Let's say you make lots of money and retire old, say age thirty-five. What are you going to do then?"

Without hesitation I replied, "See the world!"

He smiled and said, "Okay, let's say you see the world and you're thirty-eight. What are you going to do with the rest of your life? What is your *goal in life*?"

I suddenly flashed back on the experience I had teaching my friend to read and remembered the great sense of accomplishment that I had felt. It was at that moment that I realized what my goal was. I wanted to help others. And I wanted to do it in a way that I knew how.

"Brad," I said thoughtfully. "I want to write a book and help my peers." I am always so frustrated with the unfair portrayal of all teenagers as lazy, unintelligent and violent. What about the millions of us who work hard to get through school, hold steady jobs, support our families and stay clear of trouble?

He replied, "So, why don't you write now? Share with them the methods you've learned to succeed. You can help a lot of people. Share your knowledge."

That night I couldn't sleep. Brad's question about my life mission kept repeating in my head. I made the toughest decision of my life. I decided to follow my heart and jump into life not knowing where I would land.

After a great deal of research and hard work, my book about a career and life success for young people was complete. But I still had a problem. I realized that the very people I would be trying to sell my book to, would probably not be able to afford it. To solve this problem, I created an educational publishing company, designed to get my book into schools across America, where students could read the book at no cost and learn the skills needed to reach their dreams.

While I was not an overnight success, I am happy to say

that my book did eventually catch on with students, educators and business leaders. It is most rewarding to know that I got to help so many people realize what they can do to make their lives successful, especially teenagers, who have been constantly reminded of their weaknesses.

I've learned firsthand that every person holds limitless potential and passion waiting to be unleashed, and I am living proof that goals really can be achieved. Truly anything is possible when you follow your heart. The sky is no longer the limit.

Jason Dorsey

A Challenge That I Overcame

I was nervous as I sat waiting in the hospital room, unsure of what Dr. Waites, the pioneer of diagnosing developmental dyslexia, was telling my parents about the test results.

It all began when I moved to Dallas in the fourth grade, and I noticed that I was behind in my reading at Saint Michael's School. Reading out loud, I had difficulty with half the sentences. My teacher, Mrs. Agnew, said my reading comprehension and ability to pronounce words was at a lower lever than other fourth graders. I was scared every time she called on me to read aloud because, although I would try my hardest, she would always have to help me with the words. Mrs. Agnew suggested that I be tested for dyslexia.

At first I was confused about why I was being tested; I had been in all honors classes at the public school I had previously attended. The test made me feel uncomfortable, and I was scared to answer the questions, in fear of facing failure.

The test results showed that I had developmental dyslexia. At first I felt discouraged by this diagnosis, but eventually, I became determined to master my disability. I got tutors and speech therapy. I even tried to conquer the disability myself. I would read difficult books, hoping to increase the confidence I had in myself. I began to read and comprehend the readings better. I even began to love reading, which is kind of ironic since I had once detested it so much.

I had finally overcome my learning disability. Dr. Waites confirmed this when I was tested again. He said that my dyslexia was at a minimum. I was overjoyed. But even though I had conquered one of the biggest challenges in my life, I still felt like something was missing.

The missing link was filled when I put on my candy-striped uniform for the first time and walked down the halls of the hospital as a volunteer, the same hospital where I had once sat, nervous and confused. Because I felt so lucky to have had access to this facility that had helped me so much, I wanted to give back by being a volunteer.

One day a little girl in a wheelchair asked me to read a book to her. I read the book very slowly so that she could understand the story and the words. When it became time for me to leave, the girl thanked me for reading to her. I walked out of her room with a huge smile on my face. Eight years ago I would have hesitated in reading a book to this little girl, but now I was confident. I had overcome my disability and was helping others to overcome theirs. I am determined to succeed in life, and in the process, help others face and conquer the challenges that I have overcome.

Arundel Hartman Bell

A Street Kid's Guide

When I was asked to address a high school graduation in a nearby community, my mind boggled.

"Me!" I gasped. "You want me?"

After they assured me they did, I felt honored. Just think of it! Me! A guy who never went to high school was being asked to speak to a group of kids on such an important occasion.

What will I say to them? What profound words can I impart that would stay with them, and perhaps help them with life's choices? The more I thought about it, the more I realized that if I was not careful, I stood a good chance of adding my name to a long list of boring, over-the-hill, has-been speakers that came before me. These kids didn't need that. They didn't need any more long-winded speeches of how it was done in the past, nor did they need to be deluged by a barrage of useless platitudes.

I thought and rethought all sorts of ideas, but came up with nothing. It wasn't until the night before the address that it suddenly dawned on me. *Don't tell these kids what you did. Tell them what you learned while you were doing it.*

As I gathered these new thoughts, I drifted back to my

past. I grew up—or rather, was dragged up—in dozens of foster homes and institutions. It was hard to tell where one home left off and another began. Through those same years, I fumbled my way through seven different grade schools. Somehow I missed the fourth grade entirely. But that really didn't matter. Nobody paid very much attention to me. I had no books, no pencils and no paper. And as far as anyone was concerned, I was passing through.

By the time I was eleven, I was in the fifth grade and unable to read. A nun took pity on me. She kept me after school every day to teach me what she could. For the brief time I was with her, I learned a lot. I wish I could have stayed with her, but I knew I couldn't. I was in "the system." I was sent where they wanted to send me, and stayed until they sent me someplace else. I learned early to obey any and all rules, and to never question authority. The system was designed to teach unquestioned discipline, but it was really containment and control. It worked very well.

By the time I was fourteen, I was finished with school—or, rather, it was finished with me. In either case, I was tossed out, told I couldn't be educated, and given a job.

At first this was very frightening. I was alone and on my own. There was no one to turn to if I got into trouble, no one to guide me or show me the way. It was hard. I had to become street smart in a hurry. I got tough quickly; I learned to show no fear and to keep my mouth shut. I chose my roads by trial and error. Whenever I stumbled, I got up and tried again. I was determined not to quit and not to be beaten. I did alright. I got through.

About a dozen or so years ago, a friend who knew about my past and the way I grew up encouraged me to write it down. He told me it was important for people to know what it's like to grow up the way I did. And so, with much stress and difficulty, I somehow found the strength to reach back forty years to relive all the pain and all the tears. I revisited the fear and the loneliness. I wrote my autobiography, *They Cage the Animals at Night.* It was reading this book, and responding to it, that prompted those in charge of the graduation ceremony to invite me to address their kids.

It was a warm June morning when I stood at the podium. All eyes were fixed upon me. The kids were dressed in their caps and gowns and sticky from nervous perspiration. From time to time, they'd glance over to the sections reserved for parents, family and friends. They were trying to locate the proud and smiling faces of those whom they belonged to. When they did, they would smile as a faint blush filled their cheeks. They were just as proud as their parents.

I began to speak. I told them I was honored to be addressing them, but not having been in high school, or graduating from anything, I didn't feel qualified. I then made an unusual request. I asked them if there was any way in which I could take part in their moment, if they might let me be one of them: a graduate. Their applause took me into their ranks, and their eyes took me into their hearts.

I choked back my tears as I said, "This is a street kid's guide on how to get from here to there." Maybe a word here or a line there that might help you get through a rough time: I hope so. . . .

A Street Kid's Guide
(How to get from here to there)

It's hard to get from here to there
If you never get out of bed.
You lie a lot to fool your friends
But you fooled yourself instead.

It's harder to get from here to there
If you set your goals too high;
Then nothing ever works out right;
Too soon, you no longer try.

But the hardest way to get from here to there
Is when all you ever do
Is count up the years, and miles to go.
Then you're through before you're through.

So how do you get from here to there?
Well, you first must believe you can
Let no one tell you differently—
It's your life and it's in your hands.

Then turn your dreams into your goals
And see what you need now
To satisfy the requirements:
The why, the where and how.

At first you're overwhelmed, of course;
There is so much you don't know.
But keep your faith, be strong and sure,
For you do have a way to go.

Take careful steps and do them right,
Take pride in each thing done.
Don't look too far ahead of yourself,
Just that next step yet to come.

Before you know it you'll be there, friend,
Your dream will then be real.
And you'll be standing where I am now,
Telling others how good it feels.

You'll tell them not to quit themselves,
To have faith, though it's hard to bear.
So they will know it can be done—
They, too, can get from here to there.

Jennings Michael Burch

Teenagers Today

I can't count how many times people have uttered, while shaking their heads in obvious disappointment, "I just don't know what is with teenagers today."

The other day I was in my car on my way to the farmers market with my friend Jan when we passed two teens standing by the side of the road with a car wash sign. My car was filthy and my heart was full, so I pulled over. There were teenagers everywhere. There was a group directing the cars and another group spraying them down. As sponges were wiped over every square inch of my dirty car, I sat enjoying the little water battles and the many silent scenarios that were so obviously taking place. I couldn't help but wonder how many crushes, how many new friendships and how many little insecurities were in the air on this beautiful Saturday afternoon. I was amazed at how forty to fifty teenagers had devoted their Saturday to washing cars, and I was curious what their motivation might be.

At the end of the assembly line I handed them a twenty-dollar bill and asked what they were raising money for. They explained to me that a friend of theirs,

C. T. Schmitz, had recently died of cancer. He was only fifteen years old and six-feet-two. He had gone to school with a lot of the teenagers who were there that day and each of them had memories of a boy sweeter than any they had known. His friend Kevin had decided to put this car wash together because he wanted to honor his friend and also bring together his classmates with his boy scout troop. He told me that they wanted to plant a tree in front of their school and if they raised enough money they would put a plaque there also. Both would be in memory of their friend C. T.

They handed me a bag of homemade cookies with my receipt and we drove away. I asked Jan to read to me what the tag that was tied to the bag said. It said simply, "Thanks for helping us plant a tree for C. T."

Yeah! I don't know what *is* with teenagers today!

Kimberly Kirberger

An Open Heart

We had to take a malaria pill every week for eight weeks and get a shot of gamma globulin. We were told to bring old clothes, flashlights, bug repellent and an open heart.

I think the last item was the most important: an open heart. That is what those kids really needed.

Honduras is a small country in Central America. The majority of the population is dirt poor, hungry, homeless, parentless and in need. This is where I, along with eighteen of my peers, had committed to spending two weeks of our summer vacation.

I am sixteen years old. This trip was not the vacation trip most teens dream of. It was sponsored by Mrs. Patricia King, whose two sons were adopted into her family from this third-world country. Through her love we were able to help those in need.

We spent our time at an orphanage with children who won our hearts the very moment we met them. How could you not adore a child who wants only a multi-colored pen for his fourteenth birthday? For two weeks we shared our souls with these children. We lived in their world, relying only on bare necessities. The heat was often unbearable and the smell of raw sewage was constant. Dirt clung to everything and we had to close our eyes and hold our breath to shower in the contaminated water. It was our job to repaint the boys' room and the hard iron bunk beds. We washed and braided the girls' hair and painted their nails. We exchanged hugs, high fives, kisses and eventually good-byes. We came home different—better.

We learned that the best of all blessings is to be able to give to others. I feel lucky that I'm sixteen and I know that we can make a difference. That's not just something that celebrities say on TV. Every day I am grateful that I learned an open heart is a happy heart.

Sandy Pathe

8

GROWING UP

My mother always used to say: "The older you get, the better you get . . . unless you're a banana."

Rose Nylund

Wonder, to Me

One morning, I woke up later than usual. The night before had been difficult. My eldest daughter, Carla, and I had exchanged harsh words. At sixteen years old, she was challenging my parenting skills. I'm sure that I must have scolded her about the type of friends she was hanging around with, her choice of social activities, even the clothes she wore.

When I walked into the kitchen, I saw an unfamiliar piece of paper on the kitchen table. Carla had already left for school. I thought maybe this was some homework that she forgot. Instead, it was a poem she had written:

Wonder, to me,
Is the worst place to be.
Situations get complex,
You're afraid of what's next.
Starting out fresh and brand-new,
Stepping in another shoe.
Wondering how you'll turn out,
Having all sorts of doubt.
Turning over a new leaf,
Sometimes wanting to leave . . . sometimes do!

As I read her words, my heart ached for the pain she was feeling. I recalled my own youth and teenage struggles. Now I felt that I had let her down somehow. A single mom, raising five children on my own and working two jobs, I was dealing with my own set of problems. But she needed me! How could I reach her?

Suddenly, all my own selfish worries left me. I grabbed a piece of paper and penned a reply that I hoped would bring her some comfort.

That afternoon while I was at work, she came home and found the poem that I had left. That evening there were hugs and maybe a few tears. It seemed that perhaps I had made some progress in narrowing the generation gap.

Days and months passed. We still had the typical mother–daughter disagreements, but with a special bond of respect and understanding for each other. It wasn't until a year later that I realized the full impact of our special relationship.

It was Carla's graduation. I was sitting in the bleachers, so very proud to see my own daughter's name on the program for the class speaker. As she approached the podium, I felt a sense of accomplishment in knowing that, through it all, I must have done something right to have such a vivacious, beautiful daughter who was providing her classmates with advice for their future.

She talked about leaving the security of school and venturing out on your own. Then I heard her share the story of her own struggles, doubts and fears. She was telling the entire audience about that difficult day when she left the poem on the kitchen table. And then, the words of advice to her classmates ended with the reply that I had given her so many months ago.

Dearest Carla,

Wonder, to me, is a good place to be.
It helps you to think, it helps you to see.
Life's full of twists and turns will abound,
But wonder and insight can guide you around.
Explore what you may and fill up your mind,
And hold in your heart the mysteries you find.
Wonder is only saying you yearn
To know and select the things that you learn,
And making a choice in which way you turn.
The best path you take will always be right,
'Cause if you were wrong, you CAN make it right.
Each new step you take when you listen and hear
Will give you more courage and freedom from fear.
So wonder my child, rid of your doubt,
And you will rejoice with how you turn out.
And though you may fall and struggle, too,
Know that I've been there, and will always love you.

I sat there, stunned. The entire auditorium was silent, listening to her message. My eyes welled with tears; everything was a blur. When I finally blinked, I saw the entire roomful of people on their feet, cheering and applauding. Then she ended her speech with her own inspired summary of "You can turn YOUR wonder into wonderful!"

Jill Thieme

RUBES By Leigh Rubin

How Much Does It Cost?

The six teenagers sank onto their beanbags in the group counseling room. Today there was none of the usual raucous punching and good-natured exchange of insults. I knew they didn't want to be at school this week any more than I, their counselor, did.

For three days they had received counseling, comfort, sympathy and lectures. Ministers and psychologists had come to the school at a time when the kids' world seemed to have ended. It had indeed ended for four of their schoolmates, who had died in a car accident on the way home from a keg party in celebration of graduation.

What was there left for me to say? Only that these six would go on living, barring a tragedy like this one—a tragedy that didn't have to happen.

My mind searched for words to fill the silence. Finally I said, "I remember a day when I was about your age, seeing a fancy Levi's jacket and jodhpurs in a store window. Since I was to be riding in the girls' rodeo competition the following month, I figured I simply couldn't live without that outfit. I went into the store, found the garments in my size and bought them without asking how much they cost. I practically had a heart attack when the clerk told me the price. There went all the spending money I had saved practically forever. In fact, I had to go home and rob my piggy bank and then go back to the store for my purchase."

At that point in my story, I paused long enough to note that the group members were staring at me with questioning eyes. After all, what did a stupid rodeo costume have to do with their grief?

So I babbled on. "Was the outfit worth that much? No way, I concluded during the following months, when I had to do without several things I needed or wanted, including a class ring."

My counselees continued to look at me with a so-what? expression.

"I did learn from that experience," I said finally. "I learned to ask, 'What does it cost?' before buying. During the years following, I've learned that looking at price tags is a good idea when it comes to actions, also."

I told them about a time when I went on a hike with friends without telling our parents where we would be. The price was heavy. My fellow hikers and I got lost, and it was many terrifying hours before we straggled back to town to face our frantic parents and the drastic punishments they decided we deserved.

Now it was the kids' turn to talk, and they did, relating some of the times when their bad judgment had not been worth the cost of the consequences.

I gently reminded the students at this point that their friends' graduation celebration had cost too much. I mentioned the frequency of teen tragedies, many involving alcohol and other drugs. Then I read them parts of an editorial about an accident that had occurred a few months earlier. The article had been written by the town's chief of police:

Close to a thousand people were there that day, all sitting in front of a smooth casket topped with flowers and a high school letter jacket. Jason was president of the senior class, a star athlete, a popular friend to hundreds, the only son of successful parents, but he drove into the side of a fast-moving freight train at the city square on a beautiful Sunday afternoon and was killed instantly. He was eighteen years old. And he was drunk.

You never get accustomed to or forget the horror on the faces of parents when you break the news to them that their child is forever gone from this earth.

We know there will be both youth and parents who don't like our enforcement posture. There will be verbal and maybe physical abuse against the officers. Some parents will complain about our enforcement of underage drinking laws. But we can live with that a lot easier than telling parents that their son or daughter has been killed.

Four of the six students were crying by the time I finished reading the editorial. Crying for Jason, crying for their dead schoolmates and their families, crying because of their own loss.

Then we talked about the four friends they had just lost.

"Can any good come out of our tragedy?" I asked. "Or do we just let it end like a sad movie?"

It was Mindy, the shyest member of the group, who suggested in a wispy voice, "Maybe we could make a pledge or something."

Ordinarily, the three boys in the group would probably have ridiculed the idea, but this day was different.

"Hey!" Jonathan said. "Not a bad idea."

"Something like pretending there's a price tag on things grown-ups think we shouldn't do, then maybe deciding if we're ready to take the chance anyway," Laurel added.

Paul said, "The problem with that is, we can't know for sure what that price would be. Maybe nothing bad will happen even if we take the risk."

"That's a point," I admitted. "Suppose instead of 'How much *will* it cost?' we asked ourselves, 'How much *might* it cost?' Then we'd at least look at the possible outcomes."

"I'll buy that," Kent said.

A week ago, these kids would have shrugged off such suggestions, but today—well, today they weren't quite the same people they had been last week.

Margaret Hill

Image Isn't Everything

On the first day of school, after I got out of my mom's car and mumbled a good-bye, I stared in awe at the huge buildings that seemed to tower over my head. This high school was definitely bigger than the one I had previously attended. Over the summer I moved from Midland, Texas, to St. Louis, Missouri. I had lived in Midland all my life, until the move.

This was my second year of high school, but my first year of school in St. Louis. I was really nervous about starting a new school and having people like me. I had decided the night before, while lying in my bed trying to fall asleep, that I would be much happier in a new school if I made friends that were so-called "popular." Getting in with the right group of people would make my life a whole lot better. I had to project the right image to the people at this school. I didn't care how much money it cost me, I was determined to buy an outfit everyone else would want to have. I bought a new outfit, new make-up, got a manicure and had my hair styled just so the first day would be perfect. I had the chance to start over in a new school, make new friends and build an image for myself. I wasn't going to waste this opportunity.

Scared, yet anxious to begin my new life, I walked up the stairs to the front door. The halls were packed with kids yelling and laughing and telling stories of their summer adventures. I found my way to the main office where I was to receive my schedule and fill out forms. I was on my way. *My first class was geometry, but where was that?*

I was standing in the hall looking confused, when a short, blond girl wearing glasses came up and asked, "Are you new? You look lost. Do you want me to help you find your class? My name is Diane. What's yours?" Even though she seemed a bit strange, definitely not the kind of person I wanted to be associated with, I decided to answer her anyway. I was, after all, lost.

After exchanging names, I followed her up the stairs and down a hallway on the right, making polite conversation the whole way.

When we reached my room she said, "Well, here you are. It was nice meeting you. I hope I see you again. Welcome to JFK, and I hope your day goes all right."

I said thanks and waved good-bye. Once inside the classroom, I saw one big group of people huddled around someone who seemed to be telling some sort of story. I walked over and got close enough to overhear. All eyes were glued to the guy in the middle of the circle who was wearing a letter jacket covered with patches. I decided that this guy was popular. He was talking about how he and some of his friends had gone up to someone's ranch outside of St. Louis and done some pretty wild and crazy things. A few minutes later the teacher told everyone to break it up and go find a seat. I managed to get one right next to the guy wearing the letter jacket. I said, "Hi, my name is April and I'm new here." He said, "Hi, I'm Johnny."

That class dragged on and on. Finally the bell rang. I turned to him and asked, "I'm not sure where my next class is, could you help me find it?" He looked at me and then said a quick no, turned back to his friends, and walked out of the classroom. As they were walking out I heard him say, "Did you guys see that new girl trying to get into our group? That outfit was way too weird." They all laughed and some of them turned around and stared at me. I slowly gathered my stuff, not believing what had just happened. I walked out of the classroom and found my next class, bewildered that I could have cared so much.

The same type of thing happened all day in all of my classes. At lunch, I ended up sitting by myself because I had snubbed people who had been nice to me and I had been snubbed by people who I had tried to be nice to. I didn't realize it then, but I had been really shallow just wanting to be friends with popular people.

Finally, sixth period came around and I was ready to go home and never come back. Before class started, someone came up behind me and said, "Hi, again. How was your first day?" It was that same girl who had showed me to my first class.

I told her my day had not been so great. She said she was sorry and offered to walk me outside. At that moment I realized how wrong I was in wanting to only be friends with popular people. Those people weren't even going to consider being my friends, but there were some other people who I'd already met today and liked and they liked me. Maybe I shouldn't decide whether a person is worth being my friend or not by their reputation, but by who they are. I said, "Thanks, I'd like that. I'm sorry I was kind of rude this morning." She said it was okay, she was new at school once, too. Walking with Diane made me realize how nice it would be to have a friend like her. On the way to class she asked me if I wanted to go out after school to hang out with some of her friends and get to know them better. I did go out with Diane and had a lot of fun.

As time went on I made friends with lots of different people, some of them from "the popular crowd" and some not. My standards were different though. The people I sought out for friends were the nice ones—period.

Jamie Shockley

Hi There, Ugly!

It wasn't easy to pay attention in French class. Our yearbooks had just been passed out, so while the teacher droned on, we were quietly signing books and passing them around the room.

Mine was somewhere at the back of the class. I couldn't wait to get it back. What would my friends say of me? Would there be words of praise? Admiration? When class was over, I quickly found my yearbook and flipped through it with anticipation. And then it caught my eye: someone had written large words across the last page of my book: HI THERE, UGLY!

I had never really considered whether or not I was 'good looking,' but now I knew. I was ugly. If someone at the back of that grade-seven class thought I was ugly, there were probably many others who agreed. I studied myself in the mirror: big nose, pimples, slightly over-weight, not muscular. Yes, it must be true, I thought. I'm ugly. I told no one any of this. There seemed to be no need. It was a fact: I was ugly.

Years went by. I married a woman who is a very beau-tiful person—inside and out. I would tell her, "You're the most beautiful girl in the world!" and I meant it. She would reply, "And you're so handsome." I never looked her in the eyes when she said this. I felt it was one of those things wives "have to say" to their husbands. I would simply look down and remember that the true verdict on my looks was tucked away in my grade-seven yearbook.

Finally one day my wife asked, "Why is it that you never look at me when I say that you're handsome?" I decided to tell her about the yearbook and my conclusions. "You can't believe that! It's wrong! Somebody who didn't even know you in grade seven can't be taken that seriously! I know you, I love you and I chose to marry you. I think you're handsome and I think I've proved that." So, was I going to believe my wife . . . or that old graffiti?

I thought about that question for a long time and about how God doesn't make junk. Who was I going to believe? I chose to believe my wife and God.

I still have a big nose. At age thirty-four, I even still get pimples! My hair has begun to recede and you could probably find people who would say that I am ugly. But I'm not one of them! As time goes on and I listen more and more to those who love me, I know that I am beautiful . . . or should I say, handsome.

Greg Barker

Imprints

When I resolve into the essence
That I most truly am,
I feel a deep connection
With every living thing.
For that which most imbues me
With my identity
Is somehow in the other, too,
So that when I look around
I see myself—reflected.
Hidden in this union
Is the wonderful discovery
That if indeed the angels
Have wings—
Then so do I.
And if the essence of a flower
Drifts out on a gentle breeze—
Then so do I.
And if the midnight sky
Is radiant with light—
Then so am I.
And if the silent mystery

Somehow becomes revealed
In tiny dewdrops fair—
Then so will I.
For every lovely thing
Manifests the essence
Of which I am a part,
So beware, my soul, beware,
And move with gentle heart
Throughout this mystic veil.
For if Love has left its imprint here—
Then so have I!

Donna Miesbach

I Won't Be Left Behind

I run my fastest
But still get beat.
I land on my head
When I should be on my feet.
I try to move forward,
But I am stuck in rewind.
Why do I keep at it?
I won't be left behind.

The harder I am thrown,
The higher I bounce.
I give it my all,
And that's all that counts.
In first place,
Myself, I seldom find.
So I push to the limit—
I won't be left behind.

Some people tell me you can't,
Some say don't.
Some simply give up.
I reply, I won't.

The power is here,
locked away in my mind.
My perseverance is my excellence,
I won't be left behind.

Make the best of each moment,
The future is soon the past.
The more I tell myself this,
The less I come in last.
Throughout my competitions,
I've learned what winning is about.
A plain and clear lesson—
Giving up is the easy way out.

So every night before I go to bed,
I hope in a small way I have shined.
Tomorrow is a brand-new day,
And I won't be left behind.

Sara Nachtman

An Athlete's Prayer

It was right before the big one and the football player said,
"Excuse me guys for just a sec while I go bow my head."
And in the quiet of that room
The football player prayed,
"Oh God if nothing hear me now
I know that fate is made."

"So help us Lord to win this game,
It's the big one, man, you see,
If we lose this game that's it for us ,
Please do this, Lord, for me."

And as his body knelt in prayer,
He looked up to the sky,
"And while I'm here, and have some time,
I need to ask you why?"

"They say you never help teams win,
Just do it once I pray,
We will pay you back in kinder deeds
Or in another way."

"The reason I can't help you win,"
The Lord just then replied,
"Is as you're asking me to win,
So is the other side."

"I'm everybody's father and
I must not take one side,
So games are played all on your own
Or they would all be tied."

"But that doesn't mean you shouldn't pray,"
He answered him with care,
"You can pray that players don't get hurt
And that all the calls are fair."

"And then I won't just watch the game,
I'll bless it with my care,
Because dear son you need to learn
That life's not always fair."

And while the player heard this voice,
He bowed his head in prayer,
"I pray for fairness," said the boy
"And for your tender care."

"You shall be blessed," the Lord replied,
"Your team and you the same,
And now will you excuse me boy,
I cannot miss this game."

Sandy Dow Mapula

The Blank Page

The pencil moved ever so slightly in my hand as I stared at the blank page that would become my completed homework assignment: a five-paragraph essay on the meaning of life for Mr. Neal's English class.

I had no idea that a person's palms could sweat as much as mine were gripping that pencil. I almost needed sunglasses to shade the glare of the blank notebook paper. I had been sitting at my desk pondering the various aspects and meanings of life for nearly an hour. Thus far, I was clueless as to what to write. *What does Mr. Neal expect?* I wondered. *I am only fourteen.*

I thought about everything that had happened previously in my life. I began high school this year, ran cross-country and played girls' soccer. However, I was sure that the meaning of life had nothing to do with any of these things.

I stretched my arms above my head and looked around the room. My room was so *me*. The mark of Jenni was everywhere to be seen, from my posters and paintings of Europe to the many vibrantly colored CDs that littered my floor. My gaze then fell upon a photograph of me standing beside a girl. Our arms are raised above our heads in an imitation of cheerleaders and we both flash blindingly bright smiles. I froze. Immediately, tears began to well in my eyes. The girl in the photograph and I had been best friends for nearly two years when a sudden disagreement planted a rift in our friendship that still had not been mended. It saddened me beyond measure that an argument could put so much distance between such close friends.

The pencil now moved fluidly across the paper.

When I again looked up, I happened to glance at the varsity *A* I had received for completing cross-country season. Memories now rolled through my mind and flooded my brain: remembrances of long, loud bus rides; water fights with our archrival; memorable trips to various fast-food eateries after the races; the stinging words of many arguments; the tinkling giggles of many laughs gone by.

Again, the lead scraped the clean white paper.

As I went to bed that night, my homework assignment still incomplete, I ran over in my mind what I had written so far. Fitful dreams revealed new stories and thoughts to be explored.

In my dreams, I remembered when my family moved to the beach—tearful good-byes rang in my ears. I reexperienced the velvety voice of my former crush during our first phone conversation, which was a major breakthrough, even though it only lasted five minutes. I remembered how excited I felt after that conversation—I drifted on cloud nine. I relived how happy and proud I felt walking across the Albemarle High School stage to receive my varsity *A*. Even in my sleep, a lone tear's salty track burned my cheek: Albemarle, my life in the past and also now, beginning anew.

I awoke early the next morning to finish my essay. When it was complete it read as follows:

> *When you asked us to write about the meaning of life in a five-paragraph essay, Mr. Neal, I wondered how I would ever fill so much empty space. I sat thinking it over for nearly an hour before I even knew how to begin. When I began to write, however, the problem became not how to fill the space, but how to make use of what little I had.*
>
> *There is so much more to life than cross-country*

meets, soccer games, and the transformation from middle-schooler to high-schooler. What matters most is what you make of your life. If how you feel from day-to-day is based upon what others think and how they judge you, then your life has no basis. If you are a person who wakes up in the morning and dreads the day ahead, then your life has no meaning.

However, if you wake up every morning eager to start the new day, then your life has meaning, for it has a purpose. My life certainly has a purpose. Every day is a struggle to survive: building new friendships, fixing old ones, learning how to deal with complicated emotions and accepting new surroundings. I find that every day is a journey of finding out who and what you are.

I believe that the question "what is the meaning of life" is too broad. I don't think that anyone will ever truly discover the exact reason why we were put here and what we must do now that we are here. Personally, I do not care to discover the reason. I prefer to leave each day to its own devices.

Every day is an adventure in discovering the meaning of life. It is each little thing that you do that day—whether it be spending time with your friends, running in a cross-country race or just simply staring at the crashing ocean—that holds the key to discovering the meaning of life. I would rather be out enjoying these simple things than pondering them. We may never really discover the meaning of life, but the knowledge we gain in our quest to discover it is truly more valuable.

My hand ached and my pencil was but a stub, by my essay was finished. I had discovered many things while writing this essay, although maybe not the exact meaning of life. *I don't need to find that out yet,* I thought, smiling. *I have things to do along the way.*

My notebook page, as well as my mind, was no longer blank.

Jenni Norman

Who Is Jack Canfield?

Jack Canfield is a best-selling author and one of America's leading experts in the development of human potential. He is both a dynamic and entertaining speaker and a highly sought-after trainer with a wonderful ability to inform and inspire audiences to open their hearts, love more openly and boldly pursue their dreams.

Jack spent his teenage years growing up in Martins Ferry, Ohio, and Wheeling, West Virginia, with his sister Kimberly (Kirberger) and his two brothers, Rick and Taylor. The whole family has spent most of their professional careers dedicated to educating, counseling and empowering teens. Jack admits to being shy and lacking self-confidence in high school, but through a lot of hard work he earned letters in three sports and graduated third in his class.

After graduating college, Jack taught high school in the inner city of Chicago and in Iowa. In recent years, Jack has expanded this to include adults in both educational and corporate settings.

He is the author and narrator of several bestselling audio and video cassette programs. He is a regularly consulted expert for radio and television broadcasts and has published twenty-five books—all bestsellers within their categories—including nineteen *Chicken Soup for the Soul* books, *The Aladdin Factor, Heart at Work, 100 Ways to Build Self-Concept in the Classroom,* and *Dare to Win.*

Jack addresses over one hundred groups each year. His clients include professional associations, school districts, government agencies, churches and corporations in all fifty states.

Jack conducts an annual eight-day Training of Trainers program in the areas of building self-esteem and achieving peak performance. It attracts educators, counselors, parenting trainers, corporate trainers, professional speakers, ministers and others interested in developing their speaking and seminar-leading skills in these areas.

For further information about Jack's books, tapes and trainings, or to schedule him for a presentation, please contact:

The Canfield Training Group
P.O. Box 30880 • Santa Barbara, CA 93130
phone: 800-237-8336 • fax: 805-563-2945
e-mail: *speaking@canfieldgroup.com*
Web site: *www.chickensoup.com*

Who Is Mark Victor Hansen?

Mark Victor Hansen is a professional speaker who, in the last twenty years, has made over four thousand presentations to more than two million people in thirty-three countries. His presentations cover sales excellence and strategies; personal empowerment and development; and how to triple your income and double your time off.

Mark has spent a lifetime dedicated to his mission of making a profound and positive difference in people's lives. Throughout his career, he has inspired hundreds of thousands of people to create a more powerful and purposeful future for themselves while stimulating the sale of billions of dollars worth of goods and services.

Mark is a prolific writer and has authored *Future Diary, How to Achieve Total Prosperity* and *The Miracle of Tithing.* He is the coauthor of the *Chicken Soup for the Soul* series, *Dare to Win* and *The Aladdin Factor* (all with Jack Canfield) and *The Master Motivator* (with Joe Batten).

Mark has also produced a complete library of personal empowerment audio- and videocassette programs that have enabled his listeners to recognize and better use their innate abilities in their business and personal lives. His message has made him a popular television and radio personality with appearances on ABC, NBC, CBS, HBO, PBS, QVC and CNN.

He has also appeared on the cover of numerous magazines including *Success, Entrepreneur* and *Changes.*

Mark is a big man with a heart and a spirit to match—an inspiration to all who seek to better themselves.

For further information about Mark, please contact:

Mark Victor Hansen & Associates
P.O. Box 7665
Newport Beach, CA 92658
phone: 949-759-9304 or 800-433-2314
fax: 949-722-6912
Web site: *www.chickensoup.com*

Who Is Kimberly Kirberger?

Kimberly Kirberger is the president and founder of I.A.M. for Teens, Inc. (Inspiration and Motivation for Teens, Inc.) a corporation formed exclusively to work *for* teens. It is her goal to see teens represented in a more positive light and it is her strong belief that teens deserve better and more positive treatment.

She spends her time reading the thousands of letters and stories sent to her by teen readers and traveling around the country speaking to high school students and parents of teens. She has appeared as a teen expert on many television and radio shows, including *Geraldo, MSNBC,* and *The Terry Bradshaw Show.*

Kimberly is the coauthor of the bestselling *Chicken Soup for the Teenage Soul,* as well as *Chicken Soup for the Teenage Soul Journal.* She worked closely with teenagers on both projects and feels her ability to listen to their needs and wants lent to the success of the teenage *Chicken Soup* books.

She started the Teen Letter Project with Jack Canfield, Mark Victor Hansen and Health Communications, Inc. The Project is responsible for answering the heartfelt letters received from teenagers and also reaching out to teens in trouble and encouraging them to seek professional help. The Teen Letter Project is currently involved in setting up a Web page that will allow teens to give help to and receive help from one another.

Kimberly is also the coauthor of the forthcoming *Chicken Soup for the College Soul, Chicken Soup for the Parent's Soul, Chicken Soup for the Teenage Soul III* and a book about relationships for teenagers.

To book Kimberly for a speaking engagement or for further information on any of her projects, please contact:

I.A.M. for Teens, Inc.
P.O. Box 936 • Pacific Palisades, CA 90272
phone: 310-573-3655 • fax: 310-573-3657
e-mail for stories: *stories@teenagechickensoup.com*
e-mail for letters: *letters@teenagechickensoup.com*
Web site: *www.teenagechickensoup.com*

Contributors

Becka Allen is a fifteen-year-old sophomore. She has always enjoyed writing and this is her first published story. She can be reached at *tallen@central.net*.

Adi Amar is a graduate of Verde Valley School in Sedona, Arizona and currently an Outdoor Education student at Garrett College in Maryland. Born in Israel, Adi (whose name means "jewel" in Hebrew) is passionate about rock climbing, hiking, sailing, journaling, and yoga. She has received considerable acclaim for her innovative photography. Her mother, Lana Grimm, coproduced and costarred in the award-winning video *The Spirit of Yoga* in Sedona, just three months before the near-fatal crash. Her mother's miraculous recovery inspired Adi to develop a new appreciation for life, and she plans to build her future career on a combination of her outdoor skills, photographic talents and genuine love for nature.

Marsha Arons is a writer and lecturer in Skokie, Illinois. She is thrilled to be associated with the *Chicken Soup* series, and her stories appear in *Woman's Soul*, *Mother's Soul* and *A 5th Portion*. She also contributes to national magazines such as *Good Housekeeping, Reader's Digest* and *Redbook*. She has authored a book for young adults and is currently at work on a collection of short stories dealing with mother-daughter relationships. You can contact her via e-mail for speaking or other assignments at *RA8737@aol.com*.

Greg Barker is currently the pastor at Grace Lutheran Church in Victoria, British Columbia, Canada. He enjoys communicating the grace of God to people of all ages, especially to his confirmation class of seventh and eighth grade students. Greg and his wife, Teresa, are enjoying their first baby, Christopher. Greg can be reached at 1273 Fort St., Victoria, British Columbia, Canada V8V 3L4 or e-mail: *glc@islandnet.com*.

Eugene E. Beasley enjoys reading, traveling, biking, walking and communicating with people and nature. After thirty-nine years of teaching communication arts, he is now presently writing, teaching drivers education, religious pursuits and gardening. There is much Eugene has learned through experience that he wishes to share. Thus, he writes and examines. At the moment, he is preparing a memoir for his children and grandchildren to explore after he goes on to the "greater" adventure.

Stacy Bennett is a resident of Los Angeles. "Not Your Typical Prom Night" was one of her first creative writing efforts, and she continues to write on a private basis. You can contact her by email at: *dacy@earthlink.net*.

Shashi Bhat is fourteen years old and a student from Ontario, Canada. She enjoys writing, reading and both playing and listening to music. Shashi has had her stories and essays published in various newsletters.

Bryony Blackwood is a Kenyan-born British citizen living in Virginia. He spent two years in a boarding school overseas before returning to the states for college. Change and adjustment have become recurring themes in his life. The most important lessons those changes have taught him are that you are free to choose your own path in life and to shape that life to fit your dreams. Life really is what you make of it.

Alicia M. Boxler is an honor roll student. She is involved with her school marching band, church, youth group and Youth Alive. Alicia enjoys spending time with her boyfriend, friends, shopping, talking on the phone and going to concerts.

Jessie Braun is currently a sophomore at Pomona College in Claremont, California. She feels privileged and honored to have been given the opportunity to work on both the first and second volumes of *Chicken Soup for the Teenage Soul*.

Melissa Broeckelman is a student in Rexford, Kansas. She participates in track, cross-country, forensics, band, choir, scholar's bowl and school plays. Melissa is a member of NHS and is editor of the school anthology. She can be reached at HC1, Box 30, Selden, KS 67757.

Jennings Michael Burch is an internationally recognized author and speaker. His autobiography, *They Cage the Animals at Night*, chronicles his childhood experiences living in orphanages and foster homes. He speaks to children and adults about family, values, kindness and honor. He strives to eliminate the ridicule of children by other children and succeeds. He can be reached at 2 Elm St., Chappaqua, NY 10514 or call by calling 914-238-3031.

Cambra J. Cameron is a sophomore at Lubbock Christian University where she is involved in Kappa Phi Kappa and Acappella Chorus. She is grateful to God, her family and her friends for their continuing to help and encourage her. And to "David" who will always hold a special place in her heart. Her e-mail address in *jcameron@itl.net*.

Martha Campbell is a graduate of Washington University School of Fine Arts, and a former writer-designer for Hallmark Cards. Since she became a freelancer in 1973, she has had over two thousand cartoons published and has illustrated ninteen books. You can write her at P.O. Box 2538, Harrison, AR 72602 or call 870-741-5323.

Dave Carpenter has been a full-time cartoonist and humorous illustrator since 1981. His cartoons have appeared in *Barron's*, the *Wall Street Journal, Forbes, Better Homes and Gardens, Good Housekeeping, Woman's World, First*, the *Saturday Evening Post* and numerous other publications. Dave can be reached at P.O. Box 520, Emmetsburg, IA 50536 or by calling 712-852-3725.

Don Caskey writes a column for the *Gwinnett Daily Post* in Lawrenceville, Georgia, and develops training and performance support systems for Synesis Corporation in Roswell, Georgia. For more of Don's stories and columns, visit *www.nbdigital.com*. Letters are welcome at 2180 Pleasant Hill Road A5-271, Duluth, GA 30096 or *caskey@nbdigital.com*.

Terri Cecil has always been driven by challenges and that is how she looked at the car accident in 1983 that left her unable to walk. Since that injury, Terri has graduated from the University of Louisville, maintained full-time employment, served as a community volunteer, competed on the 1996 Paralympic Fencing Team and earned the national title of Ms. Wheelchair America for 1998. She enjoys traveling and speaking on the joy of diversity, the triumph of the human spirit and the need to eradicate what Terri considers to be the strongest handicap of all—prejudice of any kind. Terri can be reached at 596 Plymouth St., Apt. 1, Wilkes-Barre, PA 18702 or by calling 717-820-3272 or by e-mail: *TerriMWA98@aol.com*. She can also be reached at Pride Health Care, Inc., at 800-800-8586.

Diana Chapman has been a journalist for fourteen years, having worked at the *San Diego Union*, The Los Angeles Copley Newspapers and the *Los Angeles Times*. She specializes in human interest stories and is currently working on a book involving health issues, since she was diagnosed with multiple sclerosis in 1992. She has been married for nine years and has one son, Herbert "Ryan" Hart. She can be reached at P.O. Box 414, San Pedro, CA 90733 or call 310-548-1192.

Dan Clark is the international ambassador of the "Art of Being Alive." He has spoken to over 2 million people worldwide. Dan is an actor, songwriter, recording artist, video producer and award-winning athlete. He is the well-known author of seven books, including *Getting High—How to Really Do It, One Minute Messages, The Art of Being Alive* and *Puppies for Sale and Other Inspirational Tales*. He can be reached at P.O. Box 8689, Salt Lake City, UT 84108 or by calling 801-485-5755.

Melissa Collette is most happy when she is spending time with her friends, listening to music, writing poetry and acting. She hopes to one day become an actress and work her way up to directing and producing. She lives by the saying, "Everything happens for a reason."

Cheryl L. Costello-Forshey is a poet who offers her original poetry to the public through her business, Photographic Verse. She is currently finishing up her first book of poetry. Cheryl can be reached at 36240 S. 16th Rd., Barnesville, OH 43713-9504 or call 740-757-9217. Please send a SASE for information on Photographic Verse.

Elisa Donovan first garnered the attention of filmgoers when she co-starred as the tippity, completely misguided slave-to-fashion, Amber, opposite Alicia Silverstone in the feature film *Clueless*. She also stars in the television series "Clueless" that airs on UPN. Next, Elisa will emerge in the Paramount feature *A Night at the Roxbury*, slated for release in October. Elisa was born in Poughkeepsie, New York, and raised on Northport, Long Island. Elisa began acting at the age of seven and became engrossed with New York theater. Some of her theater credits include *The Baby, Mad Love, Mad Forest, Dark Hours, Chamber Music* and *Treading the Boards*. Other credits in television and film include *Blossom, Encino Woman, Beverly Hills, 90210* and *Powder Burns*. Elisa currently resides in Los Angeles.

Jason Dorsey is one of America's leading young speakers. Each year he reaches over 100,000 people of all ages, backgrounds and aspirations. His first book, *Graduate to Your Perfect Job*, and integrated curriculum are used across America. You may reach him by phone at 512-442-5170 or at *www.jasondorsey.com*.

Kristina Dulcey goes to a Catholic high school and enjoys playing softball. She dreams of becoming a plastic surgeon so that she can help people whose external appearances do not conform with what society deems as acceptable. She would like to specialize in reconstructive surgery rather than cosmetic as she feels cosmetic is "superficial." "After all," she says, "it's what is on the inside that counts."

Alison Mary Forbes is a sixteen-year-old high-school junior. She plans to pursue a long-awaited theater degree in college. Much thanks to the wonderful Barry Weber for submitting her poem when she was too chicken to do it herself! Alison can be reached at P.O. Box 26353, Wauwatosa, WI 53226.

Carol Gallivan lives in East Hartford, Connecticut, with her husband, Kevin, and their two teenage daughters, Kelly and Tracy. The greatest joys in her life are her relationships with God; her family; her niece and nephew, Renee and Eric; her dear friends; and the teenagers in her neighborhood.

Jessica Gardner is an eighteen-year-old from Warwick, Rhode Island, who is currently a musical theatre performance major at the University of Central Florida in Orlando. She would like to thank her family, especially her papa for the motivation, Mrs. Jean Robinson and Ms. Betty Challgren for the early encouragement, her friends and sisters for the support, and her two very best friends, Holly Langton and Shawn Carvalho, for giving her a shoulder to cry on, strength to make it through and the courage "to go out and do it." Nana, we miss you. You can reach Jessica at 401-461-3971 or e-mail her at *jessie136@aol.com*.

Kelly Garnett is currently a sophomore, majoring in Elementary Education at Oakland University in Michigan. She would like to thank her family and friends that have always been an inspiration—and true "chicken soup" for her soul.

Lia Gay is eighteen and is leaving in the fall to start college at the University of Kansas, where she will major in journalism. Lia is a talented writer, whose stories in the first volume of *Chicken Soup for the Teenage Soul* were favorites with readers. Lia is certain to succeed at any writing project she undertakes and she is certain to succeed equally well at living life to the fullest. She would like any correspondence to be sent to her care of Kimberly Kirberger, by regular mail to: P.O. Box 936, Pacific Palisades, CA 90272 or by e-mail to: *letters@teenagechickensoup.com*.

April Joy Gazmen is an eighteen-year-old Filipina-American attending University of Houston-Downtown. Although she participates as a volunteer and in school activities, writing and reading are her passion. She is inspired by the following people who are always in her heart: Mama, Cza, Hawke, Chino, friends and teachers. To be published in *Chicken Soup for the Teenage Soul II* is a dream come true. She can be reached at *irelandnikita@hotmail.com*.

Katie Gill had Hodgkin's disease when she was sixteen. She is now twenty-four and pursuing a graduate degree in education. Presently she is working on a book for teens with cancer and trying to establish support networks for adult survivors of teenage cancer. Katie can be reached at 4520 Ashbury Park Dr., North Olmsted, OH 44070.

Randy Glasbergen is the creator of the cartoon *The Better Half*, which is syndicated to 150 newspapers by King Features Syndicate. More than twenty thousand of Randy's cartoons have been published in magazines, books and greeting cards around the world. Look for Randy's daily cartoons online @ *www.norwich.net/~randyg/toon.html*.

Luken Grace is currently serving a two-year mission in Venezuela until August of 1999. He is a 1996 graduate of Sinagua High School in Flagstaff, Arizona. As the third child of six children, he has always enjoyed writing stories and drawing. After he graduates from college, he plans on becoming an English teacher.

Cindy Hamond is a freelance writer. This is her second story for *Chicken Soup*. She enjoys her school visits, especially when the children react to that "A-ha" moment in a story. She and her husband, Bruce, have five children and one grandchild. Cindy volunteers at St. Henry's as a teacher and lector and visits the homebound. She can be reached at 1021 West River St., Monticello, MN 55362 or call 612-295-5049 or fax 612-295-3117.

Jennifer Love Hewitt is best known for her starring role as Sarah Reeves on FOX's Golden Globe-winning drama series, *Party of Five*. Love has starred in such big-screen hits as *I Know What You Did Last Summer* and *Can't Hardly Wait*. Her upcoming projects include *I Still Know What You Did Last Summer*, *The Suburbans* (with Ben Stiller), and an ABC movie-of-the-week in which she will play her idol, Audrey Hepburn.

Margaret (Meg) Hill writes articles, short stories and young-adult books. Recent titles are *Coping with Family Expectations* (Rosen, 1990) and *So What Do I Do About Me?* (Teacher Ideas Press, Libraries Unlimited, Englewood, Colorado, 1993). Kirk is the pen name she uses when writing from the viewpoint of a teenage boy.

Ashley Hiser is a seventeen-year old senior in high school in Morristown, New Jersey. She is involved in many activities through her school such as president of the French Club, member of the French Honor Socdiety, secretary of the Junior Statesmen of America, coeditor in chief of her school newspaper and manager of her cross-country team. Ashley has achieved perfect attendance throughout her three years of high school and has also been on the honor roll. She volunteers through her church's youth ministry and she makes a trip to Appalachia every summer. Ashley also works part-time at GapKids twelve to fifteen hours per week.

Wil Horneff has made a name for himself on stage, screen and television. After beginning his career on Broadway, Wil starred in the feature films *Born to Be Wild, The Sandlot* and the upcoming *Harvest.* On television, he gave an award-winning performance as Jody Baxter in the CBS remake of *The Yearling* and costarred in Stephen King's *The Shining.* Wil is currently a freshman at the University of Pennsylvania.

Katie E. Houston is a sophomore in Santa Barbara, California. She loves acting, singing, dancing and has been taking piano lessons for eight years. She enjoys writing, especially realistic fiction and poetry. Katie runs track (hurdles) and she would someday like to perform on Broadway or be an English/drama teacher.

Robin Hyatt was eighteen years old when she went to Camp Virginia Jaycee for the first time. She learned a lot from that experience and was also given a wonderful chance to broaden her horizons. It was the first time that she had ever worked with people of any mental handicap. She volunteered three more times at Camp Jaycee until she graduated from Lynchburg College in 1996 with a Bachelor of Arts degree. Each time she went she looked at the world a little differently. She is currently working as the special events coordinator at the Alexandria Chamber of Commerce.

Amanda Johnson is sixteen years old and a junior in high school in Placerville, California. This is her first published work but she has been writing poems and children's stories for years. Aside from writing, she also takes Jazz and Ballet and performs in school and community theatre productions. Amanda loves children.

Andrew Keegan is one of Hollywood's most popular young actors. Last television season, he had roles on both *Party of Five* and *7th Heaven.* Andrew will star in the upcoming Touchstone Pictures film *Ten Things I Hate About You,* which is based on William Shakespeare's *The Taming of the Shrew.* In his free time, he donates countless hours to charities that help critically and terminally ill children.

Heather Klassen writes fiction for children and teenagers from her home near Seattle. She has written a number of book manuscripts, ranging from picture books to young adult novels, and is very interested in finding publishers for those works. She can be reached at 26 150th Pl. SE, Lynnwood, WA 98037 or by calling 425-742-7407.

Theresa Jensen Lacey is a freelance writer who has authored four hundred newspaper/magazine articles and two Native American history books: *The Blackfeet* (1995) and *The Pawnee* (1996, Chelsea House). Lacey is the author of two YA novels (available), is working on a children's book and one on Native

American women. The author is of Comanche and Cherokee descent. She can be reached at 112 Carney Rd., Clarksville, TN 37043, or by calling 931-358-5511, or by e-mail: *tcjl@hotmail.com*.

Medard Laz is a popular speaker and author of the international bestseller, *Love Adds a Little Chocolate: 100 Stories to Brighten Your Day and Sweeten Your Life*, as well as nine other books. Medard was instrumental in the development of Marriage Encounter and he cofounded (with Suzy Yehl Marta) Rainbows for All God's Children, a support group for children and teens who have experienced a divorce or death in their families. This group has ministered to over 600,000 children in sixteen countries. He also founded Joyful Again! (with Charlotte Hrubes), a support weekend for widowers and widows. Med is a highly sought-after speaker, giving presentations and workshops on a variety of marriage and family issues, as well as topics related to emotional and spiritual growth. Med lives in Chicago and is a priest of the Archdiocese of Chicago. He can be reached at 3600 S. 57th Ct., Cicero, IL, or by calling 708-656-9216, or by e-mail: *MedardLaz@aol.com*.

Jason Leib is twenty years old and an upper junior at Yeshiva University. He was born and raised in the Chicagoland area. He is legally blind. Despite the vision problem, he played six years of Little League. He also attends the Special Olympics where he competed in several different sporting events and won gold, silver and bronze medals in the events he played in. He attended Ida Crown Jewish Academy for high school where he played one year of junior varsity basketball and two years of varsity basketball. He received the Sportsmanship trophy award as well as an award from B'nai B'rith for basketball. Jason played basketball in the Maccabee games and won a silver medal. He also participated in intramural softball all four years of high school. Jason can be reached at 4000 Enfield, Skokie, IL 60076 or by calling 847-329-7078.

Phyllis Lin is a fifteen-year-old freshman in high school in Bartlett, Illinois. An aspiring writer, Phyllis writes for both her school academy newsletter and for her own pleasure. In her spare time, she enjoys going out with friends, reading and playing the piano. Phyllis can be reached at e-mail: *Phyllis911@yahoo.com*.

Bonnie Maloney is a sophomore in high school in Attleboro, Massachusetts. She enjoys reading and writing, and plans to study these along with psychology in the future. She is currently employed at a local bank that operates in and out of school, and looks forward to going somewhere unexplored for college.

Sandy Dow Mapula is a native of El Paso, Texas. She is presently a nurse for Zach White Elementary School and loves to write in her spare time. Her two sons, Steven and Kevin, whom she describes as the joys of her life, provide her with the inspiration to write. She can be reached at 604 Tepic, El Paso, TX 79912 or by e-mail: *SMAPULA781@aol.com*.

Jill Maxbauer is a junior in high school. There, she is involved with theater, music, athletic training, softball and the Safe & Drug Free Schools Committee. She is the youngest of three girls and is currently deciding where she would like to go to college.

Sarah McCann is a sixteen-year-old student in Bedford, Nova Scotia. Her first love is dancing, but she also enjoys writing, watching movies and drawing.

Meladee McCarty is a program specialist for the Sacramento County Office of Education in California. She works to find educational support for students with severe disabilities. She is coauthor, with her husband, of four best-selling books, including *A 4th Course of Chicken Soup for the Soul,* which has sold over 1.5 million copies, as well as *Acts of Kindness: How to Make A Gentle Difference.* She can be reached at Learning Resources, P.O. Box 66, Galt, CA 95632, or by calling 209-745-2212, or by faxing 209-745-2252.

Paula McDonald has sold over a million copies of her books on relationships and gone on to win numerous awards worldwide as a columnist, inspirational feature writer and photojournalist. She is a highly regarded national lecturer on relationships and family communications, as well as being a popular inspirational speaker, both in the United States and abroad. Paula is available as a speaker or writer and can be contacted through Creative Consultants, 417 W. San Ysidro Blvd., Ste. L724, San Ysidro CA 92173. You may phone/fax her at (Rosarito, Mexico) 011-52-66-313173 or e-mail *102526.356@compuserve.com.*

Kate McMahon resides in South Orange, New Jersey with her parents, Vincent and Elizabeth and her brother, Luke. She is a senior in high school, where Olive O'Sullivan instructs her in English. Kate is interested in pursuing studies in creative writing as well as sociology.

Walter W. Meade started writing at the age of fourteen. His first story was published in *Colliers* magazine at the age of twenty-two. He wrote short fiction stories for the *Saturday Evening Post, Gentlemen's Quarterly* and several others. He then turned to writing nonfiction for magazines such as *Cosmopolitan, Redbook* and the *Reader's Digest.* Later he took a position in the publishing world and became the managing editor of *Cosmopolitan* and then the managing editor of the Reader's Digest Book Club. His last position in publishing was president and editor in chief of Avon Books, work which he continued to do for ten years. Today Walter is retired and writing articles for *Reader's Digest* as well as many other magazines and periodicals. You can reach Mr. Meade at 4561 NW 67th Terrace, Lauderhill, FL 33319.

Donna Miesbach has inspirational poems and articles that have been published in a wide range of magazines. Currently she is editor and publisher of *Gleanings,* a rapidly growing paper that discusses the gamut of human experience. Most of the material for this publication is written by the staff, but submissions from subscribers are considered. If you are interested in knowing more about this publication, inquiries may be sent to the editor at 2805 S. 161

Plaza, Omaha, NE 68130 or by e-mail at *gleanings1@juno.com*, or you may contact Donna directly by calling 402-330-2474. In addition to her work as a speaker for local support groups, she is currently under contract with an agent for her first full-length book. A retired organist and music teacher, she is also grandmother to "eleven wonderful grandchildren."

Shelly Miller is a freshman studying electrical engineering at UM-Rolla. She really enjoys being a sister in Kappa Delta sorority and is the founder of the Society for the Antidisestablishment of Fairy Pressing! Check it out on her homepage at *http://www.umr.edu/~michele/*.

David J. Murcott is a freelance writer who resides in San Diego, California. He has written and edited stories for *A 5th Portion of Chicken Soup for the Soul, Chicken Soup for the Teenage Soul* and *Stone Soup for the World*. He can be contacted at 619-590-1461.

Amy Muscato is a high school student in New Jersey. She has varied interests including theater, singing, politics and forensics. After her graduation in June 1999, she looks forward to attending college. Amy has aspirations of a career in either politics or television news.

Sara Nachtman is sixteen years old and is a focused student, determined athlete, with much emotional experience with trying to keep up with her competition. Sometimes she gets discouraged when her progress is slow or tiresome. These are the times when Sara writes to keep her motivation high while keeping in perspective what is really important.

Josh Nally is currently a college freshman. His story, "Making Dad Proud," was written as an assignment for his Advanced Placement English Class in high school. He says, "It's one of the most powerful pieces I have ever written. It stirred sentiment within myself and my family that was previously undiscovered."

Kent Nerburn is an author, sculptor and educator who has been deeply involved in Native American issues and education. He has served as project director for two books of oral history entitled, *To Walk the Red Road* and *We Choose to Remember*. He has also edited three highly acclaimed books on Native American subjects. Kent won The Minnesota Book Award for his book, *Neither Wolf nor Dog: On Forgotten Roads in 1995*. The story "Like People First," appeared in Kent's book, *Letters to My Son*. Kent holds a Ph.D. in both theology and art, and lives with his family in Bemidju, Minnesota.

Jenni Norman is a fifteen-year-old sophomore in Albemarle, North Carolina. In addition to running cross-country and playing soccer, she is a member of the debate club and the Albemarle athletic fellowship. She loves making her friends laugh, writing, staying glued to the TV during the World Cup, trips to the beach and traveling abroad—she has been to Austria, Germany, Hungary and the Czech Republic, and plans to travel to England and France. Most of all, she loves chasing her mischievous dachshund Oscar. She can be reached at P.O. Box 550, Albemarle, NC 28002.

Tony Overman is a nationally known motivational youth speaker. He founded the National Youth I Care Hotline and produced *Teen Talk,* a nine-part video series. Tony conducts training workshops for teachers and motivational assemblies for schools. He can be reached at 18965 F.M. 2252, Garden Ridge, TX 78266, or by calling 800-487-8464.

Sandy Pathe is a junior in high school in New Jersey. She plans to continue her trips to Honduras annually and hopes her story can motivate others to put themselves out there and lend a hand. Any questions or comments are welcome at *SungirlsR@aol.com* or call 732-449-0335.

Nicole Rose Patridge is a junior in high school in Camas, Washington. She lives with her two brothers, her dad, and her mother, who just finished battling breast cancer. She found writing stories of cancer in the family often helped ease the feelings she was having while dealing with cancer in her home. She is currently looking at colleges around the country and hopes to pursue a career in writing or journalism.

Peer Resources is a leading authority in peer helping services, programs, and resources for children, teens and adults. They can be contacted by e-mail at*helping@islandnet.com* or visited at *www.islandnet.com/~rcarr/peer.html.* Write to 1052 Davie St., Victoria, BC V8S 4E3 or call 800-567-3700.

Rochelle M. Pennington is a nationally recognized author of poetry, drama and nonfiction. She is also the originator and author of the midwestern newspaper column, *Insight and Inspiration.* As a quotations specialist, Rochelle has worked with several bestselling authors providing quote recommendations to enhance their books, including H. Jackson Brown (*Life's Little Instruction Books*) and Jack Canfield (*Chicken Soup for the Soul*). She is currently coauthoring Mr. Brown's next book, *Life's Little Instruction Book à la mode.* Rochelle, who resides in rural Wisconsin with her husband and their children, spends her free time actively involved in Christian education and in volunteering Hospice Hope care to the terminally ill. Rochelle can be reached at N1911 Double D Rd., Campbellsport, WI 53010 or by calling 920-533-5880.

Susan Record is currently a student at Brigham Young University studying humanities, music and art history. She works as an editorial assistant for the BYU Faculty Center and plans to graduate in April of 1999. She and Justin Record were married in November 1996. In her spare time she enjoys writing and working in the garden.

Daphna Renan currently attends Yale University. She moved six times before she entered sixth grade. It was during these early years that she learned the significance of deep and enduring friendships. Daphna would like to thank those who have filled her life with love, laughter and learning.

Rachel Rosenberg is fifteen years old. She wrote "Unrequited Love" in 1998 when she was fourteen. She has been writing since she was ten, and one day plans to be a writer. She also writes longer stories and poems. Rachel attends high school in Montreal, Quebec, and can be reached at *Rae_38@hotmail.com*.

Meredith Rowe is currently a member of the class of 2002 at Stanford University. However, she calls McKinney, Texas, home, and graduated in May 1998 from McKinney High School. Meredith has been writing since she was seven years old and loves to contribute to the Internet, especially by designing Web pages. She would like to thank all those who made her publication possible by adding their input. She can be reached via e-mail at *cardinal02@hotmail.com*.

Kimberly Russell would like to thank her entire family for all of the continued support they have given her. She is leaving in the fall to attend Gettysberg College where she will probably major in pre-law. She would like any correspondence to be sent to her care of Kimberly Kirberger, by regular mail to: P.O. Box 936, Pacific Palisades, CA 90272 or by e-mail to: *letters@teenagechickensoup.com*.

Jamie Shockley currently attends high school in Spring, Texas. She actively participates in band, tennis and student council. She enjoys reading and outdoor activities. Jamie hopes to attend University of Texas at Austin or A&M University at College Station after graduating high school. She plans to major in business or engineering.

Harley Schwadron is a self-taught cartoonist living in Ann Arbor, Michigan and worked as a journalist and public relations writer before switching to cartooning full-time in 1984. His cartoons appear in *Barron's, Harvard Business Review, Wall Street Journal, National Law Journal* and many others. He can be reached at P.O. Box 1347, Ann Arbor, MI 48106 or call 313-426-8433.

Patty Anne Sluys is an eighteen-year-old Christian homeschool graduate residing in Chilliwack, British Columbia. She enjoys hockey, people, photography, hairdressing, desktop publishing and especially writing. She has put out a teen magazine called the *Penpal Scene* for three years. (It features inspirational articles, poems, stories, advice and more. Send $1 for sample issue.) Patty can be reached at 49950 Patterson Rd., Chilliwack, BC V2P 6H3, Canada.

Karina Snow lives with her husband, Mark, in Oceanside, California. She is a recent graduate of Brigham Young University and volunteers with the youth group in her church. Karina enjoys reading, cooking and playing with her two young children, Tori and Brett.

Constance Ananta Sobsey is a high-school student in Edmonton, Alberta, Canada. Outside of school, she enjoys spending time with friends, listening to semi-obscure music and writing. This poem is dedicated to her friend, Emily Johnson, who never ceases to inspire. Connie can be reached at *conniecas@hotmail.com*.

Marc St. Pierre is a seventeen-year-old high school senior. He enjoys listening to music and hanging out with his friends. Thanks, Aunt Linda.

Jill Thieme. Turning "Wonder into Wonderful" was only one of the many lessons in life that Mom taught us. When we didn't have money, Mom would tell us to "Make a Memory." For several years now our holidays and birthdays have become a tradition of special activities. We'll be happy to share our creative family outings with others if you write to us at P.O. Box 381, Bridgeport, MI 48722.

Erica Thoits is the *Teen People* contest winner. She loves to horseback ride and swim. Her favorite pastime is going out on the family's boat. She is an avid reader and has been writing ever since she could type. Her handwriting is too sloppy to handwrite things. She loves dogs and couldn't live without her thirteen-year-old dog, who is only one year younger than she is.

Becky Tucker is eighteen years old and leads an active life in her hometown of Lebanon, Oregon. She believes in God and thanks him for all the inspiration he has placed within her.

Camden Watts will graduate from high school in 1999. Camden enjoys staying busy with difficult courses, running cross country, swimming, playing soccer and dancing. She writes and draws for her school newspaper and for her nationally acclaimed literary magazine, *Opus*. Her best work comes from experiences written late in the evening.

Digby Wolfe had a writing career of fifty years that has been divided equally between theatre and the media. British-born Digby Wolfe is perhaps best known for being the co-creator of the landmark television hit, *Laugh-In*. A multiple Emmy nominee and winner, Digby is now the tenured Professor of Play and Screenwriting at the University of New Mexico in Albuquerque.

Becca Woolf is a junior in high school and wrote this story at age fourteen after her first heartbreak. Poetry is her passion and she is presently working on a collection of poems based on teen angst, which she hopes to publish soon. Besides being a writer, she is also an aspiring actress.

Permissions

We would like to acknowledge the many publishers and individuals who granted us permission to reprint the cited material. (Note: The stories that were penned anonymously, that are in the public domain, or that were written by Jack Canfield, Mark Victor Hansen or Kimberly Kirberger are not included in this listing.)

Starlight, Star Bright; The Right Thing and *The Player.* Reprinted by permission of Kelly Garnett. ©1998 Kelly Garnett.

Seven Minutes in Heaven. Reprinted by permission of Andrew Keegan. ©1998 Andrew Keegan.

Practical Application and *Pay Attention.* Reprinted by permission of Dan Clark. ©1998 Dan Clark.

A Geek, a Nerd, a Bookworm. Reprinted by permission of Kimberly Russell. ©1998 Kimberly Russell.

My Angel Has a Halo. Reprinted by permission of Amanda Johnson. ©1998 Amanda Johnson.

A Cool Drink of Water. Reprinted by permission of Camden Watts. ©1998 Camden Watts.

Unrequited Love. Reprinted by permission of Rachel Rosenberg. ©1998 Rachel Rosenberg.

Gray. Reprinted by permission of Constance Ananta Sobsey. ©1999 Constance Ananta Sobsey.

Starting a New Path. Reprinted by permission of Jessie Braun. ©1998 Jessie Braun.

Discovery. Reprinted by permission of Eugene E. Beasley. ©1998 Eugene E. Beasley.

Hopscotch and Tears. Reprinted by permission of Becca Woolf. ©1996 Becca Woolf.

Inside. Reprinted by permission of Melissa Collette. ©1998 Melissa Collette.

Lost Love and *Love and Belonging.* Reprinted by permission of Theresa Jensen Lacey. ©1998 Theresa Jensen Lacey.

Love Is Never Lost. Reprinted by permission of David J. Murcott. ©1998 David J. Murcott.

David's Smile. Reprinted by permission of Cambra J. Cameron. ©1998 Cambra J. Cameron.

The Rift. Reprinted by permission of Erica Thoits. ©1998 Erica Thoits.

Donna and Claudia. Reprinted by permission of Carol Gallivan. ©1998 Carol

The Ones in Front of Me. Reprinted by permission of Lia Gay. ©1998 Lia Gay.

Role Reversal. Reprinted by permission of Adi Amar. ©1998 Adi Amar.

Snowdrops. Reprinted by permission of Sarah McCann. ©1998 Sarah McCann.

My Most Memorable Christmas. Reprinted by permission of Reverend Robert Schuller. ©1998 Reverend Robert Schuller.

My Real Father. Used with permission. Author wishes to remain anonymous.

Making Dad Proud. Reprinted by permission of Josh Nally. ©1998 Josh Nally.

The Perfect Family. Reprinted by permission of Marc St. Pierre. ©1998 Marc St. Pierre.

Making Sarah Cry. Reprinted by permission of Cheryl L. Costello-Forshey. ©1998 Cheryl L. Costello-Forshey.

Andrea's Fresh Start. Reprinted by permisson of Peg Verone. Excerpted from *Woman's World Magazine.*©1998 Peg Verone.

A Lesson for Life. Reprinted by permission of Medard Laz. Excerpted from *Love Adds a Little Chocolate: 100 Stories to Brighten Your Day and Sweeten Your Life.* ©1997 by Medard Laz.

Remember Me? Reprinted by permission of Ann Landers and Creators Syndicate. All Rights Reserved.

A Wider Classroom. Reprinted by permission of Kate McMahon. ©1998 Kate McMahon.

The Bat. Reprinted by permission of Bryony Blackwood. ©1998 Bryony Blackwood.

Myself. Reprinted by permission of *Peer Counsellor Workbook.* ©1988 *Peer Counsellor Workbook.*

Firmer Ground. Reprinted by permission of Diana Chapman. ©1998 Diana Chapman.

What I Wish I'd Known Sooner. Reprinted by permission of Meredith Rowe. ©1998 Meredith Rowe.

My Most Embarrassing Moment. Reprinted by permission of Rochelle M. Pennington. ©1998 Rochelle M. Pennington.

Call Me. Reprinted by permission of Cindy Hamond. ©1998 Cindy Hamond.

For You, Dad. Reprinted by permission of Bill Holton. Excerpted from *Woman's World Magazine.* ©1998 Bill Holton.

Somebody Loves You. Reprinted by permission of Wil Horneff. ©1998 Wil Horneff.

Share with Us

We all have had Chicken Soup for the Soul moments in our lives. If you would like to share your story or poem with millions of people around the world, go to chicken-soup.com and click on "Submit Your Story." You may be able to help another reader, and become a published author at the same time. Some of our past contributors have launched writing and speaking careers from the publication of their stories in our books!

Our submission volume has been increasing steadily — the quality and quantity of your submissions has been fabulous. We only accept story submissions via our website. They are no longer accepted via mail or fax.

To contact us regarding other matters, please send us an e-mail through webmaster@chickensoupforthesoul.com, or fax or write us at:

Chicken Soup for the Soul
P.O. Box 700
Cos Cob, CT 06807-0700
Fax: 203-861-7194

One more note from your friends at Chicken Soup for the Soul: Occasionally, we receive an unsolicited book manuscript from one of our readers, and we would like to respectfully inform you that we do not accept unsolicited manuscripts and we must discard the ones that appear.

Improving Your Life Every Day

Real people sharing real stories — for nineteen years. Now, Chicken Soup for the Soul has gone beyond the bookstore to become a world leader in life improvement. Through books, movies, DVDs, online resources and other partnerships, we bring hope, courage, inspiration and love to hundreds of millions of people around the world. Chicken Soup for the Soul's writers and readers belong to a one-of-a-kind global community, sharing advice, support, guidance, comfort, and knowledge.

Chicken Soup for the Soul stories have been translated into more than 40 languages and can be found in more than one hundred countries. Every day, millions of people experience a Chicken Soup for the Soul story in a book, magazine, newspaper or online. As we share our life experiences through these stories, we offer hope, comfort and inspiration to one another. The stories travel from person to person, and from country to country, helping to improve lives everywhere.

Teenage years are tough, but this book will help teens as they journey through the ups and downs of adolescence. Teens will find support and inspiration in the 101 new stories from teens just like them. Stories in this book serve as a guide on topics about daily pressures of life, school, love, friendships, parents, and much more. This collection will show readers that as tough as things can get, they are not alone!

978-1-935096-72-6

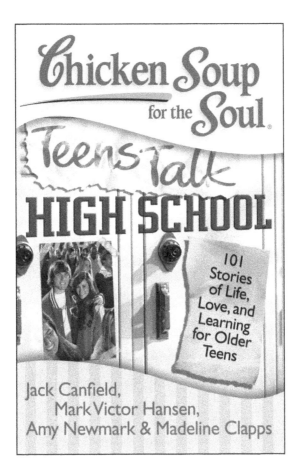

Chicken Soup for the Soul

Teens Talk

HIGH SCHOOL

101 Stories of Life, Love, and Learning for Older Teens

Jack Canfield,
Mark Victor Hansen,
Amy Newmark & Madeline Clapps

Teens in high school have mainly moved past worrying about puberty and cliques, so this book covers topics of interest to older teens -- sports and clubs, driving, curfews, self-image and self-acceptance, dating and sex, family, friends, divorce, illness, death, pregnancy, drinking, failure, and preparing for life after graduation. High school students will find comfort and inspiration in this book, referring to it through all four years of high school, like a portable support group.

978-1-935096-25-2

Chicken Soup for the Soul
for the Soul®

Teens Talk
Growing Up

Our 101 BEST STORIES

Stories about Growing Up,
Meeting Challenges, and
Learning from Life

Jack Canfield
& Mark Victor Hansen
edited by Amy Newmark

Being a teenager is hard -- school is challenging, college and career are looming on the horizon, family issues arise, friends and love come and go, bodies and emotions go through major changes, and many teens experience the loss of a loved one for the first time. This book reminds teenagers that they are not alone, as they read stories written by other teens about the problems and issues they all face every day.

978-1-935096-01-6

The teenage years are difficult. Old friends drift away, new friends come with new issues, teens fall in and out of love, and relationships with family members change. This book reminds teenagers that they are not alone, as they read the 101 best stories from Chicken Soup for the Soul's library written by other teens just like themselves, about the problems and issues they face every day -- stories about friends, family, love, loss, and many lessons learned.

978-1-935096-06-1

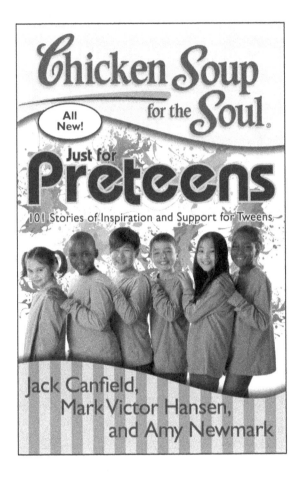

Chicken Soup for the Soul
All New!
for the Soul
Just for
Preteens
101 Stories of Inspiration and Support for Tweens

Jack Canfield,
Mark Victor Hansen,
and Amy Newmark

Being a preteen is harder than it looks! School is more challenging, bodies are changing, relationships with parents are different, and new issues arise with friends. But preteens can find encouragement and inspiration in this collection of stories by other preteens, just like them, about the problems and issues they face every day. Chicken Soup for the Soul: Just for Preteens will help readers as they navigate those tough preteen years from ages 9 to 12 with its stories from others just like them, about the highs and lows of life as a preteen. It's a support group they carry in their backpack!

978-1-935096-73-3